ESTEBAN CANTÚ

and the Mexican Revolution in Baja California Norte 1910-1920

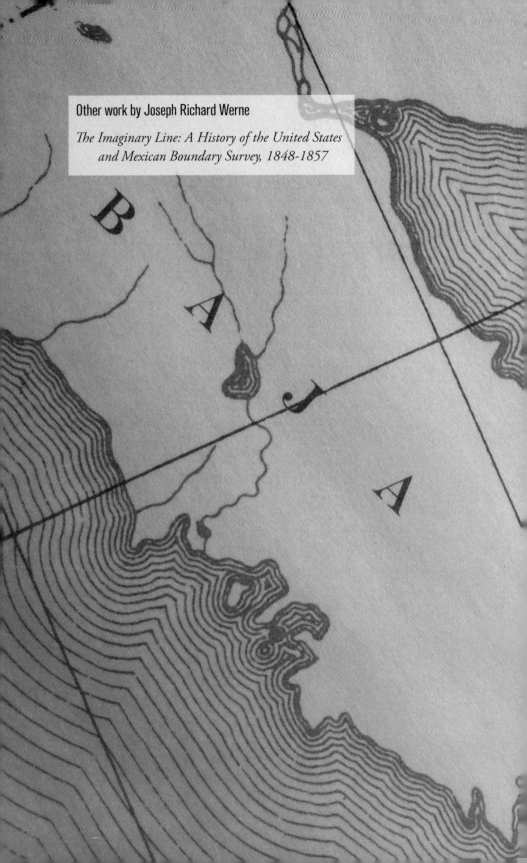

Other work by Joseph Richard Werne

The Imaginary Line: A History of the United States and Mexican Boundary Survey, 1848-1857

ESTEBAN CANTÚ

and the Mexican Revolution in Baja California Norte 1910-1920

Joseph Richard
WERNE

TCU
Press

FORT WORTH, TEXAS

TCU Box 298300
Fort Worth, Texas 76129
817.257.7822
www.prs.tcu.edu
To order books: 1.800.826.8911

Cover and Text Design by Preston Thomas

For Erika, Josef, Kirsten, and Marlene

Courtesy of Chris Erichsen.

CONTENTS

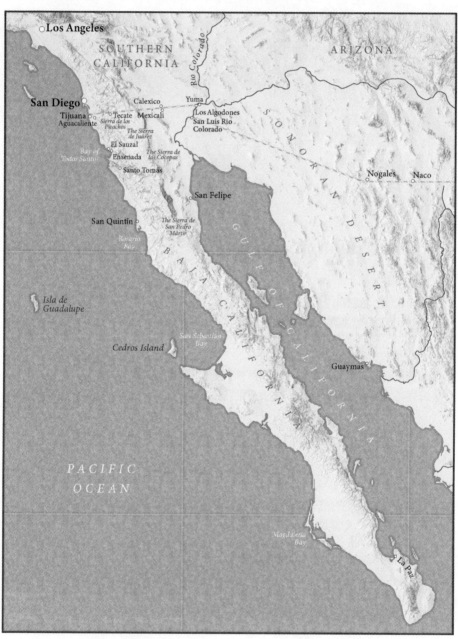

Los Angeles

SOUTHERN
CALIFORNIA

ARIZONA

Rio Colorado

San Diego

Calexico

Yuma

Los Algodones

Tijuana
Aguacaliente

Tecate

Mexicali

Sierra de los
Picachos

San Luis Rio
Colorado

The Sierra
de Juárez

El Sauzal

Bay of
Todos Santos

Ensenada

The Sierra de
las Cocopas

Nogales

Naco

Santo Tomás

San Felipe

SONORAN DESERT

San Quintín

The Sierra de
San Pedro
Mártir

Rosario
Bay

BAJA CALIFORNIA

GULF OF CALIFORNIA

Isla de
Guadalupe

Cedros Island

San Sebastián
Bay

Guaymas

PACIFIC
OCEAN

Magdalena
Bay

La Paz

Courtesy of Chris Erichsen.

PREFACE

Esteban Cantú did not play a great role in the Mexican Revolution, but he was in control of Baja California Norte during those years and definitely beyond the reach of Mexico's government until the revolt of Agua Prieta in 1920 put an end to the rule of Venustiano Carranza. Only then was the central government able to bring the territory firmly under its control. Little has been written about Cantú, and most works on the Mexican Revolution do not even mention him. Yet he maintained peace and prosperity in the Northern District of the peninsula and, while presiding over a population riddled with vice of all descriptions, managed to wring enough revenue out of the vice trade to build a considerable infrastructure that had not been there before. The peace and stability Cantú brought to Baja California Norte during the turbulent years of the revolution gave Washington little concern regarding the southern border of California, while Mexico City could only cast a watchful eye in Cantú's direction.

There was the fear that Baja California would fall to the United States, as there had been several attempts to make that a reality by purchase or filibuster since the 1848 Treaty of Guadalupe Hidalgo. These efforts continued during the revolution, beginning with the anarchist invasion of 1911, and remained a threat throughout Cantú's governorship. That much of the land in the Northern District was owned by United States interests, including the only railroad that ran through the territory, made this fear a very real and present danger. While Cantú on occasion made statements that increased this concern on the part of Mexico, he did nothing that would have caused such a loss. In the end, Cantú stepped down peacefully from the governorship of Baja California Norte, following the advice and urging of his friends when faced with a military conclusion to his rule.

This study has been supported by a number of generous grants from Southeast Missouri State University, which permitted several rewarding stays in the archives of Mexico City, Washington, and elsewhere. There is to my knowledge no body of "Cantú Papers," but there is enough archival material to justify an in-depth investigation of his governorship. No research is ever accomplished without the pleasant assistance of archivists and librarians who generously give time and insight that makes historical investigation a pleasure. I should therefore like to express my deep gratitude to the directors and staffs of: the Archivo General de la Nación; the Archivo Histórico de la Defensa Nacional; the Archivo de la Secretaría de Relaciones Exteriores; the Centro de Estudios de Historia de Mexico; the Fideicomiso Archivos Plutarco Elías Calles y Fernando Torreblanca in Mexico City; the Archivo Histórico del Estado de Baja California in Mexicali, B.C., Mexico; the National Archives in Washington, DC; the Library of Pomona College, Claremont, California; the Benton Library, the University of Texas, Austin; and Special Collections, the University of Arizona, Tucson.

Joseph Richard Werne

INTRODUCTION

One island of peace during the violent years of the Mexican Revolution was the Northern District of Baja California. Suffering almost none of the destruction and bloodshed which fell upon other parts of the nation, Baja California Norte enjoyed comparative calm and prosperity. Partly responsible for this situation was the geographical isolation of the Northern District from Mexico proper, an isolation imposed by distance, desert, and a dearth of communication. Neither road nor railroad tied the territory to neighboring Sonora, and its only seaport, Ensenada, enjoyed no regular traffic with Guaymas or any other of Mexico's Pacific ports. The turmoil of Sonora during much of the revolution further isolated Baja California Norte from the mainland. The civil war that raged between Francisco Villa and Venustiano Carranza increased the Northern District's independence from the center as well. When Carranza emerged victorious as a result of Álvaro Obregón's military success, his hold on the country was not complete. As president, Carranza had to contend with a much weakened though still dangerous Villa marauding in Chihuahua, Emiliano Zapata unbroken in Morelos, Félix Díaz, who was still fighting in Veracruz, and Manuel Peláez in the Huasteca guarding the interests of the foreign petroleum companies. There was scarce time to think of Baja California Norte.

A second cause for the Northern District's seeming immunity from the revolution was the political attitude of Esteban Cantú Jiménez, first the commander of the military garrison at Mexicali and later governor of Baja California Norte. The interim government of Francisco de la Barra had sent a detachment of federal troops, among them Cantú, to suppress the Flores Magón rebellion, but before their arrival the movement had disintegrated and the *Porfiriato* had fallen. For the next several years the Twenty-Fifth Battalion of the Federal Army remained in Baja California Norte, almost entirely cut off from the ebb and flow of the revolution on the mainland. Governor Cantú's political character was anything but revolutionary, and this factor, reinforced by Baja California Norte's isolation, kept the revolution at bay in the Northern District.

After moving the territorial capital from Ensenada to Mexicali, the governor inaugurated a rather impressive building program over the next several years, creating the Northern District's first reliable infrastructure. A military road from Mexicali to Tijuana became a reality as well as one from the new territorial capital to San Felipe on the Gulf of California. The Cantú administration also built a telegraph station, schools, hospitals, an electric lighting plant, and sewer and water systems for the cities in which streets were graded and cement sidewalks were put down. Cantú gave a much-needed boost to education through the construction of a modern high school in Mexicali as well as other schools both rural and urban.

Not all of this progress was financed through local taxes. Rather, much of the territory's revenue had a tawdrier provenance. In Tijuana and Mexicali, an almost indescribable condition of graft, crime, and immorality of all kinds had sprung up and, by its flourishing nature, provided Cantú with considerable revenue. Nearly every kind of vice could be found: white slavery, prostitution, horse track gambling, opium dens, cocaine, morphine and heroin dealers, saloons and dives of all descriptions, open extortion, and gambling halls which offered a variety of seductions. Governor Cantú either licenced or was in some other way connected to this vice.

Until he was forced from the governorship in August 1920, Cantú had acted independently of the government in Mexico City. He merely made the pretense of bowing to federal authority, when in actuality he was a law unto himself. While he seemingly recognized the government of the usurper Victoriano Huerta by willingly accepting a promotion to the rank of colonel, he later had no compunctions about accepting appointment to the governorship from Pancho Villa, Eulalio Gutiérrez of the Convention government, and first chief of the Constitutionalist forces, Venustiano Carranza. Following Carranza's victory, Cantú expressed his loyalty to the Constitutionalist leadership, promulgated the 1917 Constitution in Baja California Norte, and cast that territory's vote for the first chief in the presidential election which followed. The actual condition of affairs in the Northern District was quite another matter. Esteban Cantú accepted almost none of the federal appointees Carranza sent to the territory and often ignored the laws emanating from the Constitutionalist government. He generally acted independently of

Carranza and at times made statements that should have come only from the nation's executive. Cantú was effectively out of reach of the federal government and possessed funds enough to win the good will of his troops and followers.

While he governed Baja California Norte as he pleased, the territory became a refuge for anti-Constitutionalists of all stripes who despised the first chief personally and denigrated his rule freely and publicly. Constitutionalists reporting on the situation in the Northern District found it a tyranny where the political sympathies of the territory's native sons were ignored as Cantú gathered about him sworn enemies of the Carranza government and the 1917 Constitution. He was able to build a military establishment of one thousand regular and volunteer troops, supplied with artillery, machine guns, and one million rounds of ammunition. Cantú's small army was well equipped and paid in gold. Additionally, he generally had little difficulty smuggling arms across the border from California.

Until 1920 the government of Baja California Norte maintained an attitude of independence toward the Carranza administration, but after the first chief's death on May 21 of that year, Cantú openly declared his loyalty to the regime of the assassinated president. When he refused to turn the governorship over to the appointee of interim President Adolfo de la Huerta, the leaders of the Agua Prieta revolt that ended Carranza's rule determined to unseat the insubordinate governor with military force. Although Cantú made public his intention of resisting, he had in fact lost much support in Baja California Norte and soon realized he would not be able to maintain himself in the face of the new Sonoran dynasty. On August 19, 1920, Colonel Esteban Cantú of the old Federal Army stepped down from the governorship and went quietly into exile. He was the last officer of the *Porfiriato* to lay down his arms.

CHAPTER I

CHAPULTEPEC

"Cantú es *huertista*"
—**ENRIQUE A. GONZÁLEZ**, Mexican Consul at San Diego

An American officer and five armed soldiers served as escort to the Mexican troops now crossing the desert toward California on the Southern Pacific Railroad, the surest and most rapid means of conveying them to Baja California Norte to suppress a revolt there led by the anarchists Ricardo and Enrique Flores Magón. With their own arms under guard by United States soldiers in a separate carriage, "the troops behaved with complete dignity, observing impeccable conduct."[1] On reaching Calexico, California, the Mexican corps of infantry and cavalry of the Seventeenth Battalion under command of Major Esteban Cantú retrieved their arms and mounts, including Cantú's own "El Travieso," arriving at Mexicali at seven o'clock on the morning of June 26, 1911, once more happily on Mexican soil.[2] The interim government of President Francisco de la Barra had easily obtained permission from the United States government to cross its territory, as the last thing Washington wanted was an anarchist rebellion aided by a group of International Workers of the World (IWW) *filibusteros* across the border from California. Secretary of State Philander C. Knox believed the US needed to grant the courtesy in order to protect United States property and lives in Mexico. With Cantú was Lieutenant Colonel Fidencio González, who continued on to Tijuana with one hundred troops while Cantú remained in Mexicali with the same number of men. Aside from the *Magonista* revolt, there had been no revolutionary activity in the Northern District of the peninsula, neither propaganda nor pronouncements in favor of Francisco I. Madero, who had launched the revolution which brought down the decaying dictatorship of Porfirio Díaz.[3]

By the time the troops arrived in Baja California, Governor Celso Vega had defeated the Magonista rebels and driven them across the border. Years earlier Vega had fought in various campaigns against the Seris on the Isla del Tiburón in the Gulf of California and against the Yaqui of Sonora, where he displayed such energy and dispatch that he received a decoration from the governor of Sonora. His superiors found him apt in discharging his duties and were always satisfied with his good civil and military conduct. In 1910 he was awarded the *Cruz de Honor de Tecera Clase por Constancia en el Servicio*. During the Magonista Rebellion, Colonel Vega fought the invaders in the Sierra de los Picachos between Mexicali and Tijuana, and at Aguacaliente south of Tijuana he completely defeated the *filibusteros*, retook Tijuana, and forced the rebels across the line, where they surrendered to United States military forces. He then moved on to Mexicali in early February 1911, but rain and a heavy snowfall delayed his march. When he engaged the invaders, he bravely exposed himself before the enemy, receiving three bullet wounds for his courage.[4]

When Cantú arrived in Mexicali, he found Rodolfo Gallego and 385 armed men in control of the town. According to Cantú, writing some years later, Gallego was a United States citizen and local rancher of "robust corpulence" who claimed to be a *maderista*. He also held that he was the deputy *jefe político* of Mexicali.[5] Gallego apparently had organized a group of volunteers who were equipped by the San Diego-Yuma railroad to evict the Magonista troops from Mexicali.[6] Cantú, on the other hand, believed Gallego's men to be the same *filibusteros* and Magonistas whom Colonel Celso Vega had previously defeated. Whatever their purpose, Cantú was able to disarm Gallego's followers with the aid of several inhabitants of Mexicali and a ruse. Should his officers be approached by anyone, they were to inform that person or persons that four hundred infantry had landed with two machine guns and that more troops from Ensenada and Tijuana were on the way. Gallego's men were disarmed without bloodshed, which pleased the citizens of Mexicali. Baja California Norte was pacified, and they were now able to return home from refuge they had taken across the border in Calexico.[7] The *Calexico Chronicle* reported that "Mexicali seems to be the most peaceful place on earth just now."[8]

This however was not exactly the truth. According to Cantú, Gallego managed to suborn a portion of the Seventeenth Battalion that contained a number of vile and worthless troops, ex-criminals from Quintana Roo and the prison of San Juan de Ulúa in the harbor of Veracruz. After their desertion, Cantú and Captain Gabriel Rivera, second in command, remained ever vigilant. Gallego's plan was to retake Mexicali, and he called for the assassination of Cantú and his officers. Jacinto Mora Nova, an Indian from Chiapas who was Cantú's assistant, had learned of the conspiracy as he served as Cantú's spy in the adobe building where the troops were lodged. Mora Nova informed Cantú that two sergeants and twenty men were planning to carry out the plan on the night of September 8, 1911. The plot was to begin when five pistol shots were fired in Calexico at midnight. Cantú and his officers were to be killed and the town retaken by Gallego. Major Cantú then had the sergeants and the twenty troops assembled in the station of the Inter-California Railway, which served as his headquarters, and gave them a patriotic lecture before a small Mexican flag that he had purchased in Calexico for five cents and placed in an empty inkwell on his desk. He suggested they would not wish to betray their flag or country, but as he was unarmed and was going to retire for the night, they could kill him while he slept. Then one of the conspirators declared that he now repented of his previous intentions. Cantú then ordered them to guard him while he slept, and apparently his talk with them worked, as they guarded him well and became his loyal followers. Gallego's plot to retake Mexicali had failed. The next day the Twenty-Fifth Battalion under the command of Colonel Francisco Vázquez arrived in Mexicali by way of ship from Manzanillo to Ensenada then overland to Mexicali. Colonel Vázquez became commander of the garrison at Mexicali until his departure in October, when Cantú resumed command. At nearly the same time that the Twenty-Fifth Battalion arrived, the Eighth Battalion under Lieutenant Colonel Juan Vázquez, brother of the commander of the Twenty-Fifth Battalion, reached Los Algodones on the Río Colorado near Yuma, and the Northern District was thus secure.[9]

Cantú's mounted patrols nevertheless continued to encounter small parties of armed men crossing the border. While his one hundred troops could not patrol every inch of the line, Cantú cleverly organized a "Secret Service" composed of fourteen- and fifteen-year-old boys of Mexicali who carried out their duties as spies with "intelligence and aptitude," their youth drawing no suspicion toward them.[10] In addition to the troops under his command, Cantú organized a group of mounted volunteers in Mexicali that came to be called the *Cuerpo de Caballería "Esteban Cantú,"* which aided him in maintaining order and in creating a climate of confidence and tranquility in the Northern District of Baja California.[11] Cantú also gained a sure knowledge of the topography of the Northern District in 1911, visiting Tijuana, Ensenada, and Tecate as well as Calexico and San Diego, the effort made easier thanks to his excellent horse, "El Travieso."[12]

Esteban Cantú Jiménez was born at Linares near Monterrey, Nuevo León, on November 27, 1881, to Juan Antonio Cantú and Francisca Jiménez. He entered the Colegio Militar at Chapultepec at age seventeen on December 30, 1897. The handsome young Cantú was of fair complexion, with blond hair, blue eyes, and of good, robust health when he entered the academy, though he did have a bout with the measles before graduation. During his years as a cadet he received neither merits nor demerits; his capability and application were described as regular, and his civil and military conduct good. He did well in his studies but had trouble with French.[13]

Cantú's record remained quite acceptable after leaving the academy as a lieutenant of cavalry in December of 1900. He was soon posted to Monterrey, and in 1903 to Torin, Sonora, where he fought against the Yaqui under the command of General Manuel Gordillo Escudero. By the time he was ordered to León, Guanajuato, he had risen to the rank of captain, serving under Colonel Vito Alessio Robles, his classmate at the Colegio Militar who would be sent by the federal government to relieve Cantú of the governorship in 1920. His record of service demonstrates that he possessed good intelligence and manners but was somewhat apathetic in the service. He received no admonition for his apparent apathy, and while he tried to correct this fault he had little success because it seemed to be part of his character. Captain Cantú knew his duties, carried them out aptly, and continued to demonstrate good military spirit, commanding his squadron well.[14]

His career was not entirely without incident, however. While he was Instructor of Reservists at the Villa de Guadalupe y Calvo, Chihuahua, Cantú got into a fracas with Jesús Palacios, a second lieutenant in the reserves. On leaving a dance at five o'clock in the morning on September 9, 1902, an altercation occurred, pistols came out, Cantú was wounded, and Palacios was arrested for having attacked Cantú, who soon recovered from his wound.[15] Cantú was clearly not at fault, but in another episode he behaved differently. In Ciudad Lerdo, Durango, on September 28, 1909, at 1:15 a.m., María Vera, proprietor of the *cantina* "La Puerta del Sol," asked Cantú to leave as it was past closing time. Not wishing to do so, the inebriated captain drew his sword and threatened and cursed her, but he did finally leave when a policeman, Francisco Hernández, insisted he do so. Cantú then went to the barracks and soon returned with his troop of cavalry and rode around the plaza until he encountered Hernández, whom he roundly insulted with a variety of interesting vocabulary. When confronted with the inspector general of police, Agustín Martínez, who later reported that this was not the only instance of the captain's inebriety, Cantú returned to his barracks. All this led to a military tribunal at which the captain claimed he had left the *cantina* immediately and peaceably, asserting he had been falsely accused. While there is much correspondence resulting from the tribunal, which began on October 28, the members of the tribunal claimed the documents were somehow lost and thus there was no case, Cantú being set at complete liberty. The "lost documents" are in his record of service, indicating that the tribunal opted to shield a fellow officer, a common occurrence in the Mexican Army of that day.[16]

After arriving in Baja California Norte under the command of General Manuel Gordillo Escudero, who was appointed governor and military commander of the Northern District on July 29, 1911, Cantú, now a major, continued to perform his duties well.[17] He was reported to be very attentive and respectful in handling the men in his command and used discretion, prudence, and energy in maintaining the peace in Mexicali.[18] While Cantú was tending to his duties, the governorship of the Northern District became something of a revolving door. Gordillo Escudero requested to be relieved because of the bitter attacks upon him from the municipal trustees of Ensenada, the territorial capital. He noted that the problems in Baja California Norte were grave because a small group of people were exploiting the district to the detriment of honest citizens. Huge concessions had been made to foreign companies during the *Porfiriato*, while unscrupulous North Americans were in league with local judges. He had opposed horse racing, gambling dens, saloons, and prostitution, which he called the cancer of Baja California Norte, but the local authorities permitted such vice in order to lay taxes upon it. Gordillo Escudero claimed to have a clean record but now suffered defamation and calumny, accused of being a thief and ruffian.[19] The *San Diego Union* corroborated his plea, noting the lawlessness in Tijuana and the smuggling operations along the border.[20]

Gordillo Escudero had had a clean service record for thirty years. He was born in Mexico City on December 14, 1864, attended the National Preparatory School, and entered the army as a sergeant, working his way through the ranks and making brigadier general in April 1911. He served in a variety of commands, performing his duties well in all of them, and seems to have been something of a workhorse. Gordillo Escudero was credited with valor and was respectful to his superiors, but he tended to preponderate in everything and was severe with his troops, who respected him timorously.[21]

When the general left for Mexico City to clear himself of charges of embezzlement, Carlos Ptanik became interim governor. Once exonerated of the accusation, Gordillo Escudero resigned the governorship on December 21, 1912. President Francisco I. Madero then appointed José Dolores Espinosa y Ayala governor on February 7, 1913. After the overthrow and assassination of Madero and the accession of General Victoriano Huerta to the presidency, the officers and men of the garrison of Baja California Norte accepted Huerta as the nation's leader, and Miguel V. Gómez became governor on March 17. The new governor began a persecution of all those in the Northern District who had been loyal to Madero but, as he was a follower of Félix Díaz, was replaced by Colonel Francisco N. Vázquez in October when Díaz broke with Huerta. Colonel Fortunato Tenorio, commander of the artillery at Ensenada, later claimed that Gordillo Escudero ruled Baja California Norte as he would have in the days of Porfirio Díaz and that Ptanik governed in like manner. He claimed that the other governors dedicated themselves to pilfering the public treasury and shooting prisoners, and that Vázquez was the worst.[22]

While the rest of the nation joined the Constitutionalist forces led by Venustiano Carranza against the usurper Huerta, Cantú and other officers of the Twenty-Fifth Battalion stationed in the Northern District did not. Cantú himself was reported as an "*hombre muy valiente, absolutamente leal, conocedor del terreno y verdadero soldado*"(a very valiant man, absolutely loyal, knows the terrain and is a true soldier).[23] Cantú cooperated with the United States Cavalry of seventy troops operating north of the border to maintain the peace, which effort resulted in the capture of eleven armed and mounted men in late August 1913. This was the first serious attempt of the Constitutionalists to gain control of Baja California Norte, and it was rather feeble. Colonel Luis Hernández led a small force to dislodge the Twenty-Fifth Battalion, but Cantú with 120 troops and twenty auxiliary cavalry easily defeated it on the left bank of the Río Colorado on September 17, 1913.[24]

The next threat Cantú had to face was from Rodolfo Gallego, whom he had easily disarmed when he first arrived in Mexicali. Gallego, who lived in Calexico and owned a small ranch along the international boundary a short distance from Mexicali, had feigned friendship toward Cantú but had not forgotten his disgrace at the hands of the military commander.[25] Gallego, who had joined the Constitutionalist cause, was considered a dangerous man and was reportedly hatching a plot to take Mexicali and Los Algodones on the Río Colorado near Yuma, but Cantú knew this and was more than prepared to deal with the situation. Gallego was to have no more success than Hernández, as Cantú completely defeated his force of some two hundred men in a skirmish at La Islita on the Río Colorado on November 14, 1913. Another seventy men struck at Sharp's Heading forty miles southeast of Mexicali, but they were also routed. Gallego lost a great quantity of arms and munitions, and with his force completely dispersed, he abandoned his men in a cowardly manner.[26] For his victory Huerta promoted Cantú to lieutenant colonel and awarded him *La Cruz de Valor y Abnegación*. The thirty-two-year-old *regiomontano* had done well.[27]

After the Constitutionalist forces of Venustiano Carranza triumphantly entered Mexico City, Colonel Fortunato Tenorio carried out a *coup d'état* against Governor Vázquez on August 25, 1914, put the governor in jail, and swore his allegiance to Carranza. Tenorio claimed that Vázquez had exploited the garrison at Ensenada, forcing the men to spend their money in the small shop and *cantina* which Vázquez had opened in the garrison's quarters, not allowing them to spend their soldier's pay anywhere else. This was not the only instance of such corruption in Mexico's military at the time. Tenorio forced the now ex-governor to return hundreds of thousands of ill-gotten pesos and sent him packing across the border. Carranza then appointed Tenorio military governor of Baja California Norte.[28]

Tenorio, not wishing to demonstrate any political ambition, named David Zárate *jefe político* of the Northern District and Carranza confirmed the appointment. Zárate, a graduate of Santa Clara College in California, had been mayor of Ensenada during the presidency of Madero. In an interview with the *San Diego Union*, Zárate declared that he was not seeking the governorship of the Northern District, as he was a businessman, not a politician. As he put it, "Just now I am far too busy putting down cement sidewalks, improving our municipal water supply and building up the finances of the city for similar improvements, urban and rural—crying public needs—to bother with politics."[29]

As the regime of Victoriano Huerta passed out of existence in the Northern District, the *huertista* officials of Mexicali crossed the line to Calexico as did Cantú, who later related that a delegation of the citizens of Mexicali and the Twenty-Fifth Battalion entreated him to return and take charge of the rather fluid situation. Cantú had been preparing to depart for Monterrey to visit his family, but he cancelled those plans, returned to Mexicali, and declared martial law, his troops remaining loyal to him. According to Cantú, they had not been paid for some months; therefore he levied a forced loan of $7,500 upon the citizens of Mexicali to provide the troops their back pay (United States dollars being the common currency in the Northern District at that time). Colonel Enrique Anaya y Vasconcelos arrived on August 24 and informed Cantú that he was the Constitutionalist Governor and military commander of Baja California Norte. Anaya y Vasconcelos was a native of Sonora, had taken part in the social movement at Cananea, Sonora, in 1906, for which he was later considered one of the precursors of the revolution, although the connection between Cananea and the events of 1910 have been challenged as tenuous. He later served Governor José María Maytorena of Sonora. Anaya y Vasconcelos now demanded that Cantú deliver the Mexicali garrison into his hands. Negotiations ensued to no avail, as Cantú claimed Anaya y Vasconcelos had no proper credentials. Cantú declared he would turn over command of his force to any *carrancista* commander who had them, and ordered Anaya y Vasconcelos out of the Mexicali Valley.[30]

Meanwhile the Convention of Aguascalientes had formed a new government under President Eulalio Gutiérrez, which appointed the *sonorense* Major Baltasar Avilés governor and military commander on September 3, 1914, David Zárate retiring to private life on the seventeenth. The Convention Government soon dissolved into a civil war between the followers of Venustiano Carranza and those of Pancho Villa, the real force behind President Gutiérrez, who at length capitulated to the *carrancista* government. Villa formed a pact with Governor José María Maytorena of Sonora and authorized him to arrange affairs in Baja California Norte, granting the forces there all guarantees, the officers retaining their current rank. Maytorena was also to appoint the military commandant for the Northern District. General Felipe Ángeles soon arrived in Baja California Norte. Ángeles, something of an intellectual who had studied artillery in France and had recently served as rector of the Military Academy at Chapultepec, Colegio Militar, was the political leader of Villa's Division of the North, possessed a national view of the revolution, and served as Villa's diplomatic arm in arranging alliances. He now formed a pact with the senior officers of the Twenty-Fifth Battalion, as he had with Maytorena. Parties to the agreement included Tenorio, whose allegiance to Carranza was fickle at best, and Cantú, all of whom recognized Villa's leadership, and thus the Twenty-Fifth Battalion continued to preserve its integrity from the days of the *Porfiriato*. Avilés was to remain governor of the Northern District, while Cantú became military commander at Mexicali. Villa then ordered Tenorio to Sonora with his artillery to combat the *carrancista* force under command of Plutarco Elías Calles. Tenorio, recognized by all as an excellent artillery officer, greeted Calles with a tremendous bombardment at Naco, Sonora, delaying the capture of Guaymas for twenty-three days before returning to Ensenada.[31]

The handsome Fortunato Tenorio, with black eyes and brownish hair, entered the Colégio Militar in October 1900 at age eighteen. He was found not to be the best cadet, and after receiving his commission was found not to be the best soldier, evoking a waggish character who enjoyed a good time lubricated with much drinking. His service record reports that he was insubordinate, disrespectful, apathetic, late to rise in the morning, faked illness, and often forgot to carry his pistol. He did at length mature, and in the battle of the village of El Mulato in Chihuahua in April 1911 he fought with zeal and intelligence. In Baja California, Gordillo Escudero reported that Tenorio had a good aptitude for carrying out his duties and was of calm valor and quick initiative. With age he was acquiring seriousness and circumspection, and while he remained an affable fellow he was now esteemed by his superiors, comrades, and subordinates.[32]

On November 24, 1914, the *villista* governor of Sonora, José María Maytorena, now holding the rank of general commanding the western military zone, which included Baja California, ordered Avilés to send 380 troops from the garrison at Ensenada to Guaymas. They departed the next day on the steamer *Manuel Herrerías* with Lieutenant Colonel Arnulfo Cervantes in command. After heading south some distance, the captain of a ship heading north informed them that the warship *Guerrero* was at

Magdalena Bay with orders to capture the *Manuel Herrerías*. Colonel Cervantes and his officers then decided to return to Ensenada, but Governor Avilés refused them permission to leave the ship and arrested Cervantes and the other officers of the troop. The *Manuel Herrerías* slipped out to sea on the night of November 28 and tried to let the men disembark along the coast between Ensenada and Tijuana, but heavy seas prevented this. The ship then returned to Ensenada, the men intending to attack the city. They found this unnecessary, as Major Avilés and the rest of the garrison of three hundred troops had departed for Tijuana with Colonel Cervantes and the other officers under arrest. The garrison there had revolted rather than obey orders to march overland to join Villa, orders that Avilés had received from Maytorena. Before leaving Ensenada Avilés had stripped the government offices of fifty thousand pesos, and upon arrival at Tijuana he looted the customs house.[33]

All now depended upon Esteban Cantú, the ambitious military commander of the Mexicali garrison, who had been waging a silent battle with the politically inept Avilés from the day the latter had been appointed governor. Effectively in control of the Mexicali Valley, which was rapidly becoming the economic center of the Northern District of Baja California, Cantú held the advantage in any struggle with Avilés, who maintained himself at the territorial capital of Ensenada. Avilés further weakened his position by preferring to live with his family in San Diego, California, during the greater part of his brief administration.[34] Cantú broke with Avilés in mid-November, when Avilés sent Lieutenant Rafael Guerra to Mexicali to serve as *jefe político*. Cantú refused to recognize him as such and sent him packing back to Ensenada. When Governor Avilés arrived in Mexicali on November 20 to investigate, he insisted that Guerra be accepted as *jefe político*, but Cantú refused to permit Guerra's return. While Maytorena was certain of Avilés's loyalty, he was no longer confident of Cantú's. He believed the *carrancistas* were trying to win Cantú over to their camp. Cantú had opposed sending Tenorio and his artillery to Guaymas, and when Maytorena ordered him to send some of his troops to Ensenada, Cantú refused, thereby ignoring the pact he had made with the Division of the North.[35] Within a few days, the garrisons at Ensenada and Tijuana mutinied, and Avilés found himself camped before Tijuana with three hundred men along with Colonel Cervantes and the other officers he had placed under arrest, who were now sentenced

Colonel Esteban Cantú. *Courtesy of Special Collections, University of California, San Diego.*

to be shot for insubordination. Avilés had sent the hapless Lieutenant Guerra to negotiate with Cantú, but the military commander of Mexicali was so little impressed that he placed the lieutenant in jail and ordered him to be shot within eighteen hours. Avilés lost all control when Major Miguel Santa Cruz arrested him for not having paid his troops, but Avilés slipped away to San Diego, never to return.

❖ ❖ ❖

Maytorena had ordered both Avilés and Cantú to suspend all troop movements in the hope of avoiding conflict. While Avilés agreed, Cantú once more ignored Maytorena's orders and instead ordered troops from Mexicali, Tecate, and Ensenada to march on Tijuana. Cantú then sent what appeared to Maytorena a haughty telegram requesting the meaning of his instructions and continued his march to Tijuana. Cantú arrived at Tijuana on December 9, 1914, with 175 well-equipped men, and the whole affair was settled without a shot being fired. Santa Cruz held out as long as he could despite his break with Avilés, but when Cantú cut off his only escape save crossing the border, he gave his men permission to surrender, as they had not eaten all day. Cantú provided for the troops who surrendered to him. With the garrisons of Ensenada, Tijuana, and Mexicali, Cantú now had five hundred troops under his command. Cantú assured the loyalty of the men of the Twenty-Fifth Battalion as well as the federal employees at Ensenada when he sent $8,000 in gold "double eagles" to cover their back pay. Colonel Esteban Cantú was now master of the territory of Baja California Norte. Lieutenant Colonel Cervantes and his fellow officers were given their liberty, crossed the border, and placed themselves under Maytorena's orders.[36]

While Avilés and a few hangers-on such as Colonel Fortunato Tenorio attempted to recruit Mexicans and Mexican-Americans in a vain effort to regain control of Baja California Norte and in open violation of the neutrality laws of the United States, Cantú moved the capital of the territory from Ensenada to Mexicali and declared himself governor. Maytorena had requested instructions from Villa as to what should be done in Baja California Norte but received none. Because of the fighting in Sonora, Villa could send no troops to the Northern District. In order to resolve the crisis and in the hope of keeping Cantú in his orbit, Pancho Villa soon recognized him as governor of Baja California Norte. Thus when a commission headed by Jorge U. Orozco arrived to oversee the dissolution of the Twenty-Fifth Battalion on the part of the Constitutionalist government in late December, it found Cantú in complete control.[37] Consul Adolfo Carrillo of Los Angeles placed much of the onus for the situation upon Orozco, who squandered the funds that were to be used to disband the ex-federal troops in the Northern District, but Carrillo perhaps was ignoring the troops' loyalty to Cantú.[38]

Baja California Norte in 1910 was similar to the rest of Mexico's north because of its distance from the populous center. As with the other northern states, there had never been a sedentary indigenous population in the Northern District, which in fact was sparsely populated. Just as the Sierra Madre Occidental closed Sonora off from the rest of the republic and made that state's economic ties with Arizona stronger than those with the rest of Mexico, so Baja California Norte had an economic bond with California that was even stronger. All the territory's cattle and cotton were sold to buyers north of the border, and it was no wonder that the United States dollar was the common currency.[39]

When Cantú arrived in Mexicali in 1910, the small municipality was well on its way to becoming an important agricultural hub for the Mexicali Valley, which is an extension of the Imperial Valley of California. The first water entered the irrigation works on the Mexican side of the international boundary in June 1901, and by 1910 residents were growing the first cotton, the production of which reached fifty thousand acres by 1917. Much of this amazingly fertile land was owned by the Colorado River Land Company, which had gained control of some 835,000 acres on which it planned to grow cotton by means of irrigation. The property surrounded Mexicali on three sides, making the town's growth uncertain and, in the first years of the Cantú administration, a thorn in the governor's side. The second largest holding was that of the Southern Pacific Railroad's Inter-California Line, which ran through Baja California Norte. Completed in 1909, it crossed the line at Los Algodones near Yuma, Arizona, and re-entered the United States at Calexico, California, across the street from Mexicali. The company owned the land between the railroad and the international boundary, originally 55,192 acres. The land was held in Mexico under the name of Compañía de Terrenos y Aguas, S. A. The third holding was the 16,000 acres of the Cudahy Ranch located along the Inter-California Railway between Yuma and Mexicali. These were all owned by North American interests. Another large holding was the Mexican Land and Colonization Company, Ltd., generally referred to as "The English Company." This was a large tract along the peninsula's northern Pacific coast that was not successful because cultivation there relied on the inadequate rainfall of the region rather than on irrigation.[40]

In another concession the *Porfiriato* had granted Aurelio Sandoval of Los Angeles exclusive fishing rights in Baja California waters. His company, La Pescadora, S. A., also had the right to exploit the *guano* deposits on the islands in the Gulf of California and other islands along the Pacific Coast. The New Pedrara Onyx company was given the right to extract onyx on Cedros Island in the Bahia de Sebastián Vizcaíno, while another company received whaling rights in the waters of Baja California. That these concessions were granted to foreign nationals was a great danger for Mexico.[41]

Excepting the fertile Mexicali Valley, the wheat-growing lands near Ensenada, and the Plains of San Quintín, the terrain of Baja California Norte is rugged and mountainous, though there are a few small isolated valleys in the interior. Two mountain ranges, the Sierra de Juárez, which extends to the international boundary west of Mexicali, and the Sierra de San Pedro Mártir, which runs in a line south of the Sierra de Juárez, have peaks of over four thousand feet, with the San Mártir having two peaks that are ten thousand feet above sea level. The precipitous slopes of the ranges and their limited drainage basins cause the rivers of Baja California Norte to be short in their rush to the Pacific Ocean. East of this mountain range is a level desert basin or great sink known as the Laguna Salada, which in Cantú's time was fed by the overflows of the Río Hardy and the Río Pescadero, which were actually overflow mouths of the Río Colorado. Traveling overland with Governor Esteban Cantú via automobile, the philosopher José Vasconcelos noted the hot springs and volcanic solfataras emitting vapors and sublimates and thought the area appeared to be the navel of the world. He felt lost in this land a little below sea level until arriving at the mouth of the Río Colorado, where its red waters met the blue of the Gulf of California. Vasconcelos found neither trees nor habitations as far as the eye could see, but rather the most complete serenity and solitude in a panoramic desert recalling the first days of creation.[42]

Between the Laguna Salada and the Mexicali Valley runs the steep Sierra de las Cocopas, which ends at Signal Mountain near the border just west of Mexicali. This range marked the western boundary of the irrigation system in the days of Cantú. The Mexicali Valley, which lies somewhat below sea level, is the ancient fill of the Río Colorado containing about two million acres of fertile, irrigable land. The valley lies in a great triangle running from Yuma on the northeast to Signal Mountain on the west and south to the end of the Sierra de las Cocopas. Baja California Norte's most important port was at Ensenada, which lies on the Bahia de Todos los Santos. There was not a good road connecting the port with Tijuana and Mexicali, as this topography made road building difficult in 1910, and therefore political control of the region was tenuous.[43]

The dearth of good roads was matched by a lack of schools in the Northern District of the peninsula. The first school was established by the *Ayuntamiento* of Santo Tomás, a town south of Ensenada, using export duties to establish a school as early as 1843; it is considered to be a pioneering institution of public instruction in Baja California Norte. A private school was founded in Santo Tomás in 1869, but it closed and moved to Real del Castillo in 1873. A Commercial High School was established in Ensenada in 1896, but from that year until the governorship of Esteban Cantú the development of public education saw little advancement.[44]

In 1910 the population of Mexicali was 462, while that of its sister city, Calexico, was about 800, and the vice trade that would later make Mexicali and Tijuana tourist attractions had already begun. By 1909 there were thirty-four saloons in Mexicali, each replete with either a gambling hall or brothel for the convenience of mostly North American visitors. Colonel Celso Vega, *jefe político* at the time, received a percentage of the profits for allowing the trade to exist. While the residents of Calexico and Mexicali complained, nothing was done to better the situation. The *gente decente* (decent people) also complained about Vega's lack of vigor in dealing with a local outbreak of smallpox. Ensenada, the mining center of northern Baja California, did not suffer from the vice trade, but the city's 2,170 inhabitants needed much in the way of infrastructure, as did the entire territory.[45]

The *Porfiriato* had paid little heed to Baja California, especially its Northern District so far from the metropolis, but a 1912 *Nueva Era* report, "La Situación Real de la Baja California," found the peninsula rich in mineral wealth, with onyx, mica, and gypsum, while its islands contained large phosphate deposits and its waters were blessed with pearls and bountiful fish. The report concluded that Baja California had much potential and urged the government to focus attention upon it. "No sacrifice, no hindrance, no expenditure should be curtailed, in order to make of this peninsula what it should become in fifty years." The report also noted what a perfect naval base Magdalena Bay would make, especially when the Panama Canal was finished.[46]

As David Zárate lamented in an interview with the *San Diego Union* during his brief turn as *jefe político* of the Northern District in 1914:

> Look about you on all sides. What do you see but the greatest need of wise and economical expenditure on the public service everywhere? In the last three or more years our public treasury has received literally millions from an extremely low tax rate. And what have the people received in return? Nothing except a jerry-built "opera" house, an iron statue of Benito Juárez and a so-called city hall of "dobe" and rococo plaster. Meanwhile we are pumping as much filth as water into the rotten water system; the community is but an aggregation of cesspools because of the lack of a sewer system; the ungraded streets are either dust-heaps or mud-puddles, according to whether it rains or shines; a rancher can scarcely haul his crop to market because of the almost utter absence of passable roads; there is not a civic hospital on the peninsula; and what little trade or commerce we do here is handicapped at every turn.[47]

This was the Baja California Norte that Esteban Cantú began to rule as a private kingdom in 1914. A territory with few passable roads, fewer schools, not one hospital, little infrastructure to speak of, one railroad owned by a North American company, enormous tracts of land owned by foreigners, and a tax base insufficient to effect any improvement. Under the government of Cantú all this was about to change dramatically.

CHAPTER II

"THE KINGDOM OF CANTÚ"

"Cantú es *villista*"
—**ENRIQUE A. GONZÁLEZ**, Mexican Consul at San Diego

Colonel Esteban Cantú declared himself governor of Baja California Norte in a manifesto on October 15, 1915, in which he called Victoriano Huerta a usurper and declared that the people and the garrison of the Northern District had implored him to form a government, which he organized "under the purest Constitutional regime."[1] President Eulalio Gutiérrez of the Convention Government officially appointed him governor shortly thereafter. Following the disintegration of the brief Gutiérrez regime, Pancho Villa recognized Cantú as governor on January 20, 1915, but there was some question as to his actual political adherence.[2] Enrique A. González, the *carrancista* consul at San Diego, considered Cantú a *villista*, but also stated that he would not be surprised if the governor declared himself to be in league with Félix Díaz, noting that the governor had gone to San Antonio, Texas, to confer with him. González later learned that Cantú was completely in accord with Victoriano Huerta, who had returned from exile and was on his way to confer with the governor when he was arrested in El Paso, Texas, which put an end to the former dictator's political career. On yet another occasion González held that "Cantú is nothing more than a *panista,*" that is to say, a sponger, one who hungers after money.[3]

Cantú was indeed doing all in his power to raise money for the support of his government. He renewed the exclusive fishing rights in the waters of Baja California that Aurelio Sandoval, one of the groomsmen in Cantú's wedding, had won during the *Porfiriato,* but had lost under the Carranza government, the license fee now being paid at Ensenada. Consul Adolfo Carrillo of Los Angeles urged Carranza to decree that no local *jefe* grant such rights to foreign capitalists. Other concessions to extract minerals and onyx granted under the fallen regime of Porfirio Díaz were renewed, as were exclusive whaling rights, all of which required a licensing fee paid to the government of the Northern District. Cantú licensed a United States firm to harvest sargasso in the waters of Baja California for making potash, and in the next two years potash plants were established under the aegis of the government of the Northern District on islands in the Bay of Todos Santos and at El Sauzal on the bay near the port of Ensenada. The potash plants became a very lucrative business, especially after the United States entered World War I. On a smaller scale Cantú granted a permit to a Dutch firm to explore the Isla de Cedros for the purpose of extracting meerschaum, hydrous magnesium silicate, from which a certain type of fine smoking pipe is made. Cantú granted an exclusive license to Alberto Mascareñas to exploit the *guano* on the islands off the coast of Baja California Norte, for which he received $500 monthly. Governor Cantú further increased his revenue by placing duties on the importation of alkaloids, and it was estimated that the cotton harvest of 1916 would fetch Cantú $480,000 in United States dollars from export fees.[4]

This money of course should have gone to the federal government. Teodoro Frezieres, who later replaced Carrillo as Mexico's consul in Los Angeles, noted that Cantú had no authority to do any of this and mistakenly believed that the governor realized his hold on the Northern District was soon coming to an end so that he hoped to quickly amass all the money he could under cover of claiming to be a Constitutionalist. Frezieres had been chief of police briefly in Veracruz and later served as Mexico's commercial agent in the United States. A man who easily made friends, he was remarkably clean cut and keen, speaking English fluently. "Tall, slender and fit in appearance with sharply cut features and a black eye [sic] which doesn't lack humor," Frezieres believed that Cantú had no political convictions and lacked honor, loyalty, and honesty.[5]

Fortunato Tenorio, who hated Cantú for having outwitted him in the quest for control of Baja California Norte, accused the governor of turning the territory into a center of prostitution, gambling, opium dens, horse racing, and *cantinas* that were open day and night and claimed that all this provided Cantú with revenue. Bullfights and cockfights were taxed one hundred and fifty gold pesos each, respectively, while all *cantinas* paid three hundred gold pesos each month. The governor also levied a head tax of one dollar to be paid monthly by Mexican and foreigner alike. Many members of the Russian colony of some one thousand wheat farmers near San Quintín were forced to leave because of heavy taxation, and of course Cantú controlled the customs duties, revenue that rightfully belonged to the federal government. The governor had no authority to permit the fishing and whaling monopolies which the Carranza government had previously cancelled, nor to grant any concessions or licenses, and Carranza ordered his consul general in San Francisco to notify the North American promoters of the race track in Tijuana of this fact.[6]

Perhaps Cantú's most egregious effort to raise money was his clandestine arrangement with E. K. Cassab of San Diego to sell fifty thousand of the wild goats from the Isla de Guadalupe, a small island offshore from Isla San Gerónimo and Isla Sacramento in Rosario Bay. Cassab represented a number of meat packers in the United States and agreed to pay Cantú one dollar a head. Secretary of Foreign Relations Eliseo Arredondo found this criminal. Nevertheless, hunters were sent to the island and the first shipment of 1,587 goats arrived in San Diego on the *Mary Dodge* on July 29, 1915. A determined effort was made to put an end to the scandalous business when Consul González of San Diego swore before a notary public that it was illegal and that all persons having the wild goats in possession would be prosecuted for theft. González then employed an attorney who sent a letter to Cassab to inform him of the illegality of accepting any of the wild goats and sought out a United States Marshal in an attempt to stop the illegal purchase of the goats, 3,582 of which had already been delivered. Mexico City informed Secretary of State Robert Lansing about the problem, explaining that the goats were stolen federal property, and requested that Cantú's accomplices in the United States be stopped, but at length it took the pleading of José Cantú and his sisters before their brother agreed to stop the shameless affair.[7]

Consul Manuel Paredes of Calexico, who generally referred to Cantú as a traitor, reported that Cantú was gathering much revenue, enough he believed to cause difficulties for the Constitutionalist government. Paredes urged that something be done to end Cantú's grip on Baja California Norte, suggesting that a mere fifty men could launch an attack from the United States side of the border and Cantú's disgruntled troops

Governor Esteban Cantú in his office. *Courtesy of the Archivo Histórico Estatal de Baja California, Mexicali, BC.*

would join in against him. Adolfo Carrillo of Los Angeles held that it was a matter of life or death for the territory to come under Constitutionalist rule. Consul General Ramón de Negri in San Francisco, who later served in Obregón's cabinet as Secretary of Agriculture, agreed. He believed that Cantú was a real danger and that a force should be sent to remove him, but the consuls had been misinformed. Cantú had three hundred troops in Mexicali, one hundred each in Ensenada, Tijuana, and Tecate, twenty-five at Los Algodones, and smaller forces in the lesser towns of the Northern District, for a total of about seven hundred men, armed with six machine guns, one million rounds of ammunition, and ample artillery. Moreover, the troops were well and promptly paid each day with United States gold "double eagles." They were often referred to as the best-paid soldiers in the world; they were Cantú's *gente*, his men, loyal to him and to no one else.[8]

De Negri further informed Arredondo that a *villista* consul in Calexico was in charge of the archives of the consulate and was issuing consular invoices and other documents requiring a legal certificate under the orders of Cantú. Arredondo directed De Negri to urge the respective authorities of California to close the *villista* consulate and turn the archives over to Consul Paredes, the duly appointed representative of the Constitutionalist government. The foreign secretary informed United States Secretary of State Robert Lansing of the matter, and the department notified the proper authorities that the *villista* agent had no authority to act in a consular capacity and that the archives be placed in Paredes's possession, which was soon accomplished.[9]

Cantú meanwhile was arresting anyone who claimed to be a Constitutionalist. Juan A. Mateos and Carlos Palacios, ex-consul and chancellor at San Diego respectively, were so arrested but escaped their imprisonment at Tijuana on January 21, 1915, under cover of a very dark night and heavy rain, reaching San Diego after wandering lost for thirty-six hours, ill, barefoot, and clothing torn to pieces. Celestino Ruiz, Constitutionalist consul at Calexico before Paredes, crossed the border in early January to Mexicali to greet Cantú, believing the governor to be a coreligionist, but was immediately arrested for his courtesy call. Ruiz was still in prison one month later, as he was unable to produce a letter on his behalf from someone with sufficient stature to impress Cantú. Sánchez Hernández, a former teacher in the schools of Ensenada, sought refuge in San Diego for his Constitutionalist ideas. David Zárate also sought asylum in California in December 1915 and urged Carranza to appoint a civilian government in the Northern District. Zárate remained a constant critic of Cantú and considered his government and its actions illegal. Cantú had some cause for concern as Baltasar Avilés and others were conspiring to overthrow him and had been actively recruiting men when they were arrested by United States authorities for violating the neutrality laws. Adolfo Carrillo, calling Avilés a *maytorenista* and Cantú a *huertista* and *ex-federal*, informed his government that Baja California Norte was completely outside the reach and action of the revolution.[10] To further protect himself Cantú had reached an agreement with the authorities of Calexico, who for a time in April 1915 agreed to arrest and arbitrarily extradite to Mexicali any person whom Cantú accused of having committed a crime or misdemeanor of whatever nature in Baja California Norte. Writing to Galen Nichols, district attorney for Imperial County, California, Consul Paredes declared such an agreement to be a matter for international law, requiring a treaty, and declared the agreement illegal and unenforceable. Nichols responded that he had no knowledge of such an agreement, but Paredes managed to obtain a copy of the arrangement. The youthful looking Secretary of Foreign Relations Eliseo Arredondo, who sported a bow tie and a handlebar mustache to match his thick head of hair, requested that the Department of State look into the matter and was informed that a report of such an agreement was "false and without foundation," and that the report most likely originated from apprehensive political foes of Cantú.[11] The governor also requested the director general of customs in Washington to restrain various Constitutionalists in Calexico, including Consul Paredes, and extradite them to Mexicali. Cantú was beginning to act as though he were the head of a sovereign state, or at least independent, declaring that he would aid neither Villa nor Carranza in their struggle for power.[12] In October Cantú sent a circular to all the banks, authorities, and principal merchants of Calexico informing them that he no longer recognized the Convention government and that he intended to remain neutral regarding the conflict on the mainland until the last minute, when he would recognize the government that emerged from the civil war raging between Villa and Carranza. Although Villa was his most immediate problem, Carranza's government had lost control in many regions of the country and had little power over the revolutionary generals. Cantú could survive only through an independent stance, as the *carrancistas* could not tolerate any among their midst from the old regime. *Maderistas* were also suspect for their political errors.[13]

In part because the Constitutionalist army was needed elsewhere, the Constitutionalist government was unable at this time to bring Baja California Norte under its control, but it was able to cause the recalcitrant

Fiesta in honor of Governor Cantú. *Courtesy of Special Collections, University of California, San Diego.*

governor some difficulty. As there were no banks as yet in Mexicali, Cantú had deposited customs receipts, fines, and other revenue in two Calexico banks, but the Carranza government obtained a temporary restraining order to prevent Cantú from withdrawing the money, some $60,000. The United States border patrol meanwhile kept a close watch to prevent Cantú's soldiers from crossing the border to seize the money.[14]

Cantú had an erstwhile ally in his brother, José, who was a trusted follower of Venustiano Carranza, had served on the First Chief's staff, and had thrown in with the revolution from the very beginning. After conferring with Álvaro Obregón in Hermosillo, Sonora, in December 1915, José Cantú returned with the news that Obregón had agreed to confirm Colonel Esteban Cantú as governor of the Northern District until a successor was deemed necessary, and Cantú agreed to recognize the Carranza government on December 30. He gave a grand ball in homage to the First Chief and the commissioners sent to investigate the situation in Baja California Norte. The commission's report was favorable, and Cantú remained governor and military commander in the Northern District.[15]

Obregón also promised Cantú a promotion in return for the governor's support in his campaign of shadow boxing with Venustiano Carranza. After Villa's defeat Obregón continued his allegiance to Carranza on the assumption that he would follow the First Chief in the presidency. This gentlemen's agreement served both their purposes but was rather frail, as they did not trust one another. Obregón had gained the support of Governor Plutarco Elías Calles of Sonora, among other military leaders, and it was perhaps natural to seek that of the governor of Baja California Norte as well. Since Cantú had been recognized as governor by Huerta, Villa, and Gutiérrez, he could easily accept a promotion from the hero of Celaya. As commander of the Army of the Northwest Obregón had the power to promote Cantú and promised to do so, but it seems he changed his mind on the matter and the promised promotion was not forthcoming. Cantú's reaction was bitter. In the cantina of Sr. Rivas in Mexicali on June 14, 1916, Cantú, reportedly in a state of inebriation with two companions, declared that Obregón had betrayed him and that all Obregón and Carranza wanted to do was steal.[16]

José Cantú continued to be his brother's link with Mexico City throughout Esteban's governorship. While remaining loyal to Carranza, José Cantú managed to maintain his loyalty to his brother as well, keeping him informed of events in the capital.[17] Governor Esteban Cantú was playing a game with the central government and made every attempt to pose as a sincere *carrancista*. He was apparently confident that the government believed him and always claimed that he obeyed the central government. Juan Velázquez, the representative in the Chamber of Deputies from Baja California Norte, declared in 1919 that Cantú obeyed and complied with all laws of the central government and was one of the most loyal servants of the republic.[18] The reality was that true *carrancistas* in the territory were threatened into silence, and Cantú appointed and dismissed federal post office officials and even school teachers as he saw fit. When his brother José arrived as Inspector of Customs with a group of employees, the governor refused to accept any of the appointees other than his brother, and a reading of the *Periódico Oficial* of the territorial government indicated that every employee of the Northern District was anti-*carrancista*.[19] The *Calexico Chronicle* was correct in stating that "Cantú has been largely a law unto himself in the issuance of decrees, and it is probable that an order from Mexico City . . .will have but small effect."[20] *El Heraldo de México* agreed, noting that Cantú ran Baja California Norte like a fief and only pretended to bow to the central government, accepting scarcely any of its appointees. From time to time the government sent agents to check on the situation, but Cantú showered them with banquets, dances, and trips around the countryside in his personal automobile, a Packard. On returning to Mexico City they painted a rosy picture of the situation in the Northern District.[21]

While Cantú refused to accept appointees of the Constitutionalist government, he willingly agreed to Obregón's request to send him any artillery and machine guns that he did not need and refused to accept any payment for the donation, requesting merely fifty rifles in return. This sent Consul Teodoro Frezieres of Los Angeles, who believed Cantú should be removed from his post, into a tailspin. He suggested to Secretary of Foreign Relations Cándido Aguilar that if Cantú was able to obtain artillery and was willing to pass it on to the Constitutionalist cause, the Mexican Consulate should refrain from attempting to obstruct Cantú's arms trade and should perhaps do all in his power to assist him, as the central government was much in need of artillery.[22] Despite Cantú's bitterness toward Obregón, Cantú's behavior in this was a means of feigning loyalty toward the central government.

In reality Cantú was preparing to defend Baja California Norte from any possible invasion on the part of the Carranza government, and he had the military engineers to do it. He established permanent fortifications in Tijuana; the *Sierra de Tanamá,* about five miles east of Tecate; and the pass through the *Sierra de los Picachos*, a very strategic point defended by infantry, machine guns, and two pieces of field artillery. Any force landing at Ensenada would have to take *los Picachos* to get to Mexicali. The hill of Guadalupe near the port of San Felipe on the Gulf of California was also guarded. Cantú was trying to buy airplanes and had plans to buy a ship of war in Canada and arm it. Admiral Othon Blanco was in the Northern District willing to command it, and there were enough other ex-federal naval officers to man it.[23] In the end, however, Cantú was unable to bring his plan for a little navy to fruition.

In an effort to raise his military capacity, Cantú was actively recruiting Mexicans living across the border under the guise of hiring them to pick cotton; he had considerable success, as he paid every soldier in gold. To support his cavalry he was buying the best horses from local ranchers and had obtained about one thousand, according to one report. Governor Cantú was also quite active in smuggling arms and ammunition across the border. Aurelio Sandoval paid more than a license fee to fish the waters of Baja California, as every Sandoval fishing boat carried arms to Ensenada, often successfully, as reported by United States agents. Cantú was related to Sandoval by way of the Dato family of the Northern District. Pablo Dato, a German immigrant who claimed to be a naturalized United States citizen, was Cantú's father-in-law. Dato's sons Federico, Pablo, and Guillermo were active in running guns to Baja California Norte.[24]

J. M. Arriola, chief of the Mexican Secret Service in the United States, reported that the Dato brothers had $70,000 with which to buy munitions and were planning to ship them on the *Allenaire*, commanded by James Knowles. They intended to embark for San José del Cabo in Baja California Sur. With the aid of David Gershon of the United States Justice Department, the plan ended in failure when Federico Dato was arrested for violating the neutrality laws. According to Gershon, Arriola, and others keeping watch on Cantú, the governor was planning to gain control of the entire peninsula. Frezieres reported that Cantú had numerous agents in the Southern District advertising that he paid his employees in gold and urged Carranza to send a military force to Baja California Sur. Dato's arrest and the seizure of the *Allenaire* as well as Sandoval's *Pacific* put an end to the scheme.[25]

When the Querétaro Congress finished the 1917 Constitution, Governor Cantú promulgated the document in Baja California Norte and often expressed his loyalty to the Carranza government. After Carranza was elected president in March 1917, he appointed Cantú provisional governor and requested that he repair to Mexico City to report on his long term in office. Cantú replied that he would do so when the government appointed his successor and that he would always support the constituted government of Mexico.[26] On his own ground the independent governor behaved differently. On the occasion of his return to Mexicali from California, the local authorities, their friends, and others gave Cantú a banquet to which Manuel Paredes, Mexico's consul at Calexico, was also invited. He did not wish to attend, as he knew quite well the authorities of Mexicali disdained the Carranza government and that he himself was considered *persona non grata*, but at their insistence he at length agreed to attend. The banquet, which lasted from two o'clock in the afternoon until midnight, turned into a "*tremenda borrachera*," in which Cantú, "*excitado por el licor*," brought up an incident involving an outrage against the Mexican flag in Calexico by a group of United States citizens. Paredes related that Cantú was infuriated by the incident and condemned the act stentoriously in the vilest terms. The consul tried to mollify Cantú by pointing out that a celebratory dinner was perhaps not the proper moment for such an outburst. Cantú then turned upon Paredes, insulting him in *"terminos tabernarios,"* and called him a hypocrite, which the consul thought was not the proper way to treat a guest. Cantú then offered a toast and shouted out *"Viva Chiapas,"* no doubt referring to the revolt Félix Díaz was then trying to launch in that state. The governor's toast and his attack on the consul were applauded enthusiastically by the banqueteers. This was too much for Paredes, who got up and left the festivities immediately. J. Palacio, an agent of the Mexican Secret Service who was also at the banquet, corroborated Paredes's relation of the event.[27]

On other occasions Cantú could be quite charming. On visiting Baja California Norte, the philosopher José Vasconcelos noted that while Governor Cantú officially recognized Carranza as the head of state, he was in reality an island unto himself. Referring to Cantú as an ex-*porfirista,* Vasconcelos found his host affable, discreet, and correct in his behavior and admired the governor's great liberality in permitting Mexicans of all political stripes to enter and pass through the territory at will. Cantú invited Vasconcelos to his ranch, treating him to an exhibition of roping and horsemanship, and the following day took him on an excursion south of Mexicali to the mouth of the Río Colorado, driving over trackless terrain in his Packard chauffeured by Beneto Ceseña. Cantú sought to impress men of renown with his good nature and his well-run kingdom, and in the case of Vasconcelos and others his efforts paid dividends.[28]

Cantú's support of Carranza's opposition extended to the anti-Constitutionalist press in Baja California Norte and across the line in California. He supported *El Heraldo de México* of Los Angeles to the tune of $100 each month and gave financial aid to the huertista *Hispano-Americano* of San Diego and to *El Cronista,* which he himself published in Calexico.[29] *El Heraldo de México,* which was furious in its attacks on the government, organized the *Liga Protectora Mexicana de California,* an able and intelligent political effort to capture public opinion among the thousands of Mexicans in California. Behind this movement stood not only Cantú, but also such anti-*carrancistas* as Nemesio García Naranjo, Jorge Vera Estañol, both of whom had served Huerta as secretaries of education, along with Rodolfo Reyes, Francisco Olagível, and Félix Díaz. Their efforts were supported by vice revenues from Mexicali and Tijuana.[30] This was not unusual, as Carranza's government subsidized and controlled the press according to its whim, as had the *Porfiriato* before it.[31]

Although Baja California Norte continued to be a den of all elements hostile to Carranza's government, Cantú at times gave the impression that the Northern District was autonomous and had no connection with Mexico. He did as he pleased irrespective of instructions from the federal government, which had for example removed all import duties on agricultural and mining machinery entering Baja California Norte, and yet a levy on them continued to exist. Cantú continually made statements that should have come only from the nation's executive, and never sincerely recognized any of the governments emanating from the revolution, including Carranza's. The governor dictated his own laws; appointed judges, municipal presidents, and other officials in the territory; and established such onerous taxes that mining in the district nearly ceased. As Ben Franklin Fly, editor of the *Arizona Sentinel* of Yuma put it, "Cantú is his own master."[32] Cantú's actions were not unique. Plutarco Elías Calles, then governor of neighboring Sonora, chose to ignore those orders of Carranza's of which he did not approve, while Sinaloa governor Ángel Flores printed his own paper money.[33]

Cantú meanwhile employed men in his government who were enemies of the central government, appointing *huertistas* as municipal presidents in Mexicali and Ensenada against the wishes of the people of the region, who had proposed candidates who were native to the Northern District and identified with the revolution and the Carranza government. *Carrancistas* suffered harassment and imprisonment just for being *carrancistas*. Manuel Labastida, one of the principal businessmen of Ensenada, was so harassed that he closed his establishment and moved to La Paz in Baja California Sur. Juan de la Cruz Peralta, who had been the chief of a group of volunteers that had fought against the *magonista* invasion of Baja California Norte in 1911, was incarcerated for more than three months in Ensenada for bringing in some pro-*carrancista* newspapers from San Diego. Ramón Moyrón, another merchant of Ensenada, was jailed and fined for having shouted "*Viva Carranza.*"[34] Mexican exiles in California wrote to Carranza that Cantú was a genuine representative of reaction, that anti-Constitutionalists of all stripes were finding refuge in Baja California Norte, and that they denigrated the Carranza government openly and publicly.[35] One of the Mexican exiles in San Diego, David Zárate, requested permission from Plutarco Elías Calles to raise three to four hundred men to launch an attack on the Northern District for the Constitutionalist cause. Calles responded that as he was the military commandant of Sonora, he had no authority in Baja California Norte, and no such force was raised.[36]

Orders from Mexico City had little effect, and one source notes that the territory did not pay one single peso in taxes to Carranza's treasury, although another holds that Cantú frequently sent taxes to the federal government.[37] A more serious affront was Cantú's refusal to use Mexican coinage or currency of any vintage, using that of the United States instead. As paper money had suffered from inflation, Cantú ordered in January 1915 that all commercial transactions and salaries were to be paid in gold pesos or United States dollars at the rate of two pesos to the dollar. When Joaquín Aguirre Berlanga was sent to the Northern District to introduce the new currency of the central government, Cantú refused to accept it. Thus the United States dollar remained the medium of exchange during the Cantú years. To be fair, the close economic ties between northern Baja California and the United States made the use of dollars more convenient than treasonous. Nor did Cantú permit the use of federal postage stamps but rather suppressed them in November of 1915 and issued others under the aegis of the Distrito Norte.[38]

Cantú's territory became a refuge for various disaffected groups, among whom were former *huertistas*, *villistas*, and *felicistas*. The governor corresponded with Carranza's enemies in New York who represented Félix Díaz, and with Zapata, Villa, and especially Manuel Peláez, the revolutionary leader in the Tuxpan and Tampico oil fields. Peláez's brother Ignacio and Cantú's brother José had been in close contact for some time in the United States.[39] What José Cantú's dealings with Peláez were is uncertain, since Cantú had joined the revolution from its inception, was loyal to Carranza, and with the support of the Club Liberal Juan Álvarez was elected Baja California Norte's deputy to the Chamber of Deputies in 1917. José Cantú reported to Consul Frezieres that whenever he walked into his brother's office, Cantú and George C. Carothers, a confidential agent of the Department of State attached to Villa as the Department's ears, interrupted their conversation. The thirty-eight-year old Carothers was the United States consul at Torreón as well as a former agent of an express company, a grocer, and a real estate agent who enjoyed a particularly close relationship with Villa. The portly Carothers had immediate access to Villa, who trusted him particularly because he was corrupt. Frezieres believed Cantú was making some sort of a deal with Villa.[40]

Self-preservation led Cantú to favor revolt in Sonora. He held several conferences with Miguel Tarriba, an agent of Félix Díaz, in November and December of 1916 and early 1917, but while he aided the *felcistas* with money, arms, and munitions and provided a refuge in Baja California Norte, he was in contact with almost every anti-*carrancista* rebel in Mexico. The *felicistas* did not believe they could count on Cantú's aid in a frank manner, but the governor's instinct for self-preservation caused him to agree to aid the revolutionary leaders in Sonora so Carranza would not have a base there from which to attack him. Cantú made it a practice to aid any revolutionary group in that northwestern state. Sonora's isolation due to its distance from the center, the protection that the Sierra Madre Occidental afforded, and the disruption to its economy during the revolution was itself a bulwark against any effort on the part of the central government to gain control of Baja California Norte as troops could only be sent by sea or by rail through the United States.[41]

Frezieres informed Carranza of Cantú's association with this rebel group, expressing his opinion that Cantú was its leader. Frezieres also claimed that before his appointment the governor controlled the Mexican Consul at San Diego, and that the same was true of the consul at Los Angeles, both of whom spent the greater part of their time in Mexicali. The consul believed Cantú to be especially dangerous because he was out of reach of the government and possessed the necessary funds to win the good will of his followers.[42] Cantú openly admitted to P. M. Godchaux, who was an agent of the Bureau of Investigation of the United States Justice Department, that he intended to begin a revolution against Carranza in league with Villa and Peláez. The governor expected complete cooperation from Washington and believed he would have no difficulty importing the arms to secure the success of his revolution, which he predicted would be the largest Mexico had ever seen.[43]

This was not actually true. Cantú purchased ten machine guns in 1916 from Julio M. Trens and Samuel M. Vázquez, employees of William Hogge and Company of Los Angeles, which trafficked in arms. The guns were to be shipped to Mexicali when the United States arms embargo against Mexico was lifted, but Cantú had no success. Carranza had given orders to the Mexican consuls in Los Angeles, San Diego, and Calexico to prevent any shipment of arms or artillery to Baja California Norte. Trens

Plaza and Palacio Municipal in Mexicali. *Courtesy of Special Collections, University of California, San Diego.*

and Federico Dato were later arrested trying to move the contraband, which was shipped back to the company where it remained until 1919. United States authorities merely wanted to know who actually owned the machine guns. Cantú then hoped to sell them to the government of Mexico, which did not wish to become involved in the matter, and the whole affair was dropped at a cost to Cantú of $34,000 in United States currency. Consul Ramón de Negri considered Cantú very dangerous and wondered at the complete distraction of Carranza and his government regarding Baja California Norte with its ex-federal and reactionary officials both military and civil. He believed the situation was growing more grave day by day, and urged an immediate change in the territorial government.[44]

CHAPTER III

CANTÚ AND THE THREAT TO MEXICAN SOVEREIGNTY

"Cantú *es traidor*."

—**RAFAEL E. MÚZQUIZ**, Inspector General de Consulados

During his years as military commander and governor, Esteban Cantú successfully developed a strong friendship and fellowship with the citizenry of California, who included capitalists he invited to invest in Baja California Norte. Cantú made frequent visits to San Diego, Los Angeles, and San Francisco, always giving the impression that the Northern District was autonomous and had no connection with Mexico.[1] He gained the appreciation of United States' growers in the Mexicali Valley when he cut the tariff on the importation of cotton seed in half, to one-half *centavo* per kilogram, and later lowered the export duty on cotton that had to cross the line into Calexico to be ginned.[2] Cantú, acting as though he were a head of state, accepted the Pan American peace plan for bringing an end to the war in Europe, and when the United States entered World War I Cantú donated $500 to the San Diego chapter of the Red Cross.[3] These gestures were well received in neighboring California.

The United States government and the growers in the Imperial Valley of California requested permission from Cantú in 1915 to construct a nine-mile-long levy near Cerro Prieto. Cantú readily acquiesced to the project, which was intended to protect the Imperial Valley from the flood waters of the Colorado. The levy would be of benefit to growers on both sides of the line, but all the work was being done on Mexican territory without any agreement from Mexico's government. To inspect the work, eight United States senators and representatives arrived in Mexicali to confer with Cantú on March 17, 1915, among them Senator Edward Taylor of Colorado, who noted that the United States' interests were very large in Baja California Norte. Twelve days later Secretary of the Interior Franklin Knight Lane, along with General William Louis Marshall of the United States Army Corps of Engineers, who was in charge of the Cerro Prieto levy, arrived in Mexicali to a fine welcome from Cantú. The governor then accompanied them on a tour of the project in his Packard, and took with him the Twenty-Fifth Battalion's band to enliven the festivities. Secretary Lane later praised Cantú for his efforts to improve Baja California Norte.[4]

With the Constitutionalist government fighting for its life in Veracruz, Mexico could only express its concern over this apparent infringement of Mexican sovereignty. Antonio Prieto, the Mexican director of the International Boundary Commission established jointly by the United States and Mexico to oversee and make adjustments caused by changes in the courses of the Rio Grande and the Colorado, faced a different problem. On receiving his appointment on December 5, 1914, he learned that the previous director, Fernando Beltrán y Puga, had delivered all the archives of the commission into the hands of the *villista* consul at El Paso. Prieto lamented that he could not do the work of the commission without the documents and maps which locate the boundary monuments and urged his government to apprise Washington of this. General William Marshall explained to Prieto that the work on the levy to control the Colorado was in strict accordance with the arrangements made in 1910 with Alberto F. Andrade, trustee of the Sociedad de Yrrigación y Terrenos de la Baja California, S. A. Under the agreement, all funds were in Marshall's care as agent of all public and private parties involved in the work on either side of the border. He explained that the work was intended to protect the lands watered by the Alamo canal from the flood waters of the Río Colorado. Antonio Prieto recognized the need of the United States to protect the Imperial Valley, and Marshall insisted there was no intent to violate Mexican sovereignty. Marshall further explained that, "Inasmuch as Colonel Cantú actually governs this portion of Lower California . . . it has been necessary to confer with him and obtain his assent to the works in progress. . . . I must bear witness that I have found him equally zealous in maintaining the integrity of the territory of Mexico, and equally strict in seeing that all laws governing works executed by foreigners in the Republic of Mexico as any patriotic Mexican official can be."[5]

At the same time Consul González of San Diego wrote the Secretary of Foreign Relations that the "traitor Cantú" was negotiating an agreement with United States authorities under which they could cross over the boundary line to arrest any Mexican or United States citizen wanted for crimes committed north of the border. González rightfully argued that Cantú as a mere governor had no such authority to agree to a convention of that sort, which violated Mexican sovereignty. Only the national government had such power. He held that Cantú was a danger and should be removed from the governorship of the territory.[6] With the civil war raging on the mainland at this time, however, nothing could be done about Cantú, who continued to ingratiate himself with his neighbors.

When the organizers of the Friendship Fiesta of June 21-24, 1917, in San Diego invited him to attend as the guest of honor, he warmly accepted. The *San Diego Union* reported that much good will resulted from the fiesta, and Cantú invited everyone to a barbecue in Tijuana the day following.[7] Cantú was also a member of the League of the Southwest and regularly attended its meetings.[8] Antonio León Grajeda, a personal friend of Theodore Roosevelt and Cantú's secretary, declared in a public meeting in San Diego that "Everything that is accomplished for the progress of San Diego is celebrated by us with the same enthusiasm as if it had been accomplished in Lower California," and referred to the boundary between the two Californias as merely "an imaginary line."[9] The *San Diego Union*, which regularly praised Cantú, agreed with Grajeda that the two Californias were interdependent, editorialized that Baja California Norte was a good neighbor, and praised the cordial relations that existed between the people and authorities on both sides of the border. When there was a fire in Mexicali the firemen of Calexico always came to assist. Cantú was determined to maintain good relations, and on one occasion early in his administration was rumored to have given orders to arrest anyone who offended the dignity of United States citizens.[10]

Governor Cantú cultivated good relations with United States officials at all levels and perhaps saw this as a safeguard for his position. When Carranza's Secretary of Fomento, the erudite civil engineer Pastor Rouaix, who had joined the revolution from its inception and played a prominent role in drafting the 1917 Constitution, made a visit to Ensenada, Cantú kept such a close watch on him that Rouaix found it impossible to talk to anyone alone during his stay. Although Cantú received Rouaix with considerable warmth at Mexicali, he took every opportunity to be seen with the United States Consul at Ensenada in order to impress upon the secretary his purported close ties with the United States government.[11] On leaving Ensenada, Rouaix went to San Diego, where the chamber of commerce entertained him at a luncheon to which Governor Cantú was also invited but sent a representative instead. In the speeches following the lunch, members of Rouaix's delegation failed to mention Cantú, and the representative from Baja California Norte failed to pay any tribute to Rouaix or to mention Mexico or its president but confined himself to speaking of the cordial relations between Cantú and the State of California.[12]

For several years Cantú was able to maintain the impression among the people on both sides of the border that he enjoyed a rare prestige in Washington. This prestige, so United States Consul Walter F. Boyle claimed, was due to his employment of United States citizens of great political prominence to act as his representatives before the United States government. While Boyle did not relate who these persons were, he noted in his dispatch to the Secretary of State that another policy of Cantú's was that of transacting business directly with the local representatives of various branches of the United States government, such as Military Intelligence, the Departments of Justice, Agriculture, and Customs, leading each representative to believe that he had a special influence with Cantú not enjoyed by that of any other branch of the government.[13]

Washington was more concerned with the activities of German agents operating in Baja California during the war. The Zimmermann telegram, a secret communication that proposed an alliance between Germany and Mexico, was not quickly forgotten, and United States suspicions were heightened by the knowledge that Cantú's father-in-law Pablo Dato, who claimed to be a naturalized United States citizen, was an active German agent. There were also fears that Germans working in the Mexicali Valley might sabotage the irrigation works. Most of these Germans were laborers who had fled across the border when the United States entered the war. Cantú did deliver to United States authorities German officers who had operated in the United States as espionage agents, but only those who were of no use to him.[14]

The United States was also concerned with persistent reports of a German radio station in Baja California and the existence of a route of travel over which German agents might proceed from the California border to

Guaymas, Sonora. Although Cantú may have been aware of such a radio station, several efforts on the part of United States intelligence officers failed to discover its location. Cantú claimed that his own agents had investigated rumors of such wireless plants, but found none.[15] While sending search parties into the interior of Baja California had proved difficult and fruitless, Lieutenant Joseph K. Hutchinson of United States Naval Intelligence attempted to discover the location of the wireless from Cantú. A plausible excuse for direct negotiation with the governor lay in the Department of State's request that the Office of Naval Intelligence investigate the merits of the application for the commutation of the prison sentence being served by Cantú's brother-in-law, Federico Dato, who had been convicted in the United States for violating President Wilson's prohibition against the exportation of arms and munitions to Mexico. On the grounds it was desirable to know Cantú's version of the Dato case, Hutchinson began a series of conversations with Cantú with a scope at first limited to the Dato case, but later broadening to other questions of interest to the US.[16]

Although the radio was never found, these conversations led to Cantú's proposal that the United States modify, revise, or remove the embargo on exports from the United States to Baja California Norte, in consideration of which Cantú would: at once disclose information concerning the existence of important German activities in the United States; deliver into United States custody any persons in the Northern District connected with anti-United States activities; suppress all forms of anti-United States agitation; confiscate or destroy all radio stations offering aid to the enemies of the United States; and stop all traffic in narcotics and women at the border.[17] In return, Cantú wanted a license to import everything from tea to asphalt. This was an honest request, as the territory's economy was intimately connected to that of the United States. Cantú lamented that the United States' embargo was effective all along the border, which hurt the economy of the Northern District, as did Mexico's high tariff on the export of food stuffs, sinces the United States was the district's only market. Baja California Norte was practically isolated from the rest of Mexico by a mountainous desert and the Gulf of California, nor was there a seaport from which anything could be shipped to Sonora or elsewhere unless it be transported overland to Ensenada on the Pacific. There was little opportunity for anything exported to Baja California Norte falling into the hands of the enemy.

Practically everything that entered the Northern District came from the United States, and everything raised there was shipped across the line to California. There was indeed a dearth of communication between the mainland and Baja California. The telegraph was most unreliable, mail was very irregular, and there was no scheduled steamer between La Paz and the mainland in these early days of the Northern District's economic growth. Getting anything overland to La Paz at the tip of the peninsula was an impossibility in any case. Given this reasoning, the Office of Naval Intelligence was in favor of granting an export license to Cantú, and the State Department agreed to Cantú's request with the stipulation that the arrangement would be merely temporary, that no record would be kept, and that either side might withdraw therefrom at any time.[18]

Cantú apparently kept his part of the bargain by turning over to United States authorities slackers (draft dodgers), deserters, and German spies, but in reality he delivered only those who were of no interest to him. Even before his arrangement with the Department of State, the governor was reported as having expelled some three hundred slackers from the Northern District but refused to turn over any United States-born Mexicans. After his arrangement with the United States he continued to refuse any aid to slackers and willingly agreed to deliver into that government's hands any slackers who were so identified by authorities on the other side of the border.[19] These efforts to accommodate the United States aided Cantú in another way. He had for some time been trying to get an export permit for two portable wireless radios, which he had purchased in San Francisco in 1917, to be used to improve communication between the towns in Baja California Norte. The Department of State now had no objection to granting the governor a license to import his radios.[20]

Governor Cantú was not averse to usurping the authority of the central government. When two United States aviators from Coronado, California ran out of fuel over Mexican territory and were purportedly forced to land in Baja California some one hundred miles south of the border, the United States embassy requested permission from Mexico's Foreign Secretary, Cándido Aguilar, on January 14, 1917, to search for them. The embassy noted that a rescue party might be needed, and could Aguilar advise Governor Cantú that this was a purely humanitarian effort to save the downed fliers. Permission to search for the pilots was given on January 16, and the governor of the Northern District was so authorized, but in fact Cantú had allowed a party of twenty United States rangers to cross the line in search of the missing men the day before and even cooperated with his own cavalry. Cantú had not bothered to inform the Secretary of Foreign Relations of his actions. He also authorized four planes from San Diego, six motorcycles, and ten automobiles to seek the fliers, who were believed to have gone down near the Río Colorado. It is not known whether the fliers survived their forced landing, but the United States later requested and received permission from Mexico City to land a salvaging party near Bahía de Adair, Sonora, where the planes were found.[21]

In August 1919 Cantú again permitted two United States aviators to fly over Baja California Norte to search for a missing third aircraft, but this time he informed Secretary of Interior Aguirre Berlanga that he did so for humanitarian reasons and that he hoped the president would approve. Because of the special circumstances of the case the president did approve, but there was concern in the Mexican Senate regarding the continued operation of United States aircraft around San Quintín as late as early October 1919.[22]

These were not isolated instances of Cantú's cooperation with United States authorities. Aviators from the United States naval air station at North Island, San Diego, made hundreds of reconnaissance flights along the coast of Baja California making maps of the peninsula's coastline. This was done quietly and unofficially with the permission and tolerance of the territorial governor for his own personal and political convenience, as he prided himself regarding Baja California Norte's good relations with its northern neighbor. Cantú did not bother himself to inform the central government.[23] These flights of United States aircraft over Baja California were known in Mexico City and excited fear that this might be a prelude to an assault on the peninsula.[24]

The periodic reports that Baja California Norte had broken away from Mexico made this anxiety seem quite justified. Mexico City had not forgotten the *magonista* attack on Baja California Norte in 1911, not to mention previous threats to Mexican sovereignty over the peninsula emanating from the United States, and rumors of secession persisted thereafter. Throughout the better part of 1914 there were reports that Governor Baltazar Avilés, Colonel Fortunato Tenorio, and Cantú were governing the Northern District independently of Carranza and Villa, and that Baja California Norte had seceded from Mexico. The *Los Angeles Tribune* reported that Colonel Cantú had denied the rumors that he, Avilés, and Tenorio were planning to form a triumvirate to separate the territory from Mexico. There was of course much truth in what Cantú had told the *Los Angeles Tribune*, as he was soon to maneuver Avilés and Tenorio into exile and become the sole military and civilian authority of the Northern District. In October 1915 Cantú announced that he had withdrawn any recognition of the Convention Government, that Baja California Norte was neutral in regard to the conflict developing on the mainland, and that it would recognize no government until such government established absolute peace in verified presidential elections. Consul González urged Carranza to send loyal constitutionalist troops to throw Cantú and his following out of the northern territory.[25]

This Cantú wished to prevent, and from time to time he made gestures to prove his loyalty to the central government. In January 1916 he gave a grand ball in honor of Carranza and three of the First Chief's representatives from Hermosillo, Sonora. The governor used the occasion to show his guests his accomplishments during the time he had been in office, accomplishments that included a new bridge over the Río Colorado, new schools, a sewage system, and water works; he also pointed out his complete harmony with the North American ranchers in the Northern District. In March, however, he wrote to Obregón of the persistent rumors of United States aggression against Mexico, expressing his fear that this would lead to the loss of the peninsula, and suggested that Obregón increase the number of troops in Baja California Norte.[26]

After Álvaro Obregón had thoroughly defeated Pancho Villa in a series of pitched battles beginning with that of Celaya, reducing Villa once more to *guerrilla* warfare and ultimately to banditry, the former general of the Division of the North felt betrayed by Washington, whose good will he had courted to the point of cheering on the landing of the Marines at Veracruz in 1914. Incensed by Woodrow Wilson's recognition of the Constitutionalist government and allowing *carrancista* troops to use United States railways to reach Agua Prieta, causing him another bitter defeat, Villa threw his wrath at the United States and its citizens on January 9, 1916, by pulling fifteen mining engineers off a train at Santa Ysabel, Chihuahua, and murdering them. More infamous was Villa's raid on Columbus, New Mexico, on March 9, leaving eighteen United States citizens dead and the town a smoldering ruin. One result was the Punitive Expedition led by General John J. Pershing into Chihuahua, which ended in a failure to capture *el Centauro*, who was on his home ground and knew it like the back of his hand. A second result was yet another rumor that Cantú would declare Baja California Norte neutral in any conflict with the United States. The *San Diego Union* reported that James Coffroth, the president of the Lower California Jockey Club of Tijuana, claimed he had heard the story directly from Governor Cantú. Foreign Secretary Cándido Aguilar, Carranza's son-in-law, informed Obregón that he did not believe Cantú told Coffroth any such thing, while the governor denied having indicated to Coffroth that he would declare the Northern District neutral, declaring in May 1916 that he never made international statements.[27]

The *Calexico Chronicle,* however, reported that the independent governor declared that the Pershing expedition "does not concern the people in this part of the country. Our attitude is to maintain peaceful relations at all times for the common interest of the Americans and the Mexican people on this border."[28] Consul González believed that Cantú had indeed declared the Northern District's neutrality and once more urged the government to send a force to dislodge him. Consul Teodoro Frezieres requested Cantú make a statement to the press that he had not said anything regarding the territory's neutrality, and for this received a reprimand. Aguilar informed the consul that he should only keep watch and report on Cantú and not make suggestions to him. In these difficult times, noted the foreign secretary, Mexico needed harmony.[29] Regarding the flurry in the United States press about Cantú's expression of neutrality, Aguilar opined to Obregón that the Sandoval brothers were behind it and had paid for the press releases in defense of their fishing rights, which they felt were threatened by a concession Carranza had granted to a Japanese company. The last thing the United States wanted, suggested the foreign secretary, was a Japanese presence in Baja California, and Aguilar believed Cantú hoped his purportedly neutral stance would garner support for him in Washington. The *El Paso Democrat* perhaps put it correctly, stating that Cantú would declare neutrality only to protect his income, which mostly came from United States concessionaires. This was the general opinion of both United States citizens and Mexicans along the border.[30]

Consul De Negri, who suspected Cantú of treason, alerted the central government in late 1917 that the recalcitrant governor had for some time been holding secret meetings with powerful capitalists and high functionaries of the United States government. The consul offered no names, but said that Cantú had held a conference with the higher officials of

Baja California Norte with the possible intention of declaring the territory independent. This would reopen the border and renew Cantú's revenues. In several extended interviews with United States Consul Sidney Smith of Ensenada, the exact dates of which cannot be ascertained, Cantú intimated his desire to incorporate Baja California Sur under his own administration. He also indicated his desire to secede from Mexico and would do so immediately if assured of United States protection. Cantú held that he wanted to be friendly with the United States and cut adrift of Carranza. British Vice Consul W. D. Madden, also of Ensenada, corroborated this report.[31]

Speculation regarding the annexation of Baja California by the United States had been in the air from time to time since before the signing of the 1848 Treaty of Guadalupe Hidalgo and naturally reemerged during the *magonista* revolt. *El País* expressed the fear in 1911 that Baja California would be the next object of Yankee avarice now that Puerto Rico, the Philippines, Panama, and Hawaii had recently fallen to the imperialist power. Consul Paredes of Calexico reported a strong movement in the Imperial Valley for annexation, supported by governors George Wiley Hunt of Arizona and Hiram Johnson of California. The Los Angeles Chamber of Commerce was in favor of the idea, and many meetings in support of annexation were held in the Imperial Valley, while the *Los Angeles Times* and the *Examiner*, two newspapers which Paredes considered enemies of Mexico, also supported annexation.[32]

Perhaps the loudest voice in favor of annexation was that of Senator Henry Fountain Ashurst of Arizona, who introduced a resolution in the Senate on January 1, 1919, directing the president to begin negotiations for the purchase of Baja California and part of Sonora. Ashurst declared that the Mexican Government was unable to control the territory or protect it from foreign invasion and expressed his fear that Japan would gain control of the peninsula, which he held was "the vermiform appendix of Mexico and the Achilles heel of the United States."[33] While Ashurst's resolution, the first of many he was to introduce over the coming years, got no further than the Committee on Foreign Relations, it was considered a very real threat in Mexico. In an editorial the *Arizona Republican,* clearly in support of Ashurst's resolution, considered Mexico uncontrollable. *El Heraldo de México* noted that one hears every day in the United States that the mouth of the Río Colorado must be under that nation's control, that Arizona must have a coastline, and that all of Baja California must fall to the United States. The newspaper held this to be a danger for Mexico and reported the rumor that Cantú would separate the Northern District from Mexico. The *San Francisco Bulletin* found Ashurst's resolution absurd and that it merely unsettled good relations with Mexico. It found the California legislature's call for the purchase of the peninsula equally absurd and disruptive of United States-Mexican relations.[34]

Governor Esteban Cantú, who was definitely in control of Baja California Norte, was the first to condemn Ashurst's resolution, which consolidated opinion in the Northern District against annexation.[35] All this created something of a sensation in Mexico. *Excelsior* believed that the United States' fear that Japan would acquire territory on the coast of the peninsula was due to the yellow press, which indeed seems to have been the case. William Randolph Hearst was largely responsible for inventing a threatened Japanese takeover of Magdalena Bay, a threat which in fact did not exist. Meanwhile Mexico's Secretary of Foreign Relations calmly explained that the 1917 Constitution forbade sale of coastal lands to foreigners. This being the case, the United States should have no cause for alarm, but Mexican fears were not allayed. *El Correo de la Tarde* of Mazatlán reported widespread rumors of an impending invasion and noted United States cavalry crossings on the Rio Grande. While no intervention was planned, there were enough threats public and private to justify such fears. When inspecting the levy near Cerro Prieto in 1915, Senator Edward Taylor of Colorado declared, "These works must pass under the American flag."[36] No less a figure than the governor of Texas, William Pettus Hobby, urged intervention upon Secretary of State Robert H. Lansing as "an act of wisdom, of justice and of humanity on the part of our government."[37] Minus the patriotic pablum, but much closer to home was the resolution introduced in the California State Senate on January 13 calling for the purchase of Baja California to bring the Río Colorado entirely under United States control. Indeed, some voices called for the annexation of all Mexico's northern states. The fact that Lansing seemed to be moving toward a military solution to the issues causing irritation between Mexico and the United States and that Senator Albert B. Fall's committee was about to begin its investigation into Mexican affairs did little to soften the impact of such statements and rumors.[38]

The idea of simply purchasing the peninsula was not new. As early as 1913 the *San Diego Union* reported a proposal by unnamed capitalists and landowners in Baja California to buy the territory for twenty-five million dollars, with money that was secured by a New York bank. Such overtures were made to President Francisco Madero, so the newspaper claimed, but his fall from power and Washington's refusal to recognize the usurper Victoriano Huerta put an end to the scheme. A similar plan emerged in 1915, as reported in *El Centro Progress* of El Centro, a town in the heart of the Imperial Valley, to purchase the territory for the same amount and spread the money among the Mexican generals. Harrison Gray Otis, editor of the *Los Angeles Times,* was the head of a committee called The Knights of Honor, whose sole purpose was the purchase of Baja California. Otis was also the head of the Colorado River Land Company, which owned 835,000 acres of land in the Northern District. Consul Frezieres held that Otis was an enemy of Mexico who sought the annexation of Baja California to protect his investment. *El Heraldo de México* editorialized that Otis and his control of so much land in the Mexicali Valley was the real enemy and danger for Mexico, not Cantú. The governor, who had the company's holdings reevaluated from the original $797,848 pesos to $6,886,335 pesos in 1915, demanded $10,000 in land taxes from the company and threatened seizure of the its land and cattle if payment was not forthcoming. The company paid "that scoundrel Cantú" $6,000 in gold to satisfy him for the time being. In 1918 Cantú again reevaluated the company's worth, this time to $16,579,257.39 pesos. According to Governor Cantú, in 1915 the company went so far as to organize a troop of 120 men who crossed south of the border a mere twenty meters in an effort to bait Cantú into attacking them, knowing that a force of nine hundred United States cavalry were then on the line at the same point. Cantú approached them with a force of fifty men, at which point the would-be *filisbusteros* opened an irrigation ditch and flooded the area surrounding an adobe building they were using as a base. Cantú ordered his men to roll up their trousers and advance upon the building, which the invading force then abandoned and went back across the international line. In the adobe structure Cantú's men found eighty Winchester rifles, twelve pistols, and thirty thousand rounds of ammunition. The invaders then began firing their rifles into the air from the other side of the line, and Cantú ordered his men to the ground. Soon the captain of the United States cavalry troop arrived and asked them why they were firing their rifles in the air, and the pathetic attack came to an end. The next morning Cantú met the captain of the cavalry at the line and thanked him for putting an end to what could have been an international incident, which is probably what Harrison Gray Otis wanted.[39]

A more comic episode occurred in December 1917 when Fielding J. Stilson, the son of a millionaire lumber and real estate operator and a cousin of Secretary of State Lansing, announced that Cantú had declared Baja California Norte an independent state and was sending Stilson to Washington as his diplomatic representative. Stilson was in a state of inebriation at the University Club of San Francisco when he announced that Cantú wished to declare in favor of the allies in war-torn Europe and desired the protection of, and possible annexation to, the United States. Stilson declared that the project would be well received in Washington, where Cantú had solid connections with unnamed capitalists and members of the government and was hoping for aid against the Carranza regime.[40]

More serious was a conference of the executive committee of the League of the Southwest held in El Centro, California, April 25-27, 1919, for the sole purpose of discussing the possibility of purchasing Baja California. In the friendliest manner Arnold Kruckman, secretary of the League of the Southwest, even presented Cantú with a questionnaire regarding the social, political, military, industrial, and economic facts regarding Baja California Norte as a basis for discussion at the conference. Cantú, who was a member of the league, complied, but later took umbrage at the league's resolution: "The inclusion of Baja California within the American Union will augment in a notable manner the prosperity of the Southwest and will enrich Baja California materially, socially and culturally."[41] Consul De Negri wrote to his government that the situation in Baja California Norte was so dangerous it could lead to war and that the Northern District needed a patriotic governor. Always Cantú's enemy, De Negri urged the removal of the truculent military commander and governor of the Northern District. He reported that Senators Henry Ashurst of Arizona and James Duval Phelan of California were trying to arouse public opinion in the United States in favor of annexation.[42]

A year later De Negri, now Consul General in New York, reported a movement developing in California to seize Baja California Norte led by such anti-*carrancistas* as Armando Borboa, Fernando Espinosa de los Monteros, Dr. Ramón Puente, and Octavio Paz. The conspiracy also involved the principal shareholders of the California Land and Cattle Company, namely Harry Chandler; Lycurgus Lindsay, a Los Angeles banker and proprietor of large stretches of land in Chiapas and Sonora; and

O. F. Brant, another Los Angeles banker and the president of the Los Angeles Tittle and Insurance Company. De Negri believed the movement involved Cantú, who he claimed had protected the California Land and Cattle Company in the past. On the other hand, a rumor circulating that the movement was against the governor of the Northern District caused De Negri some doubt about Cantú's connections to the conspirators, so he suggested that an investigation be launched to determine whether Cantú was indeed in league with the conspiracy. It is unlikely that Cantú was involved in these secret discussions to seize Baja California Norte, as he was already in control of the Northern District and considered the California Land and Cattle Company his enemy.[43]

Governor Cantú's relations with the company had been uneasy. When he came to power the economic resources of the Northern District were under foreign control, the largest holding being that of the Colorado River Land Company. In order to provide revenue for his government in its early days he raised taxes by one thousand per cent, which enabled him to maintain the peace. While the company complained, its officers realized that the tranquility Cantú provided enabled them to expand their cotton cultivation without political interference. Cantú's adherence to a belief in private property freed them from any fear of land reform or confiscation while he was in power. For his part, Cantú was indignant with the hostility the company showed toward the few Mexican nationals who had taken up residence on company land. It had burned their *cabañas*, run them off the land, and despoiled them of the few cattle they had. According to Cantú the company annually drove 100,000 head of cattle across the line into the United States without paying any export duties. Cantú hoped to limit these practices, and for this reason the company, he later claimed, put a price on his head of $30,000. The hostility between the governor and the company subsided in 1916 when Cantú continued to permit the exportation of cotton after the Carranza government had prohibited it and cooperated in bringing Chinese laborers into the Northern District to work in the company's cotton fields.[44]

Despite the flurry in the California press concerning the possible secession of Baja California Norte from Mexico and its purchase by the United States, Federico Dato, who was now out of prison and apparently serving as Cantú's press agent north of the border, denied that he or Cantú supported secession.[45] When the Mexican ambassador in Washington, Ignacio Bonillas, asked Cantú if the rumors in the United States press of the secession of the Northern District and the lease of Magdalena Bay to Japan to finance an independent republic were true, the governor immediately declared such rumors false. Cantú believed the rumors were ridiculous. He stated in San Francisco that the 1917 Constitution forbade the sale of national territory and protested his loyalty to the government.[46] In an "Open Letter to the People and Government of the United States," Cantú protested the continual schemes to purchase or seize Baja California on the part of citizens and elected officials of the United States, who even went so far as to spread such propaganda in the Northern District itself.[47] Consul Frezieres believed Cantú was incapable of leading such a movement. Deputy Juan Velázquez of Baja California Norte protested Ashurst's contention that the territory was practically independent from the central government and declared that Governor Cantú had always followed the laws and orders emanating from the government. Nevertheless in September 1919 *El Heraldo de México* reported a rumor that Cantú might separate Baja California Norte from Mexico.[48]

Yet Cantú himself was partly responsible for the belief in the United States that Baja California Norte was independent of Mexico City. He had declared the Northern District neutral during the civil war involving Carranza and Villa and again during the Pershing-Villa chase. United States Consul William Burdett of Ensenada reported that in July 1920 copies of R. Velasco Ceballos's *¿Se apoderará los Estados Unidos de América de la Baja California?* were distributed among the government offices in Mexicali and Ensenada. Ceballos voiced the threat of a United States seizure of Baja California and praised the governorship of Esteban Cantú in laudatory terms. When Ceballos was in the Northern District, Cantú tendered him every consideration. Burdett suspected that Cantú financed the publication of the book and was certainly responsible for its distribution.[49] In an interview with *Excelsior*, Plutarco Elías Calles expressed his opinion that Cantú never sought annexation to the United States, that he had created a kind of island in Baja California Norte where he ruled like a monarch. If the peninsula were annexed, Calles pointed out, Washington would surely replace him, and Cantú could gain nothing from that.[50]

Adding to the fear that Baja California might fall to the northern colossus was the fact that much of the Northern District was owned by North American capitalists who employed Chinese laborers. There were frequent demands that Baja California Norte be populated with Mexicans in order to save it from United States aggression. The military governor of Sonora, Plutarco Elías Calles, reported that a group of *rancheros* in the Northern District organized by one Rafael Conrado Silver were planning to overthrow Cantú. They were not opposed to the central government, but were agitated over Cantú's leniency toward Chinese immigration and his pointed protection of United States citizens. Calles believed they might succeed, and this would pose a problem for Mexico in that two thousand American troops were in the vicinity of Calexico and any such disturbance might cause them to cross the line to protect United States interests. As it was difficult for Mexico to control events in Baja California Norte, those troops might stay indefinitely. Calles suggested that a battalion be sent to the Sonoran side of the Río Colorado just in case such a revolt occurred. Calles noted that it was good that Cantú was on good terms with the Americans, on the other hand, because Baja California Norte was full of traitors. There were other calls for the removal of Cantú, whom many considered to be a real danger to the territorial integrity of the nation. Others desired Cantú's removal because of the tyranny and abuses the people suffered under his rule.[51] The Carranza government was never able to act effectively against Cantú, whose removal from Baja California Norte would have to wait until the next administration in Mexico City.

One might make a comparison with José F. Gómez, the mayor of Juchitán during the Madero revolution, who took umbrage at Governor Benito Juárez Maza's attempt to centralize authority in Oaxaca. Gómez was believed to be fomenting independent rebellion, and a federal force was sent against him but faced strong resistance from the Juchitecos. What was at play was the desire for local autonomy, but Gómez was charged with ambitions toward creating an Isthmian state independent of the nation. At length President Madero gave Gómez safe passage to Mexico City to explain his actions, but he was arrested on the way by order of Juárez Maza, and reportedly was shot some fifty-two times when dragged from jail by a mob. Gómez and the Juchitecos had wanted only self-governing autonomy, while Governor Esteban Cantú enjoyed actual independence, which he intended to keep. Although the central government requested on more than one occasion that he journey to the national capital to justify his position, he had always found some excuse not to comply. Cantú was too clever to leave his sanctuary for the lion's den.[52]

CHAPTER IV

GERMAN SPIES, CHINESE FARMERS, AND JAPANESE FISHERMEN

"Cantú *es bribón.*"
—**EL PRIMER SECRETARIO** de la Embajada Mexicana

In 1913 Cantú married a *bajacaliforniana,* Ana Dato Félix, the daughter of Pablo Dato of Mexicali, who soon became Cantú's *padre político.* Dato had lived in Baja California Norte and Guaymas, Sonora, from 1875 to 1906, when he moved to Calexico, California. He claimed to be a United States citizen and even voted in all the elections, although he was not in fact a naturalized citizen of the United States. Dato married a Mexican and assumed the name Pablo, but according to his birth certificate, Adolph Paul Dato was born in Grossner, Germany, on June 11, 1840. Dato had served as Prussian Consul in Paris and in China before emigrating to Mexico, and when World War I broke out he became the head of the German Information Bureau in Baja California Norte.[1]

Those close to Cantú, Eusebio Calzado, Jacinto Barrera, Ramón Guerra, his private secretary, and others held that Pablo Dato made Cantú, that the governor did nothing without his father-law's approval, and that Dato had always been the brains and executive force behind the scenes. Dato was active in the Verband Deutscher Reichsangehöriger (Union of Subjects of the Empire), which subsidized a number of newspapers in Mexico such as *Boletín de la Guerra, Crónica Alemana,* and *Deutsche Zeitung von Mexiko,* to name only three. Pablo Dato and his sons, Federico, Pablo Jr., Guillermo, and Gustavo, all of whom had been born in Mexico, operated the German spy network along the California line after the outbreak of the war. Of the three Gustavo, or "Gus" as he was usually called, was a charming, bilingual product of the border known for the elegance of his clothing and manners.[2] Cantú was close to the German consul in Mexicali, who was also an intimate friend of the elder Dato. Cantú was playing a double game, attempting to convince the Department of State of his friendship for the United States, while allowing the Datos to carry on their espionage efforts in the Northern District. Cantú and the Datos were also rather persistent in their efforts to smuggle guns into Baja California Norte. The Dato family owned a cotton plantation about five miles from Mexicali that was very close to the border and served as their arms smuggling point.

The State Department knew that Cantú and the Datos were smuggling arms and ammunition across the border, as did Mexico City, which had a superb intelligence organization in the United States. Federico Dato was arrested and placed on $5,000 bond for violating President Wilson's prohibition against the exportation of arms and munitions to Mexico. He was soon indicted and convicted on a charge of conspiring to ship ten machine guns south of the California border. Cantú's attitude was not unique. When Plutarco Elías Calles was the strong man of Sonora, he also allowed German espionage agents to do as they pleased.[3]

The United States was concerned about pro-German feeling south of the border. In an interview with General Pablo González, held at González's request, the general told United States Ambassador Henry Prather Fletcher that if Washington would only lift the arms embargo, Mexico's lenient policy toward German propaganda would change immediately, the embargo being Germany's main argument for Mexico to continue this leniency. The astute Fletcher, a professional diplomat, recommended that the United States release the five million rounds of ammunition already bought and paid for by Mexico, as that government was in dire need of this war materiel. He further argued that quiet in Mexico was in the interest of the United States and believed turmoil in Mexico could adversely affect the conduct of the war in Europe. Fletcher also noted that Carranza found the embargo difficult to understand in view of the resumption of normal relations between the two neighboring countries. Fletcher also expressed his anxiety regarding Germans in the Southwest crossing the line into Mexico for the purpose of holding meetings, which Mexican authorities freely permitted. He was concerned with difficulties for the United States in Mexico, should war break out with Germany.[4]

After entering the war the United States became decidedly more concerned about activities of German agents operating in Baja California and Mexico. The United States suspicions were heightened by the knowledge that Cantú's father-in-law was an active German agent. There were persistent suspicions that a German radio station had been established in Baja California Norte to keep watch on ship departures from the naval base at San Diego. The wireless radio was believed to be located at Punta Prieto at latitude 29° north. Cantú claimed that his secret agents investigated the rumors of wireless radio stations, but found none. Confirming Cantú's claim would entail sending search parties into the peninsula to determine the location of any such radio, a problem for the US since this would be a violation of Mexican sovereignty. Lieutenant Joseph K. Hutchinson of Naval Intelligence was able to arrange a series of interviews with Governor Cantú in March and April 1918. The ostensible reason for the meetings was the State Department's request that the Office of Naval Intelligence investigate the merits of Federico Dato's application for commutation of his prison sentence for smuggling arms. According to the US, Cantú's version of the Dato case was desirable to help the State Department make a decision regarding his application. Thus a series of conversations began, at first limited to the Dato case, but then broadening to other areas.[5]

Meanwhile, plans were formulated for sending a search team into Baja California between latitudes 28° 40' and 30° north, where the radio station was believed to be. Ralph Chase, owner of the Williams Chase Canning Co. of San Diego, and one of Chase's most reliable fishermen, Bob Israel, a United States citizen of half Mexican parentage, were deemed best suited to the purpose of the expedition. For several years Chase had had a large fleet of fishing boats operating in Magdalena Bay, possessed a wide knowledge of the coast of Baja California, and often made trips which caused no concern to local authorities.

It seems that Cantú either took a liking to Lieutenant Hutchinson or simply played along with him to gain favor with the United States, on repeated occasions offering him permission to hunt, fish, prospect, or seek information in Baja California whenever he wished. Cantú therefore knew of the expedition, but did not know of its nature or when it would take place, Chase, Israel, Hutchinson, and a boatswain from the USS *Oregon* carried out the mission in the area where the radio was suspected to be, but found nothing. Radio observation by United States ships off the Baja California coast also discovered nothing. There may have been a wireless radio station in the past, however. This view was "self-incriminatingly [sic.] corroborated by Cantú, who asserted that at the village of Patrocinio in the Southern District, there was stored a German radio plant which had been used in 1915-16 when German raiders were abroad in the Pacific."[6] The mystery of the wireless radio station was solved when Consul Ramón de Negri reported the trial in San Diego of a number of German spies who had been operating out of that city, among whom were Gustav Köppel and E. H. von Schack, who had tried to erect such a radio at El Álamo in Baja California Norte, somewhat southeast of Ensenada.[7]

There was also concern over the maintenance of a route over which German agents might follow from the California border to Guaymas, Sonora. Hutchinson had little doubt that such a route of travel existed, since from time to time Germans or Austrians would appear at Ensenada when it was reasonably established that they had not crossed the California border to get there. Often they would disappear from that Pacific port, but their departure was not over the Mexicali or Tijuana roads. Cantú was very cooperative on this issue and at times sent detachments of his soldiers to apprehend the agents in question, even requesting Lieutenant Hutchinson's assistance in delivering captured German agents and escaped naval officers to the United States Navy. Cantú did deliver to United States authorities German officers who had operated north of the border as espionage agents, but never agents of any importance. To enhance Cantú's cooperation it was suggested that instructions be sent to the immigration officer at Calexico to permit Cantú's mother-in-law, Ana Dato, and his wife Ana Cantú to cross the border as freely as they wished.[8]

While Cantú cooperated with the United States in various ways he was probably pro-German during the war. Rumor had it that he and Federico Dato had toasted Kaiser Wilhelm II during a banquet held at Cantú's ranch in Baja California Norte during the 1918 German drive on the western front in Europe. Consul Samuel G. Vázquez at San Diego hotly denied that the territorial governor and his brother-in-law had done any such thing or that they were pro-German in the slightest way. If Cantú was not pro-German, Vázquez was certainly pro-Cantú. The consul established a monthly magazine in San Diego to be published in the interest of the governor of the Northern District. Vázquez had received financial backing from Cantú for the venture, which was to develop and spread propaganda promoting the governor as a presidential candidate.[9] Consul de Negri reported that Cantú had covered Vázquez with honors in order to gain his confidence, and he did not believe Vázquez could any longer be trusted by the central government.[10]

Another concern of Washington was that Germans working in the Mexicali Valley might sabotage the irrigation works that watered the rich agricultural fields north and south of the line. Most of these Germans were laborers who had fled across the border when the United States entered the war. Cantú, however, received $6.00 export duty on every bale of cotton exported to the United States and could be expected to earn a gross income of $600,000 from these duties in 1918 alone. This was one of his principal sources of revenue, and it was therefore unlikely that he would permit sabotage to the irrigation system. President Carranza himself permitted the German secret service to operate in Mexico in the expectation that German sabotage in Mexico would be held to a minimum. In reality, German agents in Mexico were so hunted by Allied counterintelligence during the last months of the war that they were not able to undertake even one operation of importance, and the irrigation works were never really threatened.[11] Moreover, the majority of laborers working the irrigated cotton fields were Chinese immigrants.

The xenophobia that the Mexican Revolution exacerbated found expression in anti-Chinese agitation in Sinaloa, Sonora, Baja California Norte, and elsewhere. It is interesting that this xenophobia fell primarily upon the Chinese and Spaniards, but not against the citizens of the United States or the United Kingdom. Rather there were many attacks upon the persons and property of the Chinese during the revolution. As early as 1911 the Club Democrático Sonorense took an official stand against the immigration of Chinese.[12] At the same time, an editorial in *El Diario* declared the colonization of Baja California should be of Mexicans only. *El Heraldo de México* some years later lamented the numerous Chinese in the Northern District who controlled commerce and monopolized the restaurant trade and agriculture. The newspaper added that many Mexicans left Arizona and California when the United States entered the war, but this great opportunity to populate Baja California Norte with repatriated Mexicans was lost. Rumors that there were more Asiatic adult males than Mexicans in Mexicali increased anti-Chinese feeling. There were an estimated 70,000-plus Chinese in Sonora and Baja California.[13]

The residents of Pueblo Nuevo in the Northern District vowed not to rent or sell houses, buildings, or land to the Chinese, and thirty of Cantú's troops revolted in September 1919 at Los Algodones over the issue of too many Chinese in the area. An effort on the part of loyal troops to restrain the insurgents from hanging several Chinese laborers caused the revolt. The leaders of the rebellion made off with some horses and arms, but were soon captured by loyal troops, brought to trial, and executed.[14] This anti-Chinese feeling continued after Cantú's removal from power. One complaint was that there were so many Chinese in Baja California Norte that Mexicans were unable to find work in the cotton fields.[15] This was not actually true. The Mexicali Valley possessed ideal conditions for the cultivation of cotton, but there was a dearth of Mexican workers in the area. Anti-Chinese agitation in Baja California Norte never approached that of Sonora, which in time expelled all Chinese from the state, let alone that in Torreón, Coahuila, where on May 14 and 15, 1911, over three hundred Chinese were murdered while shops were looted and burned to the ground by *maderista* troops. Following Torreón, violence befell Chinese in Sonora, Chihuahua, Sinaloa, and Durango. Villa regularly killed Chinese when he took a town or city during his campaigns. After his capture of Chihuahua City in 1916, *villistas* hunted down and massacred the Chinese. Cantú would never have permitted such outrageous activity, as it would have been detrimental to the economy of the Northern District as well as to his personal finances. Moreover, the Chinese in Baja California Norte were involved in a variety of economic activities and were not stigmatized by involvement in one particular type of employment or business. Because they were more integrated into the economy they provoked less animosity among the Mexican populace than was the case elsewhere in Mexico.[16]

One tragedy did occur in 1916 when seventy-five Chinese, fleeing the persecution in Sonora by boat for Baja California Norte, disembarked at La Bomba, a short distance up the Río Colorado. The captain of the vessel informed them that Mexicali was but a short distance beyond and that they could easily walk to their destination. The immigrants continued along the road for about fifty kilometers, by which time they had run out of water, nearly all of them perishing one by one in the desert. A few of them found water at the Grivel mine and were able to push on to Mexicali. The dead were later found by passers-by who buried them at a place since known as "El Chinero," or "El Cerro de los Chinos."[17]

When asked years later in a conversation in 1966 whether he favored the immigration of Chinese laborers over the employment of Mexican workers, Cantú replied that this was never his preference. Rather, the problem was one of attracting Mexican farm laborers to the cotton fields in the Mexicali Valley when they could find much easier work in the Imperial Valley north of the border. The dearth of Mexican workers made the immigration of Chinese imperative if the cotton fields were to thrive. Cantú held the Chinese colonists in the highest regard for their hard work, their high spirit of solidarity, and the respect they always maintained for the laws of the territory. In the same conversation Cantú was asked if he levied a *per capita* tax upon the Chinese in the Northern District. To this he explicitly replied no, but the truth of the matter was that everyone, Mexican, Chinese, and other foreigners, paid a monthly head tax of one dollar during Cantú's governorship.[18]

One of the monuments left by Cantú was a Chinese colony of seven or eight thousand adult males residing in and near Mexicali. The lack of economic opportunity in southern China led to an impressive emigration of Chinese to the Americas, drawn at first to the California Gold Rush and then to the building of the transcontinental railroad in the United States. The large number of immigrants, 148,000 in California alone by 1877, caused a reaction in the United States that culminated in the 1882 Chinese Exclusion Act, which closed the US as a haven for Chinese except for certain merchants, Chinese of Mexican citizenship, and undetected illegal entrants. While the gates to the United States were being closed, the door to Mexico was being opened wide. Mexico's Secretary of Finance under Porfirio Díaz, Matías Romero, proposed the immigration of Chinese laborers to till the lands, work the mines, and tend the machines of factories in Mexico's sparsely populated northern borderlands and tropical coasts. At length his efforts bore fruit, and the Treaty of Amity, Commerce, and Navigation between Mexico and China was signed in 1889, leading to a significant increase in the number of Chinese leaving the Celestial Empire for Mexico.[19]

The rise of the Chinese colony in Mexicali alone was notable, for while in 1904 there were but six adult Chinese males in the town, by 1914 their number had risen to over one thousand. According to United States Consul Walter F. Boyle, who was no friend of Cantú's, each paid from $135 to $140 to the territorial government for the privilege of entering Baja California Norte—$100 to the territorial government and the remainder to Cantú's pocket. Consul Ramón de Negri on the other hand produced a document bearing Cantú's signature that called for bringing in two thousand Chinese colonists at $160 each in gold. Pablo Dato was involved in this as well. This colony "fulfilled all expectations in supporting an uncomplaining, hard-working, wealth-producing subject of exploitation. The favorable condition being that the Chinaman expects to be exploited and will stand for any degree of exploitation just so long as it did not exceed a 'fifty-fifty' sharing of his profits with the exploiters." In an official report in 1919, Cantú reported charging $200 per Asian immigrant, but did not mention how much went to his government and how much to himself.[20]

The Chinese borrowed immense sums of money for the purpose of financing their cotton cultivation. United States financiers gladly lent this money at the rate of 24 percent per annum, with the additional stipulation that the borrower donate as a bonus 25 percent of his cotton seed to the lender and have his cotton ginned at the lender's gin. The financiers regarded the colonists as quite honest in meeting their obligations, but felt more secure with Cantú's unwritten guarantee that he would use all legal and illegal means at his disposal to force the Chinese to meet their obligations. These financial interests were solidly in support of Cantú.[21]

There was an advantage in using Chinese labor in that they had a system of organization amongst themselves undertaking the cultivation of large tracts of land under the leadership of one of their own. The Colorado River Land Company preferred to use Chinese laborers because they organized cooperatives to bring undeveloped land under cultivation at their own expense. The company thereby earned a profit from leasing the land to the Chinese cooperatives and was saved the expense of developing the land itself. The Chinese colonists formed their own association for mutual understanding and protection with regard to business, marketing, and labor, and were closely associated with the Chinese of San Francisco and Los Angeles. Each Chinese colonist contributed to the cooperative what he could afford and worked for a share of the crop rather than for wages, receiving merely food and clothing during cultivation. In this way he had a stake in the success of the cooperative. By 1920, 80 percent of the cotton crop in the Mexicali Valley was raised by the Chinese.[22]

All of the Northern District's cotton production was shipped to the United States, and most of it was then exported to Japan. While exporting the cotton was in contravention to Mexican federal law, Cantú explained the situation to Carranza by noting that Baja California Norte was cut off from the rest of the republic. There was no road or rail line to neighboring Sonora, nor was there a bridge across the Colorado, on the other side of which was a trackless desert. There was no good road to San Felipe on the Gulf of California, and there were no port facilities in that small village had such a road existed. There was a road to Ensenada, which did have a port, but there was no regular shipping from there to the Pacific ports of Mexico. In addition, there was no cotton gin in the Northern District, making the United States the only market for this valuable commodity, which was the economic lifeblood of the territory. Moreover, the growers borrowed money for their operations from banks in Los Angeles, San Francisco, and Calexico, further tying them to the economy of the United States. Thus the cotton could only be shipped across the international border. While Cantú requested that the prohibition against the exportation of cotton be lifted, Carranza's answer is not known. In any case all the cotton production of the Mexicali Valley was sent to the cotton gins of California.[23]

The colonists had little contact with Mexican nationals except over the counters of their stores in Mexicali. In that city the stores of the Chinese merchants were the largest and handled certain foods imported from Hong Kong, machinery and materials for planting cotton, and a great variety of general merchandise. Of the forty stores in Mexicali fourteen were Chinese owned, most notable of which was the Compañía Chino Mercantil Mexicana, owned by an association of Chinese merchants residing in San Francisco. The company offered general merchandise, especially foreign goods such as preserves and other food products imported directly from China and the United States. Most of the hotels in Mexicali were owned and operated by the Chinese, the most prominent of which was the Hotel Imperial. The hotel was constructed by a cooperative association of Chinese, some of whom lived in San Francisco, in other cities in the United States, and even in China, each owning a share of the investment. A number of restaurants and bars were operated by the Chinese, among them The Palace Bar, reputedly a most elegant café and cabaret. There was also the Asociación China de Mexicali, a popular meeting place of the Chinese colonists. The club had its own building equipped with comfortable meeting rooms, while next to the club was a modern, well-equipped hospital that saw to the well being of the Chinese colony.[24]

Clearly, the presence of the Chinese colonists could not be ignored, and their dominance of local business was something of an embarrassment to Mexican nationals. Chinese merchants tended to live in back rooms in their stores and keep their stock there as well, rather than maintain a separate residence for themselves and a warehouse for their merchandise. The employees in Chinese enterprises were usually family members or unsalaried partners. These practices, along with subsisting on their own inventories, kept overhead low, enabling the Chinese to offer merchandise to customers at lower cost. Their plans to return to China after sufficient capital had been accumulated made such sacrifices bearable.[25]

Unfortunately, agitation against the Chinese in Mexicali was so disturbing that Cantú felt compelled to issue an open letter to the citizens to reassure them that his intent was to populate the territory with Mexicans.[26] At the same time, the governor refused to close the door to more Chinese immigrants. Anti-Chinese feeling may have made the exploitation of the Chinese colonists easier, and even popular. It also forced United States growers in the Mexicali Valley to accept Mexican laborers. For his part, Cantú insisted it was not true that the Chinese were mistreated in the Northern District; rather they were simply a hard-working group of people.[27]

Cantú's policy regarding Chinese immigration was somewhat whimsical. Sols Simon, a United States citizen who had considerable agricultural interests near Mexicali, complained that the governor would not let him bring in Chinese or Japanese laborers to work his fields. He stated that Mexican workers from the interior would not stay in Baja California Norte because of their fear of Cantú, and that they also crossed the line into the United States because agricultural work there was easier. While Simon's protest caused a flurry of notes between him and the Mexican government, it is not known whether he was able to bring in Chinese or Japanese workers.[28] Perhaps Simon was trying to get around Cantú's immigration fee, which was illegal in any case.

On another occasion, after having granted permission for 1,500 Chinese immigrants to enter Baja California Norte as agricultural workers, Cantú rescinded the agreement, which left 330 Chinese stranded in San

Francisco. Fong Tsiang Kwang, China's *chargé d' affaires* in Mexico City, pointed out that Cantú's action violated the 1917 Constitution and contravened the Treaty of Amity, Commerce, and Navigation between Mexico and China. Orders were then sent to Mexicali not to impede the immigration of the 330 colonists. Representatives of the United States and Japanese steamship lines that brought them to San Francisco asked Washington for assistance in the matter, protesting that Cantú's original promise to allow the colonists to enter the Northern District was repudiated while they were en route across the Pacific Ocean. In early November Cantú declared that he would admit the 330 Chinese because Mexican laborers could not be found to work in the cotton fields, despite the relatively high wages. His stated reason was to aid the growers, and there the matter rested.

Despite Cantú's erratic immigration policy and the anti-Chinese agitation in the Northern District and elsewhere in Mexico, the Chinese colonists established a permanent population and center of commerce in Baja California Norte which, along with Sinaloa, received the largest number of immigrants. In Mexicali today there remain some five thousand *bajacalifornianos* of Chinese decent.[29] Cantú had little choice regarding Chinese immigration. He had to deal with the Colorado River Land Company, which surrounded Mexicali on three sides, and needed the colonists to cultivate the cotton fields which were the lifeblood of the Northern District's economy. This benefitted the company, the Chinese, and the territorial government and was profitable for Cantú, but did little for Mexicans.[30]

Cantú was aware of that problem. He could do little about the Colorado River Land Company, but in 1916 he set his lawyers on the Mexican Land and Colonization Company, Ltd., "The English Company." His lawyers found that the company had failed to live up to the terms of the original grant, paying no taxes and settling no colonists on the land nor even surveying it. Secretary of Fomento Pastor Rouaix, whom President Carranza had sent to investigate the matter, found that Cantú's legal team was correct in asserting that the company had not fulfilled its obligations. Carranza then revoked "The English Company's" grant, and Governor Cantú settled nearly three hundred Mexican families repatriated from the United States on the empty tract of land which lies along the peninsula's northern Pacific coast. Cantú himself presided over the distribution of the parcels of land in the Valle de las Palmas on September 22, 1919, under a lottery system to avoid any semblance of preference being given to any particular individual. The Valle de las Palmas is formed by a large turn toward the northeast of the Río Tijuana, which unfortunately is dry most of the year. While rainfall was inadequate in the Northern District and the irrigation works did not reach that far west, water could be found by sinking shallow wells. The families received twenty *hectáreas* each, about fifty acres, with apparent enthusiasm.[31] Cantú also offered government land to any man who volunteered to serve in his reserve military force, thereby giving them a vested interest in the territory's economy and defense.[32]

Governor Esteban Cantú wished to settle Mexican nationals on the open land of Baja California Norte, but few Mexican settlers were available, and in any case the Colorado River Land Company and other United States interests controlled most of the irrigated land. Those few who wished to repatriate from the United States were freely given Cantú's assistance. On a number of occasions such repatriates were allowed to bring their agricultural equipment, livestock, and any other possessions into the Northern District duty free.[33] Cantú's immigration policy not only flouted the laws of Mexico but was erratic as well. Consul Adolfo Carrillo reported in May 1915 that Cantú had plans to bring 50,000 Japanese to Baja California Norte as colonists. Carrillo had intercepted letters to that effect from the governor to the president of the Nich Bokú Industrial Corporation and reported that Cantú was asking for one million United States dollars to complete the deal. Working through George G. Gaxiola, a *villista* agent in Los Angeles, Cantú suggested Gaxiola work with Nich Bokú agents in Villa's name. Nothing resulted from this proposal, but Carrillo continued to intercept letters from Gaxiola as well as from the *huertista* agent Jorge Vera Estañol, a noted lawyer who served as Secretary of Education under Victoriano Huerta and under Díaz before that.[34]

The following year Cantú denied permission for thirty-seven Japanese aboard the *George W. Elder* to disembark at Ensenada, thereby violating the Treaty of Friendship and Commerce between Mexico and Japan and provoking a letter of protest from the Japanese legation in Mexico City. At length an order to allow the Japanese to disembark from Secretary of War Álvaro Obregón reached Cantú, and the small crisis passed. At the same time Cantú received an order to present himself before the Secretariat of the Army of the Northeast but failed to comply, yet he remained in charge of Baja California Norte.[35]

Anti-Japanese feeling in Washington provoked fears of Japanese encroachments on Baja California. When the Japanese cruiser *Asama* ran aground in Bartolomé Bay in November 1914, it refused assistance offered by United States warships in the area and spent more than six motionless months in the bay while Japanese vessels came to assist and repair it. William Randolph Hearst's *San Francisco Examiner* claimed this was an effort on the part of Japan to obtain a naval base in the area. The *Asama* finally left Bartolomé Bay, and the incident was forgotten, but whether this was a real attempt to explore the bay or merely the result of lengthy technical repairs is not known. As the Japanese navy was at the time considering the possibility of a future war with the United States, Washington's concern was not entirely baseless. Not long after the *Asama* incident faded away, Consul Adolfo Carrillo of Los Angeles in 1915 reported that Villa had plans, somehow in cooperation with Cantú, to sell the peninsula to Japan as a means of settling the score with Mexico and the United States.[36] A preposterous idea at best.

Then there was the issue of Magdalena Bay, where the United States desired to build a naval base. Porfirio Díaz refused to allow such an infringement upon Mexican sovereignty, but had granted the United States the privilege of maintaining a coaling station at Magdalena Bay in 1883. The privilege was renewed in 1907, and when Theodore Roosevelt sent the fleet around the world in 1908, it dropped anchor in Magdalena Bay. Hearst's *Examiner* made much of the story, and public opinion was convinced that Magdalena Bay was crucial to the defense of the United States. Japan's defeat of Russia in 1904 increased concern in the United States about Japan as a rising Pacific power. Thus the issues of the Japanese menace, hemispheric defense, and Magdalena Bay became entangled. The *Examiner* held that there were 75,000 Japanese at Magdalena Bay and that most were soldiers, but when Hearst sent reporters to investigate, they found only two Japanese fishermen. Senator Henry Cabot Lodge managed to get the Senate to ask President William Howard Taft if there had been a purchase of Magdalena Bay on the part of Japan. Both Secretary of Foreign Affairs Manuel Calero and President Madero declared such information to be false, and Japan denied having any interest in Magdalena Bay.[37] The issue seems to have been one of the yellow press rather than the "yellow peril."

For years afterward the United States Office of Naval Intelligence kept close watch on Japanese operations on Baja California's west coast.

The question reared its head again in 1912, when the *Examiner* reported an attempt on the part of the Japanese to buy five million acres of land at Magdalena Bay, the effort being blocked by the Department of State as a violation of the Monroe Doctrine. Mexican Foreign Secretary Calero held that there was no foundation to the story in the *Examiner*, but that a group of Japanese fishermen had unsuccessfully tried to obtain Aurelio Sandoval's fishing rights. Calero also denied any allotment of such a large tract of land at Magdalena Bay. It seems John L. Blackman, general manager of the Chartered Company of Lower California, had been negotiating with a group of Japanese in the hope of selling them some land on the coast. Blackman's company owned a strip of land from Santa Rosalia Bay to the tip of the peninsula and was willing to sell two thousand acres to the fishermen, but only to individuals who wanted a tract merely large enough to provide them with homes.[38] Mexico's ambassador in Washington, Ignacio Bonillas, asked Cantú if rumors were true that the governor was planning to lease the bay to Japan.[39] Cantú had no authority over Magdalena Bay, which lies hundreds of miles south of Ensenada and therefore beyond his reach. It was true that the Japanese were very actively fishing off the coast of Baja California and in early 1919 increased the size of their fishing fleet in those waters, but they had no interest in gaining sole control of Magdalena Bay.[40]

In the same year a furor arose in the United States over a purported Japanese purchase of land in Baja California Norte. The *New York Times* reported that the land involved was none other than that of the Colorado River Land Company, consisting of 1,250,000 acres, and that the price was "in all probability as much as $50,000,000."[41] The fright was all the greater since the Colorado River Land Company's property, which actually consisted of 835,000 acres, was exactly on the border separating the two Californias. In an attempt to calm such fears, the Mexican Foreign Secretary calmly explained that according to the 1917 Constitution, foreigners were not permitted to purchase land within one hundred kilometers of the coast or the boundaries of the nation. Japan's ambassador to Mexico, Baron Fujitaro Otori, believed that the rumor was a political maneuver made during the current election in the United States, and Ambassador Bonillas stated to the United States press that the whole affair was due to the jingoes and the yellow press.[42] The rumor that large tracts of land in Baja California were being sold to Japanese emerged once more in 1920, and again the Mexican embassy in Washington explained that under Mexican law foreigners were not permitted to purchase land on the coast or frontiers of the republic.[43]

Cantú was very interested in building a railroad from Mexicali to San Felipe on the Gulf of California, which would give Baja California Norte much-needed direct access to the mainland. In March 1919 Cantú was giving interviews to various railroad entrepreneurs regarding his desire for a rail line to the gulf. The Hearst press, which could not let go of the Japanese threat to the United States, feared the governor would grant the construction of the railroad to Japanese interests. There was nothing to fear in this regard, because the contract of May 7, 1919, was given to José Cantú, the governor's brother, who never had the means to carry it out. José Cantú was in charge of the customs house at Mexicali, and though the post drew only a small salary, he had been able to invest in a number of ventures. Four years after the contract was drawn, however, he needed money, so he requested the grant be rescinded so that he could have his deposit returned. The government agreed to look into the matter and promised his request would result in equity and justice, but it is not known whether or not José Cantú's deposit was returned.[44] The railroad from Mexicali to San Felipe was begun later, during the governorship of José Inocente Lugo. Baja California Norte was finally linked with Sonora and the national grid at Benjamín Hill in the desert of Altar during the presidency of Miguel Alemán in 1948.[45] At the ceremony opening the new line, President Alemán, rather than cutting a ribbon with scissors, cut a chain with an acetylene torch to emphasize the difficulties that had been overcome with its construction.[46]

CHAPTER V

LA CHINESCA

"Cantú *es panista.*"
—**ENRIQUE A. GONZÁLEZ,** Mexican Consul at San Diego

What spurred the vice trade in northern Baja California was the great surge of moral fervor in the United States during the early years of the twentieth century. Citizens crusaded against gambling, prostitution, alcohol, and even boxing and horse racing, crusades that ultimately led to Prohibition. Amusement seekers of southern California could of course look toward Tijuana and Mexicali for their particular entertainments, now so discouraged in their own country. The selling and consumption of alcoholic beverages in the Imperial Valley was illegal as early as 1907. An unintended boost to the rise of the vice trade in Tijuana was the San Diego Panama California Exposition, located in what is now Balboa Park, and intended to bring tourism to San Diego. It was a great success, attracting large numbers of tourists to San Diego from 1915 into 1917.[1]

One impressed tourist was Antonio Elozúa, a brother-in-law of Francisco I. Madero, who had been partly educated in the United States and was an associate and friend of Cantú's brother-in-law, Gustavo Dato. Elozúa obtained a license from Cantú, replete with gambling concessions, to organize the *Feria Típica Mexicana* in Tijuana. The idea was to lure tourists from San Diego to a very different sort of exhibition where they could enjoy amusements denied them at the San Diego Panama California Exhibition. Available were a variety of games of chance, boxing matches, cockfighting, and that wondrous spectacle in the afternoon, the bull fight. The *Feria Típica Mexicana* also offered a casino and night clubs, and Elozúa even brought in lovely models and Ford's Circus from lively San Francisco. It was quite a success.[2]

Another tourist attraction in Tijuana was the race track and casino proposed by James Wood "Sunny Jim" Coffroth, a sports promoter, especially of boxing, and president of the Lower California Jockey Club. Coffroth of San Francisco, displaced by the increased moral conscience of California, had visited the *Feria Típica Mexicana* in 1915 and had seen great possibilities. Cantú had previously granted a concession to build a race track and a casino for every kind of gambling to H. A. Houser and H. J. Moore, both of Los Angeles, in March 1915. They were to pay $5,000 to Cantú and 10 percent of the daily proceeds to the territorial government during the first three months of operation. Thereafter the territorial government could choose to continue to receive its 10 percent or opt for $10,000 per month. There was to be a *cantina*, restaurant, ballroom dancing, movies, and music performances, at a proposed cost of $750,000. Coffroth purchased the concession for $5,000 on May 27, 1916, and formed a company, the Empresa del Hipódromo de Tijuana, S. A. The governor's brother, José Cantú, and Adolph B. Spreckels, an investor in sugar cane and railroads, were also involved in the project. The Hippodrome opened on January 1, 1916, with Governor Cantú as a guest of honor. With Cantú was the sheriff of Los Angeles, J. C. Cline, and the comedian Eddie Foy, while fifty children from the school in Tijuana formed an honor guard, each holding the national flag of Mexico. During these ceremonies Cantú received an ovation from the crowd. The Hippodrome was four hundred meters from the international border, which easily enabled more than ten thousand guests to enjoy the opening events. Most arrived by train, although two hundred automobiles brought a number of celebrants to the festivities as well. The *Feria Típica Mexicana* was such a grand success not even the rain on its opening day could dampen it. In time Coffroth's racetrack became an attraction for some of Hollywood's famous personalities, including the great Charlie Chaplin. Antonio Elozúa profited further from the success of the racetrack by constructing the Casino Monte Carlo near the Hippodrome and adjacent to the international line.[3] None of this pleased Venustiano Carranza, who ordered his consul general in San Francisco to inform the promoters of the racetrack that Cantú had no authority to grant such a concession, but his order had no effect. Perhaps more offensive was that the racetrack and the casinos did not benefit the Mexican people of Tijuana, as all the employees were United States citizens who left for their homes in San Diego when the work day was done, as did the tourists.[4]

The United States' entry into World War I caused difficulties for Tijuana, as Mexico declared neutrality in the conflict, and President Woodrow Wilson closed the border. Baja California Norte was then in the economic orbit of the United States, whose currency was the only medium of exchange, none of the several currencies of the revolutionary years being acceptable in the Northern District during the years of the Cantú regime. Closure of the border not only made it difficult to import dearly needed manufactured and other goods from the United States, but put a damper on the vice trade as well. A federal order suspending operation of the San Diego-Arizona Railroad hobbled tourism, as did the fact that no United States citizen who crossed the border to visit Tijuana could return without a passport. At the same time the San Diego Panama California Exposition, which had provided spillover tourism to Tijuana, closed its doors. This dire situation caused Antonio Elozúa to sell his gaming concession to Carl Withington who, along with Marvin Allen and Frank "Booze" Byers—all pushed out of California by the rise in anti-vice sentiment in the state—were the owners of other gambling and prostitution halls in Baja California Norte, most notably El Tecolote in Mexicali.

Elozúa had despaired too soon, it seems, as the passage of the Volstead Act through the United States Congress in late 1919 making the production and consumption of all alcoholic beverages illegal in the United States led to an unbelievable boom in the construction of breweries and wineries in Baja California Norte, particularly in Tijuana. The most notable *cantina* in Tijuana was La Ballena, whose proprietor, Miguel González, boasted having the longest bar in the world at 170 meters, about 558 feet, in length. González also owned the Cervecería Mexicali, the most prominent brewery in the Northern District. A glass of beer had previously cost nearly one dollar, but now a pint of Mexicali Pilsner could be had for thirty-five cents.[5]

The crusade against vice in the United States had its counterpart in Mexico, beginning in the *Porfiriato* and continuing under Madero and Carranza. While not much was accomplished in the years before the revolution, it was an issue in the press and the Catholic Congresses, and with the advent of *maderismo* the uplifting of public morals became an important goal of the new government. The evils of prostitution, gambling, drunkenness, and the like were to be replaced with education, the improvement of the working class, and public works. Madero hoped for education among the lower classes and the elimination of pulque, which was believed to sap the vigor and enlightenment of the humbler citizens who indulged in it. The improvement of education and public morals was as important to the revolution as were agrarian and labor reform. Although Governor Abraham González of Chihuahua had some success in controlling vice in Ciudad Juárez, these progressive ideas actually made little headway under Madero. The effort to improve public morals grew stronger with the triumph of Carranza. As police chief of Agua Prieta and later as governor of Sonora, Plutarco Elías Calles closed the gambling dens along the border. Puritanism had a following among the constitutionalists, who denounced prostitution, alcoholism, gambling, bull fighting, and other blood sports, and praised health and hygiene. After the *carrancistas* emerged victorious in the civil war, the cleansing of Ciudad Juárez, as well as in Piedras Negras, began anew. Carranza prohibited gambling as well as the importation of opium, but these efforts were as ephemeral as Cantú's occasional closing of El Tecolote.[6]

After the fall of the Carranza government, Juan B. Uribe, a San Diego attorney, lamented to interim president Adolfo de la Huerta that Tijuana under Cantú was rife with gambling, narcotics, and prostitution, and that the city had been turned into a "pigsty."[7] Very soon after the 1919 passage of the Volstead Act creating Prohibition, the frontier towns of Mexico were full of breweries, distilleries, saloons, and gambling dens, while opium production and prostitution increased as well. Prohibition also began a golden era for smugglers. The *San Diego Union* editorialized that gambling problems in Tijuana were partly due to the naiveté of people who expected to win at the gaming tables even though they had been warned that they would be swindled.[8] *Excelsior* regularly complained of the vice in Tijuana, claiming that United States citizens brought it in, which was partially true since many of the gambling dens and saloons were American owned and built. The latest vice introduced to Tijuana was dogfighting, which *Excelsior* found revolting, deploring the fact that Governor Cantú permitted the vice to continue unabated. *Excelsior* lamented that if the Yankees would simply leave, the vice would leave with them. This was perhaps wishful thinking. On a number of occasions *Excelsior* blamed Prohibition for the vice, noting in 1920 that on the Fourth of July, 25,000 United States citizens celebrated their greatest national holiday in Tijuana, Mexico.[9]

While the vice trade existed before Cantú came to power, an almost indescribable condition of immorality was flourishing in Tijuana and Mexicali by 1916, including white slavery; prostitution; common extortion; opium, cocaine, morphine, and heroin dealers; and gambling halls and saloons and dives of all descriptions. In this way Cantú supplemented Baja California Norte's revenues and his personal income as well.[10] During a two- to three-year period under Cantú, about seven hundred women from the United States arrived in Mexicali and Tijuana as recruits for the brothels, some having been transported by white slavers. There were about one hundred seventy-five prostitutes at El Tecolote, a gambling hall in Mexicali, which paid Cantú a monthly license fee of $13,000 to $15,000. An official report of 1919 held that *"una sola concesión en* Mexicali," probably referring to El Tecolote, paid a $20,000 license fee each month. At the same time it was estimated that United States citizens contributed 90 percent of the total of Cantú's vice revenues. This tainted revenue enabled Cantú to maintain peace and order in the Northern District. At the beginning of his governorship Cantú reported to Carranza that the taxes he levied on the *cantinas,* casinos, and gambling halls were a necessary support for his government, as the regular taxes in the Northern District were insufficient to support his administration. What he did not tell Carranza was that taxes were mostly paid in dollars, but recorded as pesos. At two pesos to the dollar this made fertile ground for embezzlement, as for every dollar collected one peso was recorded.[11]

There was a rather elaborate code for the Northern District covering the health of prostitutes who had to submit to an inspection by the health police (*policía de sanidad*), whether Mexican or foreigner. The health police regulated bordellos and matrons as well and did not permit children over the age of three to live in such establishments. The *casas de asignación,* hotels or other public places that were not specifically houses of prostitution but were frequented by prostitutes, also fell under the code's jurisdiction. There was a register of the prostitutes of Mexicali that included a photograph of each, specified her country of origin, and gave other information.[12]

El Tecolote was the largest of the vice dens in Mexicali, housing a *casino,* a brothel, a vaudeville theater, a barber shop, and Hop Lee's Chinese Restaurant, with opium and heroin also available. There were roulette wheels and faro tables along with thirty-five poker tables in a building that covered an entire city block, with separate entrances for *gente decente* and *gente de color*.[13] Early in his administration Cantú declared his opposition to the vice then thriving in Mexicali and Tijuana, but did not bring an end to it, which would probably have been impossible in any case. Rather than try to eliminate the vice trade, he sought to regulate and license it. Originally the dens of iniquity, including the original and much smaller El Tecolote, were lined up along Avenida Porfirio Díaz, confronting and luring the good citizens of Calexico on the other side of the street. Cantú sought to appease the concerns of the citizenry of both sister cities by moving the gambling halls and saloons to "La Chinesca," as Mexicali's Chinatown was called, where establishments such as the new and much larger El Tecolote described above would be contained within an enclosed area. To ensure that eager guests would be able to find the new location, a "string of lights" led them from the border crossing directly to the new address in "La Chinesca," thereby allowing tourists to find their way to the new habitations of delight and lead them safely home again.[14]

The *Calexico Chronicle* had complained of prostitution and white slavery as early as 1910 and in 1914 ran a series of articles regarding Encarnación Sánchez, a United States citizen of Los Angeles, who with Pablo Flores, another United States citizen, and José Valencia had come to Mexicali to rescue Sánchez's daughter Amelia, an "inmate of a Mexicali sporting house."[15] Sánchez had hoped to induce his daughter to return home and prosecute the man, Felisoldo Simmons, who had taken her to Mexicali and a life of prostitution. Adolfo M. de Pecina, the immigration officer at Mexicali, arrested Sánchez, who was brought before Judge Trinidad Meza y Salinas, found guilty of espionage, and shot *ley fuga* style while enroute to Ensenada. Sánchez, Flores, and Valencia were taken three miles south of Mexicali and shot by firing squad, but Flores, who received but a minor wound, feigned death and even escaped the *coup de grâce* pistol shot to the head. Flores stumbled back to Calexico to inform the authorities there of the incident, which evoked a request from the United States to investigate the killing of its citizens.

Encarnación Sánchez, it seems, was indeed working as a spy for one of the anti-Huerta groups in Los Angeles. Adolfo M. de Pecina, the arresting officer, had married into the usurper Victoriano Huerta's family and had been appointed immigration officer at Mexicali, but more importantly, his task was to inform the failing dictatorship of affairs in Baja California Norte. Pecina and Meza y Salinas were later arrested for theft of papers from the home of Placedio de Pizarro in Calexico, the papers incriminating them in the murder of Sánchez. Amelia Sánchez and her consort Felisoldo Simmons were also arrested by United States agents across the international line from Bisbee, Arizona.[16] All in all a tawdry story of white slavery, murder, espionage, and violation of Mexican sovereignty on the border. The white slave trade came close to Governor Cantú in July 1920, when the *San Diego Union* noted that for several months there had been a warrant out in California for the arrest of his brother-in-law, Pablo Dato, for violation of the Mann Act. After Cantú left the governorship, Dato was indicted in California for having induced eighteen-year-old Billie Palermo, a cigar worker in Mexicali, to a prostitution pit in Tijuana.[17]

Protests against the vice in Baja California Norte came from both sides of the border. Deploring the evil situation in the Northern District, which had reached alarming proportions by 1920, and the inaction of the government against prostitution and vice, *Excelsior* blamed the Volstead Act and the thousands of Yankees who descended on Tijuana and Mexicali to indulge themselves. The *San Diego Union* had earlier made a similar charge.[18] United States Consul Boyle at Mexicali asserted that many people, especially United States citizens who frequented the gambling halls in Mexicali, had fallen prey to the vice concessions. They began by losing their money, cashed checks with the gambling institution, and again lost their money. They then beseeched the establishment not to present the checks till they could make them good. As the check had cost the gambling hall nothing, the money being immediately lost back to the house, the institution readily agreed, and thereby had a club, Boyle explained, to hold over the more or less prominent citizen's head. Gambling halls such as El Tecolote were in this way agents of Cantú.[19]

While Cantú permitted and licensed the vice trade in Baja California Norte, he made a show of opposition to it in order to appease the people of California. Cantú closed all the gambling dens, saloons, dance halls, and opium dens promptly at midnight on New Years Eve in 1915, and the revelry came to an abrupt halt. In April of 1915 he arrested a number of gamblers and bunco men at the request of the authorities of San Diego, took them to the border, and gave them an opportunity to cross the street into the United States, where they were all promptly arrested. In June 1916 Cantú closed all narcotics operations in Tijuana and Mexicali, but not permanently. When Cantú's troops mutinied at Los Algodones in September 1919 against the presence of Chinese in the area, Cantú reacted by closing El Tecolote and other gambling halls in Mexicali. He announced a cleansing of all vice in the Northern District again in June 1920, but declared that he could not undertake the task until the fall because his government needed the revenue.[20]

In reality Cantú needed the vice revenue to operate his administration and build the infrastructure Baja California Norte so desperately needed. When Cantú came to power in May 1914, the $150,000 peso subsidy the federal government sent to the Northern District each month had been suspended due to the revolution and civil war and was not reinstated during Cantú's governorship. Baltasar Avilés had departed with the district's funds; the region's commerce was in a state of bankruptcy, and the troops had not been paid in nine months. Cantú reacted vigorously, imposing a forced loan on the gambling houses and other dens of iniquity, while Mexican nationals who established commercial operations were taxed at the rate of foreigners. But the biggest boost to the territorial government's revenue was from vice, at first clandestine and then licensed and regulated. From then on Cantú needed no support from the central government, as Baja California Norte could attend to all its needs with its own resources, thanks in large part to revelers from across the border.[21]

Cantú was undoubtedly aware of the possibility of personal gain from the vice that already existed in Mexicali. In the early years of the twentieth century the relative autonomy provided Baja California Norte by geography and the fact that it was a very lightly populated territory had offered the governors and their subordinates an opportunity to enrich themselves. In the spring of 1914 Cantú moved assiduously to appropriate such advantage for himself when he accused Enrique Tejedor Pedrozo, *subprefecto* of Mexicali, of irresponsibility and corruption. As the *subprefecto* answered only to the *jefe político* in Ensenada, Cantú had no authority over him, but he found another way to remove him from the path he had chosen for himself. The ambitious Cantú provided the secretary of the army and the navy testimony to the effect that for appropriate bribes Tejedor Pedrozo had interfered with all attempts to bring an end to the rampant vice in Mexicali, which at the time had more than thirty casinos and several brothels and gambling dens. These dens of iniquity attracted about 1,400 pleasure seekers during the week, their numbers swelling to about 2,200 each weekend. Cantú charged that Tejedor Pedrozo was

responsible for the growth of this industry and had also allowed the local Chinese population, then about one thousand persons, to operate a
number of opium dens in a clandestine manner. Cantú's primary complaint was that the *subprefecto* and his associates retired to their homes in
Calexico at an early hour each evening, leaving the populace of Mexicali
without law, order, or peace of mind, while scandalous activity and pistol
shots were seen and heard throughout the night. With Mexicali lacking
a police force, the troops under Cantú had to attempt to keep the peace,
but this was difficult because of the number of celebrants and the boister-
ous activity that occurred every evening. Cantú's denunciation of Tejedor
Pedrozo took place during his silent war with Governor Baltasar Avilés,
who soon found exile in San Diego, leaving the military commander of
the Mexicali garrison free to take control of the vice trade himself.[22]

Consul Manuel Paredes of Calexico reported as early as mid-May
1915 that Cantú was gathering much revenue, while publicly giving the
impression that he was a devoted *carrancista*. Paredes noted that the governor was in complete control of Baja California Norte, and that not
one man in the entire Northern District had the civic courage "to throw
down the gauntlet before Cantú."[23] Cantú's revenues were considerable.
By early 1915 he was receiving approximately $12,500 in custom duties,
as well as $4,000 from the several gambling houses, $4,000 from opium
dens, and $3,300 from the twenty-two *cantinas* every month. There was
also $1,400 from the *casas de asignación*, and $77 in taxes on the sale of
tobacco and liquor. Then there was the notorious head tax of one dollar
per month levied on every person in the Northern District, whether Mexican, Chinese, or foreigner, which amounted to $12,000 each month.
Paredes reported a monthly revenue of $37,337, all to be paid to Cantú
in advance each trimester, providing Cantú with another $112,011 every
three months. In addition Cantú imposed a 1 percent property tax on
all town lots—3 percent on commercial establishments—also to be paid
each trimester, in advance.[24] Paredes did not account for the $13,000 to
$15,000 El Tecolote paid each month, but it is difficult to reach an exact
figure, as much of this revenue was clandestine. Nor did he include revenue from Ensenada and Tijuana, which were not as lucrative for Cantú
as Mexicali.[25]

Paredes's information was incorrect, at least in regard to opium revenue. The enterprising Cantú allotted opium concessions, from which
he received an initial $45,000 and thereafter $10,000 per month.[26] The

primary producers and consumers of opium were among the growing Chinese community, located mainly in the Mexicali Valley, who worked in the cotton fields of the Colorado River Land Company. The Chinese had established semiclandestine opium dens in the principal cities of the Northern District and several laboratories for its manufacture. Cantú attempted to explain to Carranza his reasoning for allowing the commercialization of opium by first condemning its use, and then pointing out that its production and consumption among the Chinese colony was so prevalent that it would be impossible to eradicate with the limited resources and manpower at his disposal. He also noted to the First Chief that there was no federal law banning the manufacture of opium nor one to expel Chinese who were involved in this commerce. Finally, Cantú contended that his government needed the revenue. As Cantú reported to Carranza, opium factories producing over 250 kilograms per month paid a tax of $1,000 gold pesos, or $500 in United States dollars, and those producing fewer than 250 kilograms per month $500 gold pesos. These payments were due monthly in advance. In Tijuana there reportedly was an opium smoking room in every block of the city. Each of these paid a tax of $300 gold pesos per month. Cantú levied a $2 gold peso tax on every kilogram of purified opium sold. Chan Fu owned one of the largest smoking rooms in Mexicali as well as a laboratory for opium manufacture; Cantú received 10 percent of his take. After the federal government of Mexico banned traffic in opium, Cantú followed suit, seizing all clandestine opium, but rather than destroying it he either sold it himself or released it for a large fine.[27]

Huge volumes of opium left the Portuguese colony of Macau on the coast of China for San Francisco, where it was diverted to Mexico to be processed. Most of the refined opium found its way into the United States with the aid of Cantú's relatives, the Dato family. Cantú levied a tariff of $3.50 gold pesos on each kilogram of imported opium.[28] At the same time Cantú decreed duties on the importation, fabrication, and sale of alkaloids and extracts thereof. The duty on impure alkaloids, from which morphine can be produced, was fixed at $24 per kilogram and that for pure alkaloids at $72 per kilogram. Factories involved in such enterprise paid $10,000 for a permit and $4,000 each month thereafter.[29] Thus the narcotics smuggling along the border today is nothing new. It was just easier in the days of Cantú, as no tunnels needed to be dug.

Since Mexicali as yet had no bank, it was natural for Cantú to deposit the territorial revenue in the banks of Calexico, but he had other investments in neighboring California as well. Jorge González reported in September 1915 that the governor owned a plot of land in Los Angeles valued at $12,000, a house in the same city for which he paid $20,000, and a ranch of unknown value in the Imperial Valley. In addition there was $70,000 in various Los Angeles banks and another $70,000 in San Diego banks. Cantú had invested $40,000 in local California industries and held $208,000 in the several banks of the Imperial Valley, for a total of $420,000. More impressively, Consul General Ramón de Negri reported in October 1915 that the "traitor Cantú" had deposited $1,100,000 in various California banks.[30]

An effort was made on the part of the Constitutionalist Government to attach Cantú's deposits in the Security Trust and Savings Bank and the Citizens National Bank, both of Calexico. The necessary bond could not be furnished, however, and at that point Cantú had probably transferred the money to an account under his wife's name, as reported the Pinkerton Detective Agency employed to assist in the endeavor.[31] Paredes explained to Mexico's ambassador in Washington, Juan Neftalí Amador, that he could not attach Cantú's deposits in Calexico until First Chief Carranza informed the Secretary of State of the United States that Cantú was not the officially recognized governor of Baja California Norte. While the judge hearing the case against the "*infidente* Cantú" postponed the hearing until early November because Consul Paredes did not have *exequatur*, success was ultimately achieved, and Cantú's deposits in the two Calexico banks were embargoed.[32]

United States officials observing Cantú surmised that the governor was sharing in the vice profits in Tijuana and Mexicali, but Mexican authorities had a better grasp of the situation. Secretary of Foreign Relations Cándido Aguilar reported in May 1916 that Cantú received $6,000 in gambling revenue from Tijuana and a like sum from Mexicali every month, while the Hippodrome in Tijuana provided $200 daily, and all prostitutes paid a tax of one dollar each day in addition to the head tax of one dollar per month (one is inclined to cry double taxation here). This income was in addition to local federal taxes and fines, none of which was sent to Mexico City. There was honest revenue as well. Experts estimated the cotton harvest in the Northern District for 1916 would amount to

80,000 bales, all of which were to be exported to the United States, there being no cotton gin in Mexicali. The export fee was $6.00 a bale, bringing in a total revenue of $480,000 to Cantú's coffers.[33] The Mexicali Valley was ideal for growing cotton, and by 1920 United States Consul Boyle reported that the harvest for that year amounted to some $16 million, garnering Cantú $2 million in revenue. That, along with revenue from import duties, land and labor taxes, and vice concessions brought the total of the territory's revenue to $5 million in 1920.[34]

Governor Esteban Cantú did not appropriate this immense revenue to himself only. After moving the territorial capital from Ensenada to Mexicali, he inaugurated a rather impressive building program over the next several years. Before Cantú, the towns of the Northern District were connected only by means of horse or mule back, calash or cart, following the course of the flat sandy desert or the beds of arroyos, but during times of rain these were not passable as torrential waters rushed to the Pacific Ocean. By the end of the nineteenth century there was a road connecting San Diego and Yuma which touched Tijuana and Tecate, but Cantú realized the necessity of a national road linking the towns of Baja California Norte. A military road connecting Mexicali to Tijuana and Ensenada became a reality, as did one from the new territorial capital to San Felipe on the Río Colorado. The section of the road from Ensenada to Tijuana was a very old road in bad condition, having been abandoned in certain stretches; it was merely being improved. The section from Tijuana to Mexicali was a new and much more difficult endeavor. The construction of these two roads cost two and one-half million pesos. There was a five to six mile stretch over the Sierra de los Picachos that could only be completed with the use of dynamite, which Cantú managed to import from the United States despite closure of the border during World War I. Due to his close relationship and cooperation with Lieutenant Hutchinson of United States Naval Intelligence, Cantú was able to import the needed dynamite to finish the road. It was a very useful convenience and a bit of an engineering feat as well, the Sierra de los Picachos being conquered by a series of switchbacks while bridges spanned the dry river beds and arroyos. The road was seven meters wide, easily accommodating the automobiles of the day. Before completion of the Mexicali-Tijuana road it was necessary to use roads north of the international line. While Cantú received much praise for this consequential undertaking, Engineer Luis Robles Linares, drilling and blasting through live granite, made it possible.[35]

Photos showing the road from Mexicali to Tijuana. *Courtesy of Special Collections, University of California, San Diego.*

Governor Cantú inaugurating the Mexicali to Tijuana road. *Courtesy of Special Collections, University of California, San Diego.*

The road from Mexicali to San Felipe on the mouth of the Río Colorado was another remarkable achievement intended to bring Baja California Norte into closer contact with the mainland. Cantú realized the importance of communication between Mexicali and the port of San Felipe, which he believed would provide the most direct route to Manzanillo on the mainland coast. The *Calexico Chronicle* had nothing but praise for Cantú's new road to San Felipe when it was finished in 1918, heralding it as another example of the prosperity which the governor had brought to the Northern District and remarking that Calexico would also benefit from its construction. Other roads of lesser importance connected smaller towns, villages, and ranches, all of which converged on Mexicali. Cantú also had plans for a railroad connecting Mexicali with the gulf port, which would have made it feasible to ship cotton from the Mexicali Valley to Manzanillo and thence to the interior of Mexico instead of sending it across the line to California, but that project did not get beyond the planning stage during his administration.[36]

Construction of the Escuela Cuauhtémoc. *Courtesy of Special Collections, University of California, San Diego.*

Cantú made every effort to tie the Northern District together. In addition to the new road system, telegraph lines connected Mexicali with Tecate, Tijuana, Ensenada, and Los Algodones, while telephone lines were reaching out from Mexicali as well. The importation of wireless radios, the result of Cantú's cooperation with United States authorities, made possible a well-equipped radio station in Mexicali enabling communication with all wireless stations in Mexico and the United States. Cantú lowered the import duty on oil that powered the electrical plant in Mexicali, which he considered an equitable act of benefit to all citizens whether of the upper or lower classes. When Cantú seized power there was no potable water in the small community of Tijuana. To alleviate this situation he granted a concession to J.W. Hackworth, a United States citizen of California, to establish a water plant with the stipulation that all public buildings in Tijuana were to receive their water free and that all employees were to be Mexican citizens. A further benefit to the community was a concession to Manuel P. Barbachano of Tijuana to provide the town with electric lighting via the plant in San Diego, as the population of Tijuana at that time was too small to support a plant of its own.[37]

Perhaps more important for the future of Baja California Norte was the impetus Governor Cantú gave to education, his most notable achievement being the construction of a new secondary school in Mexicali, the Escuela Cuauhtémoc, at a cost of $100,000.[38] There had been previous efforts to enhance education in the Northern District with the adoption of teaching methods conforming to the laws of the nation under the leadership of Professor Luis Vargas Piñera, who assumed complete control over education in the territory in 1911. The lack of educational infrastructure was solved with the active support of Cantú, who financed the construction of a number of urban as well as rural schools in the Mexicali Valley beginning in 1915, and later constructing schools throughout the Northern District at Pueblo Nuevo, San Isidro, Colonia Castro, Colonia Rivera, Los Algodones, Hechicera, and Colonia Sonora. This spree culminated with the opening of the fine Escuela Cuauhtémoc, appropriately on September 16, 1916, to celebrate Mexico's independence day. This new secondary school, located on Avenida Porfirio Díaz, was an architectural delight that served students of the entire Northern District and was a welcome replacement of the dens of vice which had been removed to "La Chinesca." In a short time students were transferring from schools in Calexico to attend Escuela Cuauhtémoc, which years later became the Casa de Cultura de Mexicali.[39]

The institutions planned by Vargas Piñera came to full flower in 1916 with the opening of night schools for adults in Mexicali and Ensenada and the course of elementary pedagogy, later evolving into the Normal School in 1919 housed in the Escuela Cuauhtémoc. These were all made possible through the enlightened and progressive attitude of Esteban Cantú toward education. The Escuela Cuauhtémoc was an educational center of the first order for its time, and when a group of teachers from the United States toured the establishment, "the remark was made that the institution probably was supported by American funds," possibly referring to the Northern District's vice revenues.[40] Nevertheless, the Escuela Cuauhtémoc was a "modern high-school building . . . a model of its kind and well worthy of a much larger and richer community."[41]

Cantú also supported efforts to improve the quality of teaching in the Northern District when in late 1918 qualifying examinations were required for those lacking a degree in teaching or having insufficient service records.

Beginning in 1919 the remuneration of teachers began to improve, and in the same year the territorial government began sending three teachers from the Escuela Cuauhtémoc to Los Angeles each summer to further their studies in various subjects. Students in the Normal School received scholarships to aid them in their three-year course of study, resulting in an adequate supply of teachers for the Northern District.[42] Governor Cantú's efforts to support education in Baja California Norte provided a strong base on which later administrations wisely built.

One of the problems facing Mexicali as the town began to grow into a city was the hard fact that it was surrounded on three sides by the Colorado River Land Company, while the international border with the United States closed the square on the north. Governor Cantú was able to solve the difficulty by purchasing land from the company in 1918, which enabled him to begin the construction of the fine Palacio del Gobierno, an architectural achievement of the first order, which was completed after his departure from the governorship and years later became the rectory of the Universidad Autónoma de Baja California. Other accomplishments under Cantú were the new bridge over the Río Nuevo, construction of a hospital, the paving of streets, an electric lighting plant, new infantry and cavalry barracks, a customs house, a drainage system for the city of Mexicali, and the beautiful park of Los Niños Héroes de Chapultepec with its magnificent gardens. In naming the park Cantú had not forgotten his days at the Colegio Militar on the heights of Chapultepec, where several young cadets had fallen during a last desperate attempt to save the castle during the 1846-1848 war with the United States.[43]

Tijuana also benefitted from the vice revenue of the Cantú years when the principal streets of the city were paved with concrete, a vast improvement over the dirt streets, muddy when it rained, dusty during drought, and cratered with numerous potholes. The water system was also much improved, providing potable water for a larger portion of the citizenry. Other public improvements were the Casa de Gobierno, a new military garrison for infantry and cavalry, a public jail, and two new public schools. In an effort to spur the growth of the different regions of the Northern District, after becoming governor Cantú established three new municipalities, Mexicali, Tijuana, and Tecate, adding these to Ensenada, which already existed.[44]

The *San Diego Union* had nothing but praise for Cantú when he had two thousand acres of wheat planted near Ensenada in 1917 and forbade export of its harvest in order to lower the cost of bread in Baja California Norte. The newspaper also lauded the governor's efforts to enhance public works in Ensenada: "The streets have been graded, cement sidewalks built, an electric lighting plant has been erected, water and sewer systems have been constructed and extended and an ice-plant is now in full operation."[45] This sounds very much like the program of public works David Zárate had called for when briefly *jefe político* of the Northern District in 1914.

While one may condemn Governor Esteban Cantú for allowing the dens of iniquity in the Northern District to ply their trade, one must realize that the vice trade was already in place when he arrived in Mexicali in June 1911, and that by the time he assumed the governorship in 1914 that trade had grown considerably.[46] The economic disparity from one side of the border to the other perhaps made the situation inevitable. Cantú could have attempted to liquidate the vice trade, but despite his command of the garrisons at Tijuana and Mexicali this would have been difficult because of the financial distress of the gubernatorial office when he came to power. Baltasar Avilés had stripped the treasury at Ensenada and the customs house at Tijuana before his departure into exile, and Mexico City was sending no financial help because of the revolution and civil war then raging on the mainland. Rather, Cantú chose to regulate and license the vice trade, wisely moving it out of the sight of the good people of Mexicali and Calexico to "La Chinesca." As a result the vice revenues were considerable by 1916. Then came the bonanza of Prohibition in 1919, filling Cantú's private bank accounts to be sure, but also allowing him to build an infrastructure in Baja California Norte that would not have been possible otherwise. How else could he have possibly built a high school at the cost of $100,000, not to mention the other key elements of the Northern District's infrastructure?

Toward the end of 1919 the Secretary of Hacienda sent a commission led by Modesto C. Rolland, a civil engineer who had served the Constitutionalist government in various posts, to review the government and economy of Baja California Norte. Governor Cantú cooperated with Rolland, and the result was an in-depth report on the Northern District. Rolland reported that Cantú's administration was swollen with too many employees supported by taxes that were a burden on the people. Were Cantú to trim his staff, Rolland reported, the governor could save $337, 950 pesos a year, and thereby be able to lower taxes. Rolland found Cantú's military budget of $1,400,000 pesos for 1919 absurd, declaring that he could do well with half that amount, as there was no military threat to the district.[47]

On the other hand Rolland had much praise for Cantú's efforts to build the district's infrastructure, particularly the Camino Nacional from Mexicali to Tijuana and Ensenada, which, along with telegraph and telephone lines, went far to tying the region together. He also believed the governor deserved applause for his achievements in extending public education and was impressed with the Escuela Cuauhtémoc. Rolland also noted Cantú's efforts to settle Mexican nationals on agricultural land, but found the number of Chinese and Japanese in Baja California Norte alarming. Despite his praise for some of Cantú's efforts, Rolland believed the federal government should bring his oppressive administration to an end by sending a force of two or three thousand troops to the Northern District.[48]

CHAPTER VI

THE ABDICATION OF HIS MAJESTY CANTÚ

"Cantú *es rebelde.*"
—**PLUTARCO ELÍAS CALLES,** Mexican Secretary of War

Until 1920 Baja California Norte had managed to hold itself aloof from the turmoil and bloodshed of the revolution, and enjoyed unprecedented economic growth as the rest of the country seemed to be tearing itself apart. President Venustiano Carranza had finally established what appeared to be peace on the mainland when he fatally chose to impose Ignacio Bonillas, Mexico's chief diplomat in Washington, as his successor. A competent administrator, Bonillas had earned an excellent technical education in the United States and was respected in that country as well as in Mexico. Nevertheless the ambassador, who had spent so much time in the United States that he was derided as "Mr. Bonillas," was not the man the people desired to lead them; instead they wanted the real hero of the revolution, Álvaro Obregón, as their standard bearer. *El Heraldo de México*, in a front-page open letter to Bonillas, called his candidacy the triumph of imposition. More to the point Obregón had agreed to support Carranza's bid for the presidency in 1917 with the understanding that the First Chief would, in return, support his run for the presidency in 1920. The governor of Guanajuato, Federico Montes, sent a letter of invitation on January 11 urging his fellow governors to meet in Mexico City in February to discuss the peaceful transition of power. This was perhaps done at Carranza's urging. Not all the governors accepted the invitation, notably Esteban Cantú, who had no desire to distance himself so far from his power base. A trip to San Diego was one thing, but traveling to Mexico City could be fatal to

85

his hold on power. Absent also was Adolfo de la Huerta, as the Sonoran legislature did not give him permission to leave the state. In January the military leadership in Sonora, Plutarco Elías Calles, Adolfo de la Huerta, and others were throwing their support to Obregón and formalized their rebellion in the April 23, 1920, Plan of Agua Prieta.[1]

Adolfo de la Huerta had thrown his lot in with the revolution from the beginning, first adhering to the ideas of Ricardo Flores Magón, then to those of Francisco Madero. Then he had joined the ranks of the followers of Venustiano Carranza, serving in the First Chief's outer circle despite their mutual mistrust. In 1919 de la Huerta quite handily won the governorship of Sonora against Ignacio L. Pesqueira, notwithstanding the latter's substantial support from Carranza, who had broken his promise to Obregón not to impede *el Manco*'s march to the presidential chair. Carranza's attempt to break up the Sonoran leadership backfired as Francisco Serrano launched the candidacy of Obregón in Sonora, and Calles renounced his position in the government to join the *obregonista* presidential campaign. Carranza then declared he did not recognize de la Huerta as the legitimate governor of Sonora, and the northwestern state put itself on a war footing.[2]

While the Sonoran leaders marched on Mexico City unopposed and made de la Huerta the interim president (until the actual election a few months later, which made Obregón president on December 1), Governor Esteban Cantú in a rather sudden about-face declared his loyalty to Carranza, adding that friendly relations would be maintained between the United States and Baja California Norte during any resulting turmoil. This is reminiscent of Cantú's posture during the civil war between Carranza and Villa, in which he declared his neutrality. Adolfo de la Huerta held that Cantú's loyalty to Carranza was rather "*prendido con alfileras*" (attached to him with pins). After the success of the Agua Prieta revolt Cantú wrote to Obregón congratulating the new government in its efforts to realize national unification and expressed his desire to place Baja California Norte under the orders of Provisional President Adolfo de la Huerta.[3]

With the triumph of the rebellion, Obregón appointed Baldomero Almada governor of Baja California Norte in early June, to replace the thirty-nine-year-old Esteban Cantú. While Cantú declared his willingness to turn his office over to Almada, he actually placed all possible obstacles in the appointee's path. When Almada arrived in Mexicali from

Los Angeles at his invitation, Governor Cantú escorted him throughout the Northern District that he might familiarize himself with his future duties. Cantú then wrote to Obregón that he had a long discussion with Almada regarding the territory, but failed to release the governorship to him. There was concern in Mexicali that a change in administration would upset the peace that Cantú had provided for the past six years, not merely in Baja California Norte, but also with the territory's neighbor to the north. At a meeting held in the Escuela Cuauhtémoc on June 3, Cantú made a short speech introducing Almada, who in turn gave a brief address inviting comments on his appointment. Eduardo Trujillo, an engineer and graduate of the Colegio Militar in Cantú's employ, asked by what authority had Obregón appointed Almada governor, declaring the people would not accept him. Almada's response is not known, but following the meeting he returned to Los Angeles and informed the press that he and Cantú were in full accord.[4]

Cantú, on the other hand, stated to the *Calexico Chronicle* that Almada's appointment arose from his request for a leave of absence, as he very much needed the rest. A large crowd gathered at Los Niños Heroes Park in Mexicali on June 6 to voice their support for Cantú with a number of eulogistic orations in which not a discordant note was heard. When he returned from Los Angeles, Almada was greeted on June 13 by five thousand vociferous people in the plaza of Mexicali who informed him that they did not wish to lose Cantú, whose administration had been so beneficial to them. Realizing he could not take office against such opposition, Almada crossed the street to Calexico and traveled on to Los Angeles, where he informed the central government that he could not gain control of Baja California Norte with fewer than five thousand troops, and then fearing for his life, as claimed the *Calexico Chronicle,* left for Mexico City to confer with interim president Adolfo de la Huerta. According to Enrique Barrera, an *obregonista* of Mexicali, Almada had become a comical and ridiculous figure before Mexicans and foreigners alike. On his departure Almada requested $500 from Cantú to return to Mexico City, but Cantú eagerly gave him $1,000. *Excelsior* reported that the citizens of Mexicali sent a telegram containing a mass of signatures to de la Huerta and Obregón notifying them that they wished no change in the governorship, that before Cantú the territory had been a heavy weight on the nation, but in recent years the Northern District had become self-sufficient and had developed economically under the leadership of Cantú. In a second telegram the citizens informed de la Huerta that they were not participants in an unpatriotic separation from the nation and asked what were the interim president's reasons for wanting to remove Governor Cantú. Almada later charged that gambling interests had persuaded Cantú to remain in office, but one is inclined to suspect that the recalcitrant governor had orchestrated the whole affair without much influence from any quarter. On the same day at the mass meeting in Los Niños Héroes Park, Cantú informed Obregón that he was unable to turn the governorship over to Almada because of the mass opposition of the local populace to such a change. He related that groups of business leaders, agriculturalists, and *braceros* vigorously opposed Cantú's proposed leave of absence for reasons of health. Cantú assured Obregón that the actual state of affairs in Baja California Norte presented no problems for the new government in Mexico City, and that the people and administration of the Northern District sincerely adhered to the new order. In view of the situation Cantú wished to withdraw his petition for a leave of absence and remain at his post.[5]

Faced with the flurry of opposition to Baldomero Almada in Mexicali, de la Huerta withdrew Almada's appointment, confirmed Cantú as governor, and invited him to Mexico City for an exchange of views on the situation in Baja California Norte. Cantú, as was his custom, refused to accept the invitation, with the excuse that the situation in the Northern District was "too delicate for him to leave."[6] While he did not openly declare his independence from the central government and claimed that he followed its orders, Cantú had no intention of giving up his post. To underscore his attitude Cantú refused to recognize the immigration officer whom de la Huerta had appointed for Tijuana. An observer of Cantú's actions, Juan Rodolfo Platt, a Sonoran businessman, admitted that Cantú had always done as he pleased, irrespective of any instructions from the federal government. In an interview with *Excelsior,* Secretary of War Plutarco Elías Calles stated that Cantú had always controlled the officials in the Northern District, had been ignoring the government for years, and was only now forced to take off the mask of loyalty, since Mexico City intended to replace him by force, if necessary. Cantú rejoined that violence should not be used in the mounting crisis because Baja California Norte had remained tranquil during the revolution and because of the foreign interests in the district, which a military solution would adversely affect.[7]

Cantú was taking a gamble that the Sonoran Revolt would prove ephemeral, but not all in the Northern District were willing to play this game of chance. The garrison at Los Algodones, which had mutinied and murdered two of their officers the previous September, deserted Cantú and joined the Agua Prieta revolt, but this was just the beginning of the desertion to follow. President de la Huerta now determined to eliminate Cantú and began by ordering that five delegates be sent from the Northern District to Mexico City to suggest appropriate candidates for the territory's governorship. Cantú made every effort to pack this delegation with his supporters and succeeded in the selection of the three delegates representing Mexicali and Tijuana, but failed with regard to Ensenada, still chafing perhaps at its loss of status when Cantú moved the territorial capital to Mexicali. A mass meeting was held in that Pacific coastal city, and the group emphatically refused to condone any candidates favoring Cantú, choosing instead two anti-Cantú delegates who left Ensenada secretly at night as they feared arrest by the authorities. Once safely in the United States they departed for Mexico City, where they requested that de la Huerta appoint a native son, which they insisted Cantú was not, as Baja California's governor. This was the first time in years that any *bajacaliforniano* had dared to voice opposition to Governor Cantú in a public forum.

United States Consul Walter Burdett at Calexico reported that Cantú's favored candidate was Carlos Bernstein of Tecate, whom Cantú assumed would loyally continue his policies and protect his financial interests in Baja California Norte. Bernstein went to Sonora to solicit Obregón's support for his gubernatorial aspirations, but apparently without favorable result. He had acted as Cantú's confidential financial agent, receiving the governor's portion of the vice revenue which he then invested in Cantú's name. As a young man Bernstein was held to be a petty swindler who later became an official in the gambling dens of Tijuana and an associate in the Hippodrome. He had acquired a fortune and by 1920 was operating a number of enterprises in the district. Bernstein was the owner of flour mills at Ensenada and Tecate, a cannery at San Quintín, and other enterprises. He had acted as a spy for Cantú throughout his tenure, thereby gaining the protection of the governor, who aided Bernstein's rather rapid rise in fortune. Bernstein attempted to pass himself off as a constitutionalist, visiting the constitutionalist clubs of California and railing against Cantú in the office of Consul Adolfo Carrillo, who easily saw through the ruse. Bernstein had been a close confidant and front man for Cantú's own business interests, but later would betray his benefactor. Walter Burdett believed Cantú would hold on as long as possible, but that he would not resist militarily.[8]

The de la Huerta government had tried to remove Cantú peacefully, but after his refusal to meet with the interim president in Mexico City, it opted for a military invasion of Baja California Norte. Juan Velázquez, the Northern District's representative in the federal chamber of deputies, maintained that Cantú had always followed the orders of the government and that to send an armed force to the territory would be costly and futile. Cantú himself responded in a manifesto to the citizens of the Northern District that he did not recognize the authority of the federal government to disturb the reign of tranquility and peace that had prevailed in the territory, and condemned de la Huerta's decision to bring war and devastation to its people, who, he declared, would fight to the death if necessary.[9] At the same time the governor stated, "There is no rebellion against the federal government on my part."[10] In his manifesto Cantú laid the blame for the proposed invasion at the feet of Álvaro Obregón. It seems Cantú felt Obregón had betrayed him in 1916 when he had requested additional troops to safeguard the Northern District from the persistent rumors of United States aggression against Mexico, but no additional forces had been forthcoming. In October 1916 Jesús M. Garza, an adherent of Obregón, discussed with Cantú the possibility of an alliance between the independent governor and the hero of Celaya, who was gathering political support in his struggle with Carranza, but nothing came of it.[11]

Mexico's chief representative in Washington, Fernando Iglesias Calderón, a staunch liberal rather than a revolutionary, believed that while Cantú would resist the invasion, he was not trying to make Baja California Norte independent. Iglesias Calderón held that the majority of *bajacalifornianos* did not sympathize with the wayward governor. Defeated *carrancistas* such as Cándido Aguilar, Lucio Blanco, Bernardo Mena Brito, and Andrés Ortiz either sent expressions of support to Cantú or made their way into the territory, many coming from Coahuila. Iglesias Calderón and Mexico's Consul Eduardo Ruiz at Los Angeles believed the *carrancistas* in the Northern District hoped to use Cantú's rebellion to overthrow the de la Huerta government.[12] At that moment Mexico's chief diplomatic representative was correct in his evaluation of the situation, as Cantú began to prepare for imminent invasion.

Obregón, writing from Nogales, Sonora, informed Secretary of War Calles that Cantú was making an all-out effort for armed action against the government, his agents smuggling arms and artillery across the border. Cantú had earlier in his governorship sought to purchase airplanes in the United States, ostensibly to enhance mail service in the Northern District. He now attempted to buy three planes and hire foreign pilots "for mail and observation purposes."[13] As this violated the neutrality laws of the United States, Iglesias Calderón took the proper steps to prevent Cantú from procuring any arms of whatever nature from the United States. Despite the efforts of Washington and Mexico City, Cantú managed to employ three aviators, one of whom was one T. O. Paine, commissioned to purchase planes in the United States and deliver them to Mexicali. The effort was apparently successful, for in early August two planes flew over the Río Colorado on a scouting mission. Federal troops opened fire, and the planes turned away. On another occasion the two planes strafed and bombed a federal garrison on the Río Colorado, but failed to do any damage. Iglesias Calderón related that Cantú had about one thousand bombs for the defense of his kingdom. This caused the federal government to order Captain Alfonso R. Virgen and his squadron of planes based at Jiménez, Sonora, to Baja California Norte.[14]

Cantú, now in open rebellion, severed all communications with the federal government and began to make military preparations for the defense of his kingdom. All automobiles, wagons, hospitals, and hospital supplies owned by Mexicans and the Russian colony at San Quintín were requisitioned, while horses, cattle, and supplies from surrounding ranches were confiscated. He commandeered fifty cases of dynamite from the Compañía de Terrenos y Aguas, S. A., the Mexican corporation that operated the irrigation works in the Mexicali Valley under the aegis of the Imperial Valley irrigation district of California. The Mexican yacht *Tecate*, which inspected the fisheries of Mexico's west coast, was also seized. There was a report that the *Tecate*'s captain, Leonardo Zepeda, was lured ashore and killed in a fight with Cantú's soldiers, but his demise later proved a falsehood. While Cantú expected invasion from the Pacific as well as the Gulf of California, the *Tecate* would not make much of a navy for him.[15]

The beleaguered governor sent to his brother-in-law Gustavo Dato in Washington $58,000 on Dato's assertion that for such sum he could secure belligerent rights for Baja California Norte, which would enable Cantú to import arms and ammunition freely. Another part of Cantú's survival strategy was his employment of Dr. Jorge Ziegner Uriburu, whose flawless English and position as president of the University of California at Riverside made him the perfect spokesman in Los Angeles for Cantú's rebellion. Uriburu, an Argentine national who called Mexico his second country, held that Cantú's rebellion was perfectly justified, rather like de la Huerta's revolt against Carranza, whose government Uriburu had despised. Los Angeles authorities at first accepted this reasoning, but de la Huerta's consuls, Paredes in Calexico, Ruiz in Los Angeles, and Ives Lelevier in San Diego, went on the counteroffensive, informing the serious press in the United States that Cantú was merely an appointee of the president of Mexico who was in rebellion against the federal government. Iglesias Calderón in Washington informed the State Department that Cantú was a simple rebel who hoped to retain control of the vice revenue in Baja California Norte. Roberto V. Pesqueira in New York applied the same tactic, and opinion in the United States toward Cantú changed to the point that Gustavo Dato's efforts had no effect. Obregón meanwhile requested Louis Hostetter, a friend well disposed toward the de la Huerta government, to intercede in Washington. Hostetter was well acquainted with Warren G. Harding and other members of the Republican Party. He informed Obregón that the Department of State refused to listen to Dato and made it clear that the embargo on the exportation of arms applied to all political factions in Mexico and was still in force. The department also informed the de la Huerta administration that any citizens of the United States who crossed the border to fight for Cantú would have their passports voided, and that all precautions would be taken to prevent any filibustering expedition against Mexico. At nearly the same time Cantú presented to United States immigration authorities in Calexico a list of Mexican citizens he desired kept out of Mexicali. The immigration agent refused to acquiesce on the grounds that this was a function of the government in Mexico City. Consul Walter Boyle concurred in this action and opined that the request was merely an effort on Cantú's part to have his enemies discredited by United States authorities so as to impress upon the people of Mexicali that he had the support of the United States, which he did not. Cantú's relations with the authorities in San Diego and Calexico had by this time cooled completely.[16]

PELIGRO

El Tío Sam está harto de eso, señor Cantú; todo Mé-xico siente vergüenza por ello.

"Uncle Sam is fed up with this, Señor Cantú; all of Mexico is feeling shame for him," in *El Heraldo*. *Courtesy of the Archivo General de la Nación in Mexico City.*

In an effort to augment his forces Cantú forced one hundred Japanese and a number of Russian colonists to join his army, but found the Chinese not so willing when he called upon seven thousand of them to take up arms in his defense. The *Unión Fraternal China* requested Fong Tsiang Kwang, Chinese *chargé d'affaires* at Mexico City, to appeal to the Mexican government and the Chinese legation at Washington for

The caption to this cartoon titled "A Soldier to His Dog" reads "What are you: loyal or disloyal?" *Courtesy of the Archivo General de la Nación in Mexico City.*

protection from Cantú's rebellious plans, and requested that the United States grant the Chinese colonists asylum to avoid the coming conflict against Cantú, whom they had no particular wish to die protecting. In the end the Chinese colony did not have to bear arms in defense of Cantú, but the governor did manage to levy a forced loan of $100,000 upon them. *Excelsior* reported that the de la Huerta government stated that if Cantú was indeed calling on foreigners to fight Mexicans, he was committing treason. Mexican workers meanwhile were fleeing across the border to escape being forced into his army.[17]

In an editorial *El Heraldo de México* declared that Cantú was placing the entire nation in danger, that the economic interests in the Imperial and Mexicali Valleys were international in scope, and that the governor was a traitor who threatened to throw the nation into chaos just when the de la Huerta administration had brought peace. The newspaper called for a moral as well as a military campaign against Cantú. Secretary of War Calles noted that Cantú could only put one or two thousand men in the field, whereas the federal government could send many more troops than that since Villa was no longer a problem, and the difficulties in Chiapas had been resolved. In an interview on August 4 with *El Heraldo de México*, Calles stated that "Cantú *es un rebelde*," and that the only problem in bringing him down was the proximity of the United States and its troops on the border. Calles also noted that everyone knew perfectly well that Cantú was a completely immoral being who had enriched himself by permitting gambling and prostitution and granting vice concessions to United States entrepreneurs. Calles held that none who had enjoyed this corruption would fight for Cantú.[18]

Despite Cantú's feverish efforts to defend his realm, it was clear that his regime would fall without a fight. By the end of July he had no support outside of or south of Mexicali and Tijuana. His troops were deserting and crossing into the United States, his family already having departed for their home in Los Angeles. The *Calexico Chronicle* meanwhile reported that all was calm and normal in Mexicali, with business going about its pace as usual and no evidence of preparations for war were to be seen.[19] The de la Huerta administration had given Cantú ample opportunity to step down peacefully because of the delicate nature of the imbroglio Cantú had presented the government. De la Huerta's personal secretary, Miguel Alessio Robles, an eminent lawyer who had aided Obregón's flight from Mexico City when both men broke with Carranza in 1920, informed the *Washington Post* that the administration was ready to act emphatically "because it does not want what happened to Texas to happen in Lower California."[20] *Excelsior* concurred, while *El Heraldo de México* noted that the situation in Baja California Norte was very dangerous, both because of the proximity of the United States and because the irrigation works in the Imperial Valley depended on the waters of the Río Colorado flowing unimpeded through the Northern District.[21] While the central government preferred a peaceful solution to Cantú's obstinance, a military option was planned earlier in June 1920 when the secretary of war ordered Brigadier General Abelardo Rodríguez to form a column to invade Baja California Norte and bring the territory under the control of the federal government. Rodríguez had previously been part of a colonization effort in the region around San Luis Río Colorado on the left bank of the river for the purpose of establishing cotton production in the vicinity and did so successfully at El Alamar, so named after the many poplar trees there. In reality his mission was to become acquainted with the topography of the region, form an understanding of the situation in the Northern District, and study the possibility of a military incursion if one became necessary.[22]

Another member of the Agua Prieta group that had overthrown Carranza, Abelardo Rodríguez, was born on May 12, 1889, to Nicolás Rodríguez and Petra Luján in Guaymas, Sonora. The Rodríguez family included eleven children and was of modest means when they moved to Nogales, a developing commercial center where Abelardo had spent a part of his youth. There he proved an indolent student who was neither fond of books nor the classroom, but thanks to his mother learned a more than passing English in Nogales, Arizona, across the line. Rather, the young Rodríguez was a passionate devotee of athletic endeavors, especially boxing and baseball, and he developed a robust physique. He spent his early years bouncing around looking for a career, variously working in his brother Fernando's hardware store in Nogales and then with the Cananea Consolidated Copper Company, where his mastery of English stood him in good stead. Loving music and singing, he briefly sought a career as a vocalist, but after several weeks of lessons in Los Angeles his voice instructor suggested he waste no more time pursuing a talent he did not quite have. Securing employment with the Southern Pacific Railroad of Mexico, he hoped to rise to the position of conductor, but the discovery of his color blindness put an end to that attractive possibility, as he would be unable to read the traffic signals so critical to the safety of the industry. He returned to his brother's hardware store in Nogales for three years where his popularity as an athlete and his robust physique won him election to the post of chief of police. While Abelardo Rodríguez was serving in this capacity Francisco I. Madero and José María Pino Suárez were assassinated in Mexico City, and Governor Ignacio Pesqueira, refusing to recognize the usurper Victoriano Huerta as president, called all *sonorenses* to arms. Now an opportunity was open to Rodríguez, who had always wished to make something of his life, use the talents he did have, and influence the outcome of a great movement.[23]

The handsome, twenty-one-year-old Rodríguez joined the Constitutionalist Army in March 1913 as a lieutenant in the Second Battalion of Infantry in his home state, attaining the rank of colonel by 1916. He fought in many battles with recognized valor, including that of Celaya, in which he was praised for his gallantry and bravery. Rodríguez carried out his duties with energy and dispatch, Plutarco Elías Calles, under whom he had served, calling his conduct meritorious. Despite his earlier dislike of academic subjects Rodríguez's service record commends his grasp of geography, mathematics, and history, noting that his English was excel-

The caption to this cartoon titled *Popular Expressions* reads "Don't break, rope, because this is the last pull!" The word on the legs of the men who have been hanged is "Traitor," in *El Heraldo. Courtesy of the Archivo General de la Nación in Mexico City.*

lent. The young officer fought against Huerta, Zapata, Villa, and the Yaqui Indians of Sonora before being promoted to brigadier general in May 1920.[24]

Abelardo Rodríguez took command of the *Brigada Rodríguez* in Mexico City on July 20 with orders to march to Baja California Norte to depose Cantú with military force. Leaving the capital six days later, his troop reached Manzanillo by train and on July 29 embarked on the gun boat *Guerrero* and the merchant bark *Bonita* for Mazatlán, where his brigade landed on August 2. There he organized his force, now renamed the *Columna Expedicionaria de la Baja California.*[25] The original plan was to attack the Northern District on the Pacific Coast south of Ensenada at Punta de Santo Tomás and the Gulf of California, but those intentions were dashed when a hurricane drove the *Guerrero* onto a reef and the ship sank in the storm. All members of the crew were rescued, but four-fifths of the *Guerrero* lay submerged in the sea. The captain of the *Guerrero* was not on board when the ship sank, and Rodríguez held him responsible and put him under arrest. The general wondered if the sinking were indeed an accident of nature, considering the ex-federal naval officers, Othon Blanco,

Ignacio Torres, Rafael Carrion, and others were abiding in Mexicali under Cantú's protection, but weather was the more likely culprit.[26]

Secretary of War Calles now ordered Rodríguez to concentrate his troops in Guaymas, gather all the boats he could, transport his force as far north on the coast of Sonora as possible, and march to the Río Colorado, crossing the river as best he could. Mexico had requested the Department of State's permission to cross United States soil by rail to reach Mexicali in a more expedient manner, but was denied on the grounds that it was a presidential election year and the Democratic governors of Arizona and Texas and the Republican governor of California would have to agree, which would be difficult at best. It would therefore require more time to reach Esteban Cantú's capital city. His force now numbering six thousand men with a battery of artillery and a machine gun regiment, Rodríguez got his well-organized and provisioned troops to Puerto Edgardo, Sonora, on the Río Colorado on August 16 in the *Bonita* and the barks *Washington* and *Pacita* and a number of other small craft, setting up his headquarters at Rancho La Grulla. After reaching San Luis Río Colorado by forced night marches to avoid the heat of the desert, Rodríguez built a pontoon bridge across the river using materials purchased in Yuma, Arizona. Carlos Bernstein, a former trusted supporter of Cantú but now an enemy, loaned Rodríguez a motor boat to aid in the construction of the bridge. Bernstein apparently aided Rodríguez in the transport of his troops toward Mexicali in other ways, for he was later paid $3,813.55 in pesos for his efforts. The column then crossed the river on August 30, marched to Paredones Station, and boarded the Inter-California Railway the next day, reaching Mexicali at dawn on September 1, 1920.[27]

Washington was of course keeping close watch on the events that were now unfolding on the California border, which had remained an enviable scene of tranquility during most of the turbulent years of the Mexican Revolution. In an effort to keep the border calm, Secretary of State Bainbridge Colby informed Consul Walter Boyle at Mexicali that the United States would under no circumstances permit the shipment of arms or ammunition to either faction in Mexico. Boyle was instructed to inform Cantú conclusively of this and cooperate with his counterpart in Calexico to prevent any shipment of arms in accordance with President Wilson's July 12, 1919 proclamation forbidding exportation of war matériel to Mexico. Mexico City in turn informed its consulates along the border that all points of entry into Baja California Norte were closed.

Mexico's representative in Washington, Fernando Iglesias Calderón, informed the Mexican secretary of foreign relations that while Washington was in favor of the de la Huerta administration in its battle with Cantú, it could not order closure of all points of entry without an act of Congress, but would look for any breach of the neutrality laws.[28]

As the crisis neared its culmination, the *San Diego Union* reported that the Department of State had ordered the border at Tijuana and Mexicali closed to all but those having legal business, and that no tourists would be permitted to cross the line, effectively killing Cantú's revenue. The state department also ordered that any artillery experts or aviators who participated in the possible coming conflict would have their passports revoked. Iglesias Calderón reported from Washington that the United States would not aid Cantú or the Mexican government in any way.[29] There was fear that an international incident might occur if troops were sent against Cantú because of the large United States interests in the Northern District, particularly the irrigation works located south of the border, which if imperiled could cause military intervention on the part of the United States. The de la Huerta administration on the contrary did not think the obstinate stand of Cantú would in any way place Mexico in a conflict with its northern neighbor, that there would not be a separatist movement on the part of the recalcitrant governor, and that the citizens of the United States would be glad to be rid of all the vice that had blossomed under Cantú. *El Heraldo de México*, on the other hand, editorialized that General Joseph T. Dickman had orders to invade the territory if Mexico could not protect the irrigation works, which might be damaged or destroyed by an attempt to depose Cantú militarily.[30]

While at Rancho La Grulla preparing for his march to San Luis Río Colorado, General Rodríguez received orders on August 21 from the secretary of the army and the navy Calles to press forward posthaste. Cantú had relinquished the governorship of Baja California Norte on August 19, but Calles did not trust him.[31] De la Huerta regarded Rodríguez's expedition as one which would not actually engage Cantú's troops, but merely intimidate the obstinate governor and add weight to other pressures he intended to exert against him. The interim president's policy of political conciliation paid off most conspicuously with regard to Pancho Villa, who after many years of struggle had agreed to lay down his arms and retreat to the quietude of the hacienda of Canutillo. De la Huerta now sought to influence the numerous *villistas* and *maytorenistas* in the territory by enlisting the support of Villa and former associates of Victoriano Huerta and José María Maytorena, former governor of Sonora. De la Huerta sent Roberto V. Pesqueira to the United States as Mexico's financial agent in New York with the added mission of influencing the press of that country. He also requested Iglesias Calderón to obtain the moral backing of President Wilson in ridding Baja California Norte of Cantú's vice-laden regime, and further sought the assistance of Javier Fabela, then Mexican Consul at Los Angeles. Cantú now found himself attacked on all sides and unable to purchase arms and munitions in the United States. De la Huerta's personal secretary, Miguel Alessio Robles, informed the press that the conflict would be solved peacefully.[32]

As de la Huerta had imagined, the campaign against Cantú up to this point had been one of words rather than bullets. In a manifesto to the people of the Northern District, Cantú fulminated against the invasion, stating that his territory had enjoyed a reign of peace and prosperity that was now threatened by the actions of a federal government he did not recognize. He declared the people would fight to the death if necessary against this unjustified attack.[33] To this General Rodríguez responded that after Cantú had submitted to the Plan of Agua Prieta and all the nation had enthusiastically placed itself at the command of Interim President de la Huerta, the governor of the Northern District, moved only by his ambition to remain in power, had inexplicably placed himself in opposition to the federal government. Countering Cantú, Rodríguez asserted that his troops were orderly and disciplined and came only to restore order and peace to Baja California Norte, not to bring violence, as Cantú claimed. *El Heraldo de México* reported that the government had given General Rodríguez strict orders to give the people of the territory, nationals and foreigners alike, absolute guarantees of safety, and had declared that no incident should disturb the border area.[34] A third, unsigned manifesto came from a group of Mexicali residents who denounced Cantú as a traitor, laying the charge of seven years of official banditry at his feet, during which time he and the Dato family had become millionaires. Calling for the return of decency and disgusted by the licenced vice in the Northern District, they held that North Americans believed El Tecolote in Mexicali and Casino Monte Carlo in Tijuana were the peoples' only home.[35]

Governor Esteban Cantú's support in Baja California Norte continued to crumble as Francisco Javier Fernández, federal treasurer at the Tijuana customs office, arrived in San Diego with $100,000 in gold that he turned over to Ives Lelevier, the federal consular agent in that city. Fernández also brought all the documents from the customs office to keep them out of Cantú's hands. *El Heraldo de México* reported that several other federal officials had crossed the line and placed themselves at the orders of Consul Manuel Paredes at Calexico, while the *carrancistas* who had sought refuge in Baja California Norte had retreated across the line to the United States. Cantú responded by seizing the customs house at Ensenada and issuing warrants for the arrest of David Zárate, who had returned from exile in1919, Carlos Bernstein, and others deemed iniquitous to the regime. Bernstein fled to San Diego while Zárate, ever an enemy of the *regiomontano* governor, was awakened in the middle of the night by a friend who informed him that he was about to be arrested. Still in his pajamas, he fled posthaste by automobile with his wife and two children, left them in charge of his father-in-law in Santo Tomás, then took to the hills on horseback. Zárate then circled back to the seashore, where he flagged down a small launch under the flag of the United States, the *Newark*, which took him aboard. The *Newark* was searched when it put into port at Ensenada, but Zárate was hiding in a water tank and was not discovered. Thus he made it to safety in San Diego, presumably still in his pajamas. Cantú then confiscated all of Zárate's possessions, as he was reportedly doing to all who opposed him at this time, and the jails soon were filling up.

Accustomed to paying his troops and employees in gold, Cantú now began to print paper money because his government was so short of cash. Workers found the currency unacceptable; merchants closed their shops rather than accept the worthless script, and Cantú found it increasingly difficult to recruit new troops for his army. The prolongation of Rodríguez's campaign, due in part to the sinking of the *Guerrero*, seemed to be working to the advantage of the federal government. Lelevier opined that Cantú had lost all support, that the border and the casinos were closed, that Cantú was bereft of revenue, and that his troops would offer no resistance. *Excelsior* commented that Cantú would be foolish to put up a fight, as he had amassed a fortune amounting to seven million United States dollars and had a magnificent home in Los Angeles, all of which he stood to lose should he refuse to go quietly.

In a last bid to hold onto power, Cantú declared he would end his hostile attitude only when recently elected Álvaro Obregón was duly sworn in as president, again calling the de la Huerta administration illegal and un-constitutional. This would give him a chance to collect the export duties of several hundred thousand dollars on the 1920 cotton harvest, but de la Huerta refused to countenance such a compromise. *El Heraldo de México*'s correspondent in Mexicali reported on August 7 that Cantú offered to step down in two weeks if de la Huerta abstained from sending troops to the Northern District, but the president again refused to compromise. Consul Lelevier informed the press that all of Cantú's taxes on the export of cotton and the hated head tax would be abolished as soon as the fed-eral government regained control of Baja California Norte.[36] This left the cotton growers little reason to stand with the weakening governor, while lifting the head tax would be a relief to all, especially the prostitutes, for whom it amounted to double taxation since they also paid one dollar per day to ply their trade.

Cantú could expect no support from north of the border because the US would brook no violence in the Northern District that threatened the irrigation works in the Imperial Valley. Moreover, Cantú claimed he faced great pressure from the United States and a complete closure of the US-Mexico border.[37] Francisco Terrazas, a *felicista* observer at Calexico, corroborated this, noting that the governor had to bow before United States pressure. By giving in to de la Huerta and going peacefully to the US, Cantú avoided imprisonment or worse. The border was closed to all citizens of Baja California Norte, while all of Cantú's agents were placed under surveillance and several had been apprehended under the merest pretext by United States authorities. Immigration officials in Calexico told Cantú's supporters who lived north of the boundary that the United States intended to suffocate Cantú's rebellion. Finally, Terrazas claimed that a United States secret service agent told the willful governor that at the first outbreak of violence, United States forces would intervene to defend the irrigation works and the cotton fields in the Mexicali Valley. In his farewell address Cantú stated that the threat of invasion on the part of the United States was the primary factor in his decision to resign his office. Meanwhile General Rodríguez was at that moment crossing the Río Colorado with six thousand troops en route to Mexicali, with orders to dislodge Cantú from the governorship with violence, if necessary.[38]

President Adolfo de la Huerta's desire to bring the crisis to a peaceful conclusion, along with the pressure he was exerting on Cantú, began to bear fruit. Juan Rodolfo Platt, a Sonoran businessman, a friend of Obregón, Calles, and de la Huerta and an acquaintance of the wayward governor, was sent by the president to Calexico as his representative. Cantú, who had an impressive espionage organization along the border, immediately learned of his arrival and invited Platt to visit him at his residence in Mexicali. The two discussed the situation for an hour, during which Cantú tried to prevent Rodríguez's troops from reaching Mexicali, offering that he simply wanted to turn the governorship over to an honorable man. Platt then departed, but it was now reasonably clear that Cantú wanted out of the imbroglio he had created. Consul Ives Lelevier did not believe that Cantú would put up a struggle or that his troops would fight for him. On August 15 *El Heraldo de México*, having at this time a correspondent in Calexico, reported that Cantú had abandoned his hostile attitude toward the government.[39]

Because de la Huerta did not wish to dishonor Cantú by turning the territorial government over to one of his enemies, he suggested that Luis Mauricio Salazar, a confidant of both men, receive the governorship from Cantú through direct negotiation. Salazar had been friendly toward Cantú and carried out commissions for him in California, where he resided. To attempt a peaceful arrangement, de la Huerta sent to Mexicali Roberto V. Pesqueira, another friend of Cantú's whom the government had recently appointed Mexico's financial agent in New York. Obregón wrote to Governor Thomas E. Campbell of Arizona, with whom he was well acquainted, introducing Pesqueira and requesting that Campbell recommend Pesqueira to the governor of California. Obregón informed Campbell that Pesqueira and Rodríguez's troops were being sent to put an end to Cantú's vice-ridden regime. With California's permission, Pesqueira would travel to Mexicali by way of Los Angeles. De la Huerta then commissioned his friend Vito Alessio Robles, who had been a comrade of Cantú's since their days at the Colegio Militar, to aid in discussions leading to a peaceful transfer of power. Alessio Robles left Mexico City on August 13, arriving in Mexicali on the seventeenth to join Cantú, Salazar, and Pesqueira in a series of friendly conferences in which Alessio Robles pointed out the national difficulties that might arise should the crisis continue and exhorted Cantú to relinquish the governorship without strife. Cantú had another reason for agreeing to go quietly. It seems Justice W. O'Connor of the Los Angeles federal court informed Cantú

The headline reads: "Colonel Esteban Cantú finally abandons his frankly hostile attitude and hands the government of Baja California to Señor Luis M. Salazar," *El Heraldo de Mexico,* December 15, 1920. *Courtesy of the Archivo General de la Nación in Mexico City.*

that he would be arrested the moment he stepped onto California soil should he cause hostilities with federal troops in the Northern District. O'Connor was angered by Cantú's violation of the neutrality laws of the United States when he smuggled planes and other war supplies across the border. Put simply, Cantú could not blithely flee to his house in Los Angeles after having started a little war in Baja California Norte. Cantú sent his brother José to meet with Pesqueira in Los Angeles before he reached Mexicali. Pesqueira informed José Cantú that the governor would have to submit absolutely.[40]

When Salazar arrived in Calexico, Cantú immediately invited him to Mexicali and indicated that he was willing to relinquish the governorship in principle and step down peacefully. Cantú was waiting for sufficient guarantees from de la Huerta for his officers, troops, and territorial officials that remained loyal to him before making his departure final. *El Heraldo de México* correctly surmised that Salazar's government in Baja California Norte would be transitional. There had been talk of a preliminary election to determine whom the people of Baja California

Norte would like as governor. A prime candidate was David Zárate, who led a group in Ensenada which campaigned for a civilian government. While it was clear the people desired a native son in the position, the commissioners from the Northern District who arrived in Mexico City to confer with de la Huerta advised that there should not be such an election because Cantú had enough support that a victory on his part was not a remote idea.[41]

Pesqueira's mission was a success. It was agreed that Cantú would relinquish his office in a decorous manner on condition that all current employees of his government be retained in their present positions and that the officers and men stationed in Baja California Norte be retained in their posts and be given the right to join the new Federal Army. To this President Adolfo de la Huerta agreed.[42] On August 19, 1920, Colonel Esteban Cantú of the old Federal Army and governor of Baja California Norte since 1914 peacefully turned his office over to Luis Mauricio Salazar at five o'clock in the afternoon and went quietly into exile. *El Heraldo de México*'s correspondent in Calexico reported that all was now quiet in Mexicali and the political prisoners set free.[43] The Twenty-Fifth Battalion stationed in Mexicali, which had arrived with Cantú in 1911 and was the only corps of the old Federal Army still extant, was disarmed on August 28. Governor Salazar invited the men in the ranks to join the new army created by the Treaty of Teoloyucan in 1914, but not one accepted.[44]

CHAPTER VII

EL HÉROE
EMPAREDADO

"Cantú *es filibustero.*"
—**ADOLFO CARRILLO,** Mexican Consul at Los Angeles

After Esteban Cantú left the governorship of Baja California Norte, the office once more became a revolving door. After little more than a month the caretaker government of Luis Mauricio Salazar gave way to that of Manuel Balarezo, who after less than one year handed the reins of power to Epigmenio Ibarra Jr. on September 21, 1921. Ibarra was a native son from Real del Castillo, which lies to the east of Ensenada. The vice revenue that had been the base of Cantú's power continued despite the Sonoran Dynasty's dislike of it. Governor Ibarra held that the revenue gained from the sale of alcoholic beverages was critical to the Northern District's coffers and requested that the duties on their importation be suspended. He also requested that no limit be placed on the number of passports issued to tourists wishing to attend the races at the Hippodrome, as any restriction placed on passports issued would be a "*golpe muerte*" (a death blow) for the treasury. Both petitions were granted, and the per diem fee on passports was lowered to one gold peso. The vice and immorality continued, and Ibarra seems to have been in league with the vice peddlers, granting a concession to his relative Enrique Torres to operate a slot machine joint with twenty-seven machines, and receiving $12,000 in United States currency from Frank Byers, one of the owners of the famous El Tecolote, to open a gambling establishment. This the Obregón government had expressly prohibited, and José Inocente Lugo, who had joined the revolution as a *maderista,* became governor of Guerrero, and later served as

Carranza's head of the labor department, replaced Ibarra in March 1922. The vice continued nonetheless. By the time Abelardo Rodríguez became governor in October 1923, the vice and the revenue it engendered was a force to be controlled, but not eradicated.[1]

The new regime in Mexicali made an attempt to recapture the money that Cantú and his brother-in-law, Federico Dato, had siphoned off the treasury of Baja California Norte while in power, and especially the one-half million dollars taken days before Cantú handed over power to Luis Salazar. The money had been deposited in banks in British Columbia in Dato's name, but Salazar, who continued his search for the ill-gotten money after he left the governorship, did not think Cantú or Dato could access the funds because once the Obregón government was recognized by the United States, Mexico could press criminal charges and have them extradited.[2] While Salazar investigated this pilfering personally, the administration of Warren G. Harding took three years to recognize the Obregón government, giving Cantú ample time to hide his money as well as cause mischief, which he was not long in doing.

On May 3, 1921, a group of individuals shouting, "¡Viva Cantú!" made an assault on the garrison at Tijuana. After a bit of shooting they fled to the hills pursued by cavalry under the command of Colonel Anselmo Armenta, who dispersed the rebels, most of whom then crossed the border into the United States. Abelardo Rodríguez, then military commander of the Northern District, was not concerned about this *cantuista* movement known as "*Restaurador del Orden*," and while there were rumors of a Cantú comeback, Rodríguez reported that tranquility reigned in Baja California Norte. Mexico's consuls in Los Angeles, Calexico, Yuma, and San Francisco kept Rodríguez informed of Cantú's activities in California, noting that the money the former governor had pilfered was being depleted by his large family of Datos.[3]

Nonetheless he yet had ample funds to cause anxiety within the Obregón government, and a year after his downfall Cantú still had sympathizers in Baja California, where he sent emissaries to spread discontent against the government. His prestige was growing, and he increasingly represented a center of revolutionary activity in the United States, frequently conferring with fellow exiles such as Francisco Murguía, Lucio Blanco, and Manuel Peláez, and traveling to Washington, New York, El Paso, and elsewhere to maintain his circle of contacts. Meanwhile, the *felicistas* had taken an interest in his opposition to de la Huerta and Obregón, and the United States Justice Department was also keeping watch on the former governor of Baja California Norte.[4] In August 1921 Lucio Blanco organized a meeting in New York that included Cantú, Murguía, José María Maytorena, Pablo González, Manuel Calero, Jorge Vera Estañol, Nemesio García Naranjo, and others to discuss a plan of action prepared by Vera Estañol to reestablish the Constitution of 1857. Félix Díaz was invited to attend, but sent as his representative Pedro del Villar instead. This New York gathering of counterrevolutionaries left the leadership of such a revolution open, and not all of those gathered were prepared to desert the Constitution of 1917. Thus the leadership of such a movement was there for the taking, and Esteban Cantú felt he was ready. In early September 1921 Consul Enrique Ferreira of San Diego warned the Secretary of Foreign Relations that Cantú was at the head of a conspiracy to invade Baja California under the banner of the 1857 Constitution and had moved closer to the position of Félix Díaz. By the end of October Cantú was calling on his supporters to prepare for the planned revolt.[5]

Cantú began buying artillery, machine guns, rifles, and ammunition which he hoped to ship to Baja California, making frequent trips to San Francisco, El Paso, and San Antonio, Texas, to keep in close contact with his accomplices in those cities. One report held that a group of *filibusteros* had a large number of machine guns mounted on automobiles for a planned simultaneous attack on Tijuana and Mexicali. Cantú's agents were trying to deliver two thousand Mausers and 500 million rounds of ammunition from Canada to Ensenada shortly after he relinquished the governorship of Baja California Norte.[6] Whether they succeeded or not is unknown, but Cantú was not always successful, as United States authorities seized 225 rifles and 60,000 rounds of ammunition on one occasion and three trucks loaded with 250 rifles and 88,000 cartridges on another near San Isidro, California, destined for his planned revolution in Baja California Norte. While some of the arms shipments were intercepted, Cantú was occasionally successful, and with the assistance of Information Chief David Gershon of the United States Department of Justice at that. Gershon, who did not sympathize with the Obregón government, placed obstacles in the path of Mexico's consuls in California. On one occasion Gershon, working with Federico Dato, personally conducted an arms shipment across the border to Mexicali, actually brandishing his badge at the border crossing to do so. The Department of Justice later removed Gershon, who earlier had opposed Cantú, but now appeared to have become a *cantuista* sympathizer. Gershon had become an admirer of Cantú and a friend of Carl Withington, but the friendship was based on the financial benefits that might come his way. Withington aided Cantú's planned revolt in the hope of reopening El Tecolote. Governor Ibarra ordered a strict vigilance along the border, but Adolfo Labastida, municipal delegate for Tijuana, informed Obregón that there was in fact no vigilance at all on the Mexican side of the international boundary. Labastida further held that with very rare exceptions the employees of the government in Tijuana were Cantú sympathizers, which should have been no surprise, as it had been agreed that all employees of Cantú's administration would retain their posts if he quietly stepped down. Many local merchants were sympathetic as well. Carl Withington, who hoped to reopen El Tecolote, actively aided Cantú by bribing many officials in San Diego County to look the other way as Cantú prepared his revolt.[7]

It was known in Mexico City by early November 1921 that Cantú was planning a revolt and that he had recruited 150 men who were ready to descend on the Northern District. At the same time he was unloading arms along the Pacific Coast of the peninsula. This information was passed on to the United States Secretary of State with a reminder that this was a violation of the neutrality laws of that nation. A skirmish involving two hundred *cantuistas* against General Abelardo Rodríguez's troops took place on November 14, some six miles from Tijuana, and a second skirmish occurred at Vallecitos on the following day. The opposing forces met again on November 17 about forty miles south of Tijuana between Vallecitos and Santo Domingo; this time General Rodríguez completely defeated and dispersed the rebels.[8] Major Loreto Lerdo González, former commander of the *Cuerpo de Caballería "Esteban Cantú"* and *ranchero* at Tecate, led the revolt. A friend of Cantú's, he had been stranded in Baja California Norte after Cantú's fall from power, unable to cross the line into the United States because of legal charges against him there. He took refuge in mountains that he knew like the back of his hand, and with the help of some friends collected arms and about three hundred men, then waited for a proper time to rise.[9]

José Cantú, now also in exile due to the fall of Carranza, related to the press that the revolt was the work of anti-patriotic *filibusteros* and that his brother had nothing to do with it. To this Esteban Cantú responded in a letter to *El Heraldo de México* that no one, not even his brother, could make statements in his name, that he was opposed to the government of the usurper, Álvaro Obregón, and that the Constitution of 1917 had established an absolute tyranny. He declared that he stood for the reestablishment of the Constitution of 1857 and that the recent revolt in the Northern District was not the work of *filibusteros*, but the work of himself and his patriotic followers, "*todos mexicanos de sangre y corazón*."[10]

The revolt failed in part because of detective work done north of the border some months before. In August 1921 Frank C. Drew, a San Francisco attorney, loyal friend of Álvaro Obregón, and true sympathizer with his government, visited the office of Mexican Consul General Eduardo Ruiz in San Francisco with important information regarding Cantú's planned attack on Baja California. Drew had hired William James Otts of the William J. Otts International Detectives, which had resident investigators in San Antonio, El Paso, Tucson, El Centro, San Diego, Los Angeles, San Francisco, and New York, to investigate Cantú's activities. Ruiz referred to Otts as another honest man who, after a bit of sleuthing, discovered that there were traitors in the garrisons at Tijuana, Tecate, and Mexicali. Ruiz of course sent the information on to General Rodríguez and President Obregón. As Rodríguez at first refused to believe there were any traitors in his command or that there was any conspiracy in the making, Ruiz journeyed to Mexicali, and after a long conversation with the general convinced him that there was indeed a real danger. Otts had spies among Cantú's associates, as did Ruiz, and these confirmed Otts's information. On the eve of the attack there were only four hundred troops in Tijuana, Tecate, and Mexicali, while Cantú, Ruiz reported, had six hundred for the attack on Tijuana alone. Rodríguez requested more troops to meet the threat, which he now took as very real, but only 450 Yaqui soldiers were sent. Yet Rodríguez had little to fear. Cantú's commander for the Tijuana operation, Colonel Agustín Camou, failed to appear at the proper time, and most of Cantú's troops left. In addition much of the $56,000 allotted to pay the would-be revolutionaries disappeared, leaving only $20,000 to pay the remaining 260 *filibusteros*, as Ruiz called them. Thanks to Otts's information, much of the arms and ammunition Cantú had gathered had previously been seized by United States authorities. Consul Ruiz held that Drew and Otts were instrumental in foiling Cantú's plan, which was to seize Baja California Norte, after which he believed he would have the necessary funds from the vice revenue of the Northern District to begin a movement to overthrow the central government.[11]

The revolt was also to have taken place in Sonora. In January of 1910 Brígido Caro had disrupted an attempted address from Francisco Madero in Hermosillo by forming a crowd to shout him down. Caro was to have raised Cantú's banner with the support of the Yaqui chiefs. The Yaquis, ever ready to rise against any government in hopes of reclaiming their lands, had placed themselves at his orders and signed a manifesto proclaiming Caro governor and renouncing Obregón. The Yaqui chiefs had offered three thousand troops, all well armed. The Yaquis, noted as skilled, intrepid fighters and masters of *guerrilla* warfare, had joined the Plan of Agua Prieta, but generally favored any opponent of official authority, whether representing Sonora or the nation, that might threaten their communal control of Yaqui lands. Adolfo de la Huerta, like José María Maytorena before him, understood and sympathized with the Yaquis, but Obregón apparently had not carried out certain promises made to them in 1920, and the Yaqui were therefore willing to join Brígido Caro's revolt. Caro had all in readiness, but his support fell apart. Alberto Terrazas, former *hacendado* and governor of Chihuahua now in exile, did not follow up on his promises of aid. Cantú failed to send the money he had promised for the movement. Caro waited in vain. For lack of money the three hundred men recruited in Arizona were not mobilized, despite the fact that Cantú had received $40,000 from fellow counterrevolutionaries in New York. Nor were the funds promised by Manuel Peláez released in a timely fashion. While Federico Dato had been the treasurer of the plot and seems to have diverted a sizeable portion of the money to his own interests, Cantú also failed to send the money he had in his possession. The truth of the matter may never be known, as Cantú later claimed the New York group of exiles never sent the money he was promised. Loreto Lerdo González and a few others survived in hiding, but those who were captured were immediately shot without trial. Those who fled across the border were arrested for violation of the neutrality laws but were soon released.[12]

Brígido Caro believed the fiasco in Baja California Norte and Sonora was the fault of Cantú for withholding the money. He considered Cantú a perfidious coward and a traitor to the cause. Caro had informed Cantú of every detail of his planned revolt in Sonora because of its importance in the effort to overthrow Obregón, and Cantú had in turn laid all Caro's plans before Manuel Peláez, from whom he expected a large financial contribution to the revolt. Peláez, always willing to play a double game and protect his own interests, had a number of meetings with Plutarco Elías Calles, then at a sanitarium in Rochester, New York, trying to recover from a rheumatic pain in his right leg that bothered him much of his life. Peláez informed him of what was stirring in Sonora, and according to Caro, Calles, after brief visits to New York and Washington, traveled forthwith to Hermosillo, where he put himself at the head of six hundred troops, quickly ensuring the government's control of Sonora. Several of Caro's adherents were arrested and shot before *el Tigre de Sonora* could shake the dust of the journey from his clothes. Shortly after the fiascos in Baja California Norte and Sonora, Peláez informed his fellow exiles while in San Diego that he was a friend of Obregón and that he had not and would not participate in a revolution. He stated that it would be unpatriotic to launch a revolution at that moment, as that would only invite the intervention of the United States. Peláez held that the Constitution of 1857 was gone forever, and that the Constitution of 1917 gave the people all the freedom they needed to determine their future.[13] This declaration did not keep Peláez from plotting with his fellow exiles in the future, however.

Not only were Cantú, Peláez, Terrazas, and Caro involved in the conspiracy, but Terrazas's lawyer, former Senator Albert Bacon Fall of New Mexico, was as well. As a young man Fall had made a prospecting tour of Northern Mexico, acquired some undeveloped mining properties, and become acquainted with William C. Greene, the copper king of Cananea. Fall was also closely allied to petroleum interests; Edward L. Doheny and Harry Sinclair were personal friends. Known for his intelligence and determination, he was often austere and arrogant in public discussions, as his chairmanship of the Senate Foreign Relations Subcommittee on Mexican Affairs sometimes demonstrated. Fall was an opponent of the 1917 Constitution, which threatened the oil interests of the United States. He wanted a formal treaty or protocol protecting the oil interests before recognition. Referring to Fall as "*el furioso intervencionista*," *El Heraldo de México* consistently called him Mexico's greatest enemy. Cantú was in contact with Fall and visited him in Washington some months after his eviction from the governorship of the Northern District. If Cantú could mount an offensive on Mexican territory, the oil companies would back him with five million dollars. Now United States Secretary of the Interior, Fall was most eager for United States intervention in Mexico and held the Obregón government in extremely low regard. Fall had a meeting with Alberto Terrazas on September 10, 1921, in Redding, Cali fornia, and Terrazas later met with Cantú and Brígido Caro. Purportedly the movement was forged six months earlier at a meeting in San Antonio, Texas, which included representatives of three unnamed United States senators. The plan called for operations along the border of Sonora and Chihuahua as well as in Baja California.[14]

At the urging of Secretary Fall, several meetings including Félix Díaz, Samuel García Cuéllar, and Peláez were held in New York. There the participants reached an accord to instigate revolts in Mexico. Peláez was to operate in Veracruz, Díaz in the South, and García Cuéllar in the North. Cantú and Maytorena were to subordinate themselves to Peláez, who was to serve as the leader of the movement. Secretary Fall was in favor of Félix Díaz as the leader of Mexico. During the secret Committee on the Mexican Oil Industry, which Fall chaired, Fall had the *felicista* Samuel García Cuéllar in his employ. García Cuéllar had been lobbying in Washington against recognition of the Obregón government. Cuéllar had several meetings with Cantú and Manuel Peláez regarding the armed bands that had been sent into Mexico.[15]

Another player in the game was Dr. Jorge Ziegner Uriburu, president of the University of California at Riverside and thereafter a member of the Latin-American Law Offices firm in Los Angeles. Uriburu was also a proponent of Félix Díaz, whom he kept informed as to events in Baja California Norte and the actions of those surrounding Esteban Cantú. He was not of the *felicista* inner circle, but whatever his role was among the Mexican exiles, he was very knowledgeable about their activities.[16] Keeping Uriburu and other counterrevolutionaries informed about events in Mexico was the soldier of Sonora, Emilio Kosterlitzky, who spoke excellent English and now held a position as translator in the United States Department of Justice. Of Polish origin, Kosterlitzky joined the National Guard of Sonora as a soldier and rose in the ranks, becoming a lieutenant colonel in 1890. He fought the Yaqui, Mayo, and later the Apache, had served in the suppression of the 1906-1907 Cananea Copper Company miners' strike, was known for his good civil and military conduct, and carried out his duties well, gaining an inti- mate knowledge of the terrain of Sonora. He retired in 1912 as a colonel of cavalry after thirty-five years of dignified and valorous service. He returned to the service that same year, but after the Constitutionalists rose against Victoriano Huerta, he was driven out of Sonora into Ari-

Colonel Emilio Kosterlitzky of the National Guard of Sonora. *Courtesy of the Emilio Kosterlitzky Papers, Special Collections, University of Arizona, Tucson.*

zona at the battle of Nogales on March 13, 1913, by then Colonel Álvaro Obregón. Kosterlitzky and his federal troops crossed the street to Nogales, Arizona, after leaving their rifles and uniform coats and hats in a pile in the Mexican customs house. He and his men were detained at the United States Army camp at Cavalry Hill for some months before being allowed to return to Mexico.[17] After surrendering his arms, Kosterlitzky was interned under the command of Captain F. W. Benteen of the Twelfth United States Infantry, who noted that while the colonel enjoyed the privilege of parole, he never violated it. Benteen had only praise for him, finding Kosterlitzky to be "a man of the highest ideals and one that could be trusted implicitly."[18] Colonel Kosterlitzky also had a powerful friend in Harrison Gray Otis, editor of the *Los Angeles Times* and one of the principals of the Colorado River Land Company. He and Otis enjoyed a very friendly correspondence. Kosterlitzky also carried on an amicable correspondence with General Leonard Wood, who requested Kosterlitzky's opinion of the condition of affairs in Baja California Norte and Mexico generally, and remembered fondly their day-long meeting in Nogales. These connections probably aided Kosterlitzky in obtaining his post with the Department of Justice. In answer to Wood's query, Kosterlitzky found order and harmony in Baja California Norte because of Cantú and the Twenty-Fifth Battalion, which maintained the peace, while along the rest of the border the *carrancistas* maintained no order at all. Kosterlitzky, who had known Cantú for twenty years, lamented his fall from power. He considered Cantú to have been an efficient governor who had developed the territory's resources and believed he had the mettle to be a strong factor in Mexico's future.[19]

Kosterlitzky knew the movements of the counterrevolutionaries very well and was an enemy of the revolution that had forced him into exile. He was an old friend of Brígido Caro and kept him informed of daily events in Mexico from his vantage point in the Department of Justice. That is how Caro knew about Calles's conversations with Peláez and Calles's rapid response to the planned revolt in Sonora. Kosterlitzky did not give the 1921 *cantuista* invasion of Baja California Norte any real aid, but was well connected to the enemies of the Obregón government, giving them what information he gleaned from his post as translator.[20] At the dinner meeting of the League of the Southwest held at Riverside on December 9, 1921, Uriburu had a conversation with Albert Fall in which the secretary, who had no confidence in the Obregón administration, said that if the educated men who supported the Constitution of 1857 failed to unite, the United States would have to occupy Mexico for four or five years and do what the United States had done in Cuba.[21] The rumor among the expatriates around Félix Díaz held that Cantú's revolt of November 1921 had been "initiated and sustained" by Secretary Albert Fall.[22]

After the failure of Cantú's revolt of November 1921, Uriburu wrote to Díaz that if Secretary Fall had ever had any doubts as to the inabilities of the former governor of Baja California Norte, they should now be completely dispelled. Cantú, Uriburu continued, was absolutely incompetent to direct anything and lacked energy of any kind. Perhaps

Reconstruction of the Escuela Cuauhtémoc. *Courtesy of Special Collections, University of California, San Diego.*

the apathy Cantú had demonstrated as a cadet at Chapultepec was at play as well. Uriburu lamented that the whole revolt had been operated by Federico Dato, who was well known for his crass ignorance but was extremely skillful in matters of money. The recent movements in Baja California Norte and Sonora had failed for the complete lack of planning and direction. Uriburu believed faith in the competence of Cantú as the *jefe supremo* of those favoring the restoration of the Constitution of 1857 had disappeared, he now being a player of merely secondary importance. Cantú's support now began to fade away, his efforts to communicate with the authorities in Washington were frustrated, and the former *huertista* Jorge Vera Estañol, who had been the attorney for numerous foreign interests, pointedly declared that he had never been Cantú's mentor, that he had merely offered advice that was never followed. Manuel Calero, a lawyer in the Ministry of Fomento (Development) during the *Porfiriato*, then foreign secretary in Madero's cabinet and now another devotee of Félix Díaz and the Constitution of 1857, declared that he had met Cantú only once, and that had been enough to convince him that the colonel was a complete nullity. Calero perhaps was prejudiced against men from Mexico's North, as he had been aghast at Madero's decision to appoint

Governor Abraham González of Chihuahua secretary of filiation, referring to him as a callow rustic.[23]

Whatever the causes of his failed revolt, Cantú did not lose hope
of returning to his lost kingdom in Baja California Norte. He was reported to be planning a revolt near Santa Rosalia and Tecate, attempting
to suborn the troops in the garrisons of the Northern District and run
arms and munitions across the border. Manuel Cubillas, Administrator
of Customs at Tijuana, reported in March 1922 that *cantuistas* were again
active along the California line, but the immediate problem was that
Mexico's federal troops in the Northern District had not been paid for
some time. The pay of the men stationed at Ensenada was in arrears
over a month, and these were new recruits whose loyalty was uncertain.
Frank N. Thayer, an authorized representative of Cantú, and Pablo Dato
continued to smuggle arms and munitions into Baja California Norte,
their activities supported by Cantú's dividends from the Lower California
Jockey Club, in which he was a stockholder.[24] While the Department of
State had investigated the activities of Cantú and the Dato brothers, no
evidence of recruiting men, running arms, or other revolutionary activity
could be discovered.[25] Brígido Caro noted that while Cantú, Maytorena,
and Peláez, all living in Los Angeles and in frequent contact with each
other, were moving closer to Félix Díaz, he did not have much faith in
them. Nor should he have. Peláez had endorsed Díaz's political program
in 1918, but had never embraced *felicismo* with any sincerity and had
severed his relationship with him in 1920. Cantú was hampered by his
noxious relatives, the Datos, and none of the three had the capacity for
decisive action, being motivated only by wealth and power. As Caro saw
them, "There is no patriotism in any one of them."[26]

Another player was General Pablo González, who had broken with de
la Huerta and Obregón, was found guilty of rebellion and nearly shot,
but de la Huerta gave him a reprieve, upon which he retired to the United
States. Although he kept his record clean, Esteban Cantú held a conference in Los Angeles, organized by his brother José, with Manuel Peláez
and Pablo González in an effort to bring all the anti-Obregón elements
together to insure the success of the revolution that would bring them
back to power. Cantú and González were willing to contribute $200,000
each, but it was uncertain if Juan Barragán, once Carranza's chief of staff
who fled Mexico with much stolen money on the demise of the First
Chief, would contribute an equal amount. Whether the money promised

was the personal money of Cantú, González, and Barragán, or whether someone was banking them is unknown.[27]

In pursuit of this effort, Cantú launched a plan which circulated in typescript only, without a date, but probably written in March 1922 by Jorge Vera Estañol. The plan vilified the Obregón government and called all factions from *porfiristas* to *carrancistas* to unite against it. He called for the restoration of the Constitution of 1857 and the organization of *"El Ejército Nacional Reorganizador,"* which would include all elements desiring to put an end to the rule of *"el Manco"* in order to reconstruct the nation. Upon arriving in Mexico City a provisional government would hold elections for the offices of president and vice president.[28] Brígido Caro, who never forgave *"coronelito"* Cantú for his failure to support Caro's planned 1921 revolt in Sonora, now ridiculed the *"coronelillo"* and his attempt to launch himself as a national figure. Caro, an adherent of Félix Díaz, did not believe that anyone who knew Cantú well could envision him as a serious opponent to Álvaro Obregón, referring to the former governor of Baja California Norte as *"el héroe emparedado"*—a devotee who lived in a cloister without taking the vows. That is, Cantú was with Félix Díaz but would not avow it.[29]

Cantú had sound reasons for not doing so. Félix Díaz was hampered by his very name, which recalled the *Porfiriato*, and by his lack of charisma, political courage, or strength, as exemplified when Victoriano Huerta simply brushed him aside after the overthrow of Francisco Madero. Nor was he much of a military tactician, as his first attempt to take Veracruz demonstrated. In fact, he was incompetent. At Chapultepec he had spent much time studying engineering, but little in the way of military tactics. Díaz had won little success in his second effort to gain control of the State of Veracruz, and by the beginning of 1920 *felicismo* was all but dead. Esteban Cantú had no need to fall in behind a ghost *caudillo*.[30] By early 1922, following the failure of Cantú's first attempt to regain Baja California Norte, the situation had changed. There was much talk among the *felicistas* about the possibility of the unification of all the anti-*obregonista* factions. This would impress the administration of President Warren G. Harding, which looked upon the Constitution of 1917 as a threat to the petroleum interests of the United States and, as one follower of Félix Díaz put it, would be *"un golpe mortal para la horda sonorense"* (a mortal blow to the Sonoran horde).[31] Cantú and Maytorena had reached an accord with Félix Díaz, and there seemed to be growing support for the Constitution of 1857, as Cantú and Francisco Murguía, as well as a few *carrancistas*, had openly risen to its support.[32]

As late as March 1922 the *felicistas* were convinced that Washington would not treat with Obregón, but within a month there was much ado in the press concerning amiable platitudes being exchanged between Harding and Obregón, and that recognition of Obregón's government would soon follow. Uriburu related that a highly placed friend of his in Washington, possibly Albert Fall, explained that Harding wanted re-election and wanted William Randolph Hearst's support. Hearst in turn wanted Harding to end the tiff with Mexico and recognize Obregón.[33] At length the Bucareli Accords, which held that Article 27 of the 1917 Constitution would not be applied retroactively, thereby mollifying the oil interests, were signed on August 13, 1923, and recognition followed ten days later. This would make launching revolutions from United States soil far more difficult. In any case the various counterrevolutionary factions could find no common ground. For his part, Esteban Cantú stated privately that he was completely in accord with Félix Díaz, but did not know if Díaz was with him. In reality there was no unity among the anti-*obregonistas* in exile. Nor among those in Mexico, for the first leader to cross the border into Mexico would gain their allegiance; if it were Félix Díaz, they would become *felicistas*, if Esteban Cantú, they would become *cantuistas*.[34]

Consul Manuel Paredes at Calexico, meanwhile, informed Governor Lugo of the Northern District that United States Army Intelligence had orders to keep watch on any agitators operating north of the border. The intelligence service was providing Mexico's consul general at Laredo with its intelligence reports, including the information that Pablo González and Cantú's agent, John Brown, were in New York in May 1922 trying to obtain a bank loan for the planned revolt. Another report noted that Albert Fall had called a meeting with González and Samuel García Cuéllar to discuss such a revolt.[35]

Cantú was still a threat. United States Military Intelligence reported that a considerable number of revolutionary leaders residing north of the border considered Cantú as the only man who could unite the anti-*obregonistas* and that Cantú was making a determined effort to settle the differences among the various factions. He was reported to be holding a conference for that purpose with other counterrevolutionaries in El Paso on February 21, 1922. Uriburu wrote to Félix Díaz in September 1922 that only 150 troops remained in the garrisons of Baja California Norte, the other men having been posted to fight the revolt in Durango. This rebellion was raised by Francisco Murguía in August under the Plan of Zaragoza, in which Murguía repudiated Obregón and hailed himself as the chief of the movement. Murguía had remained loyal to Carranza even beyond the First Chief's assassination, the blame for which he laid at the feet of Obregón. Murguía had spent five months in prison before de la Huerta granted his freedom, at which point he fled to San Antonio, Texas, where he planned to return to Mexico and combat the government. Cantú had been in constant contact with Murguía, and Uriburu believed now was the time for an uprising in the Northern District. Uriburu had a long conversation with an unnamed confidant of Cantú's which convinced him that the *felicistas* could count on the former governor, noting that Cantú still possessed the discipline of Chapultepec and would return to his post.[36]

Murguía crossed the border into Chihuahua with a few men but was soon chased by seventy government troops into Durango. He was quickly defeated in October of 1922 at Jagüey del Huarache and soon faced a firing squad. The revolt was carried forth in Sinaloa by General Juan Carrasco. According to the report of Frank N. Thayer, one of Cantú's representatives in the United States, Carrasco now served as Cantú's field general, defeating government troops in three important engagements. Carrasco had in some way obtained twenty thousand pesos in gold from the Southern Pacific Railroad, and many government troops had deserted to the rebels, strengthening Carrasco's force by three thousand men. The rebels were held to be in possession of ample supplies and ammunition, making this, Thayer proclaimed, a real organized effort to restore the Constitution of 1857, a document more amenable to the oil interests of the United States. While this was a serious uprising involving other *carrancista* generals, it was soon crushed, and Carrasco was killed in battle.[37] Cantú's involvement in these revolts remains unclear.

Emilio Kosterlitzky was able to make an information-gathering tour of the Northern District at Uriburu's request and found sufficient artillery and machine guns and a force of four hundred well-armed men, but by mid-November 1922 the garrison at Mexicali had been reduced to a mere fifty demoralized men, with desertion being a daily occurrence. Kosterlitzky believed that with $50,000 a force could be organized to regain the territory, as he found much discontent among the people of the

Northern District. Mexico's consuls in San Diego and Calexico reported that Cantú and Peláez were planning a revolt using bands of mercenaries. The military commander of the garrison, General Jesús M. Ferreira, requested reinforcements of at least two hundred men. Obregón responded that troops would be sent as soon as possible.[38] Uriburu nonetheless believed a strong force and a strong leader would be able to take Baja California Norte, but that Esteban Cantú was not the man for the task. He had lost much prestige because of the element around him, namely Federico Dato, who only sought money. Uriburu, who now spoke of Cantú in the harshest of terms, was convinced that his lack of resolution and Dato's pilfering had caused the 1921 failure to win the Northern District. "*Dato es un completo bárbaro e ignorante en absoluto*" (Dato is a complete barbarian and ignorant in everything).[39] Uriburu was correct as to the avarice of Federico Dato, who, with his equally covetous brother Guillermo, stole the bells of San Quintín Mission in May of 1916 after hearing that they were made of solid gold. Their plan was to ship them to San Diego by sea, but the captain of the vessel, not wanting to be involved in the affair, discovered the bells to be merely copper, and during the night threw them overboard into the harbor of San Quintín. All in all a tawdry business of desecration, theft, and reprehensible greed, which left the mission without its bells and the Dato brothers deservedly fleeced of the $2,000 they paid to get them.[40]

At length the revolt in Sinaloa was quelled, and Cantú made no concerted effort in 1922 to regain control of Baja California Norte, although he continued to conspire with others into the next year. According to William James Otts, in late 1923 several meetings took place in San Francisco and Los Angeles involving some of the same conspirators, including Pablo González, Manuel Peláez, Federico Dato, and Cantú, who had plotted during 1921 and 1922. Otts believed a revolt was brewing in Baja California Norte and Sonora and informed Obregón and Governor Abelardo Rodríguez of the movement. He reported that his agents had infiltrated the conspirators and that he could bring down the intended revolt as he had in 1921 and 1922. By March 1924 the possibility of an attack along the border of the Northern District had become more serious. Governor Rodríguez meanwhile organized a service of special agents to keep a watch on the would-be rebels.[41]

An even more serious threat was the possible joining together of the anti-*obregonista* cells of all stripes. On August 10, 1923, a meeting was held in San Antonio, Texas, for the purpose of achieving that very goal. In attendance were representatives of Félix Díaz, José María Maytorena, Pablo González, Cándido Aguilar, Esteban Cantú, and others. The movement was initiated by *carrancistas* and produced an act of union which intended to restore the era destroyed by Agua Prieta, but some of those in attendance refused to sign the document.[42] The longed-for grand coalition soon fell apart as Maytorena, Cantú, and Peláez would not commit themselves, and the latter two refused to finance the effort. According to Emilio Kosterlitzky, Peláez, always landing on his feet, was invited by Obregón to return to Mexico. Peláez sold his house in Los Angeles, returned to Tampico, and was arrested and later released after the "Revolt of the Generals."[43]

Adolfo de la Huerta, Obregón's original choice as the presidential candidate for the 1924 election as Plutarco Elías Calles appeared too ill to seek the office, at first refused to accept the bid. He was at odds with *el Manco* over a number of issues, including the Bucareli Accords, in which Obregón had agreed not to apply the 1917 Constitution to oil leases granted before its adoption, giving much relief to United States petroleum interests and making Washington's recognition of his government possible. There was also Obregón's interference with the elections in San Luis Potosí and Nuevo León and a misunderstanding over de la Huerta's resignation as secretary of hacienda (treasury), but the real battle began with Alberto J. Pani's attack on him in the press, in concert with Obregón and Calles, now the official presidential candidate. Pani, the new secretary of hacienda, correctly charged that de la Huerta had left the treasury with a deficit of $42,000,000 pesos. De la Huerta entered the presidential race and later launched a revolt against his fellow Sonorans, Obregón and Calles. Lasting but a few months, the revolt was crushed, and de la Huerta went into exile in the United States.[44]

Adolfo de la Huerta's "Revolt of the Generals," which began in late 1923, provided the opportunity for Cantú to realize his dream. De la Huerta needed a front to open up in the north, and Cantú, in collusion with Maytorena and Enrique Estrada, who had joined Madero in 1910, hoped to take advantage of the situation, and plotted to regain Baja California Norte. An invasion of the Northern District was in the planning stage when it was foiled by the authorities of the United States. Estrada, a former general and the tyrant lord of Jalisco who had encouraged de la Huerta to launch the revolt against Obregón, ended up in a United States

This caption to this cartoon titled *Baja California in Danger* reads "It's a fierce one who wants to devour her!" "No, it's a dog, you!" This is a play on Cantú's name, of course. *Courtesy of the Archivo General de la Nación in Mexico City.*

jail for violating the neutrality laws, but was soon free to join the uprising in Mexico against Obregón.[45]

The "Revolt of the Generals" was a serious enough challenge that Álvaro Obregón took to the field himself and quelled the last major uprising against the central government. By this time the economy of Baja California Norte was flourishing to such a degree that Governor Rodríguez was able to loan the federal government $941,000 pesos to aid the campaign against the rebels.[46] If half the officer corps of the Mexican Army could not defeat Obregón, there was little hope that one lone colonel left over from the *Porfiriato* could regain Baja California Norte.[47]

CHAPTER VIII
EN BUSCA DE ESTEBAN CANTÚ

"Cantú *es ex-federal y porfirista.*"

—**TEODORO FREZIERES**, Mexican Consul at San Diego

Under Governor Abelardo Rodríguez Baja California Norte was able to rely on its own resources without having to depend upon the federal government for assistance. At the same time his administration was energetic and productive with regard to the growth of infrastructure. As under Cantú, hospitals and schools were constructed, and population of the territory with Mexican nationals was promoted, settling these newcomers on small parcels of land at the expense of the administration. Cotton production continued to be important for the Northern District's economy, as was Chinese labor. To promote agriculture Rodríguez established the Banco Agrícola Peninsular and began construction of Rodríguez Dam near Tijuana to capture the occasional torrential rains, provide much-needed water for irrigation, and to quench the thirst of the inhabitants of the city, now officially a municipality. The Palacio del Gobierno in Mexicali which Cantú had begun was completed, along with a municipal theater and a public library. Pavement was laid down on the Tijuana-Ensenada road. The need for public water purification plants and the generation of electricity was met, and the city's first fire department began when a fire station was constructed in Mexicali.[1] As with Cantú, Rodríguez financed his administration's progress from the vice revenue at hand. Immediately following Cantú's fall, the Sonoran Dynasty attempted to rid the border towns of this vice through Obregón's *programa moralizador*, viewing the vice in Tijuana, Mexicali, and Los Algodones as bad for Mexico's public relations with her northern neighbor, and Obregón wanted recognition of his administration from Washington. While Cantú was living off vice revenue in the Northern District, Plutarco Elías Calles, governor of Sonora at the same time, made a rigorous effort to rid that state of gambling dens and saloons. Now that Cantú was gone, this same moralizing tone, it was thought, could be played out in Baja California Norte. Governor Luis Mauricio Salazar and General Rodríguez, then military commandant, ordered the closure of all the *cantinas* and gambling halls in Tijuana, Mexicali, and Los Algodones in early September 1920.[2] Obregón soon received numerous letters from the citizens of California applauding his assault on vice. One bogus telegram, however, stated that the Bankers Association, the Chamber of Commerce, the Merchants Association, and the City Council of San Diego deplored the closing of the casinos in Tijuana and Mexicali as they were a valuable asset to the city. Obregón hotly responded that if the vice dens were such a valuable asset, they should be built in San Diego and Calexico, thereby saving their patrons a long walk.[3]

Unfortunately for the governors immediately following Cantú, the closing of the casinos proved disastrous for the treasury of the Northern District. On more than one occasion during 1921, Governor Epigmenio Ibarra reported to Obregón that the situation was difficult with the price of cotton down and unemployment rising. Revenue had fallen off drastically, making it impossible to complete the Palacio del Gobierno, much less to construct much-needed infrastructure. Ibarra noted that the penury of the treasury and the depressed economy were known to everyone. With the casinos closed, he lamented, there was not enough revenue to administer the territory, and he requested that he be permitted to establish a *casino china*, as the Chinese had all the money in the district. He promised not to let any *blancos* near it. While Obregón pondered Ibarra's request, $30,000 pesos were sent to alleviate the revenue shortfall in Baja California Norte.[4]

The Sonorans at length came to the realization that gambling would have to be permitted to enable the government of the Northern District to function. In early 1922 the Foreign Club opened in Tijuana along with a gambling establishment catering exclusively to the Chinese population in Mexicali. José Inocente Lugo, who followed Ibarra in the governorship, pointed out to Obregón the difference between legal and illegal gambling, thus giving an air of morality to casinos and private social clubs that offered only those games of chance permitted under the law. These, and in a short time others, were soon flourishing in Baja California Norte. As a result the coffers of the territorial government were no longer in a state of penury. To the contrary, Governor Abelardo Rodríguez was able to help Obregón suppress the revolt of Adolfo de la Huerta in 1924 with a loan of $941,000 pesos but could still spend $957,766 pesos on schools between 1923 and 1931.[5] Thus Rodríguez, like Cantú before him, was able to captain a flourishing economy in Baja California Norte—and perhaps enrich himself as well—because of the abundant vice revenue emanating from the casinos of Tijuana, Mexicali, and Los Algodones. Like Cantú, Rodríguez licensed the gambling dens and in this way exercised some control over them, but with the difference that he favored the larger, well-organized casinos and tended to rid the territory of the lowest dives. El Tecolote, the Sunset Inn, the Foreign Club, and the Tívoli came roaring back to life while other establishments of little importance to the treasury were denied a license.[6]

Indeed, little changed regarding the flow of vice revenue following the departure of Cantú despite the public protests against it by members of the Sonoran Dynasty. Obregón, Calles, and de la Huerta all condemned Cantú's licensing program, and General Abelardo Rodríguez had closed the gambling dens and houses of prostitution when he arrived with his troops in Mexicali. Yet they soon reopened. The newly installed Obregón administration, suffering from a depleted treasury and growing foreign debt, could not ignore the possibilities presented by the steady income that had flowed from the cabarets and saloons in Mexicali, Tijuana, and elsewhere along the border in the days of Cantú. Possibly the Sonoran Dynasty's condemnation of Cantú was misplaced.[7]

Perhaps Rodríguez admired Cantú's dealings with the vice trade, although he himself dealt with the situation with more finesse, as his close association with the casino Agua Caliente will attest. With the suppression of the de la Huerta revolt, Cantú let go of the thought of returning to his former kingdom as a conquering hero, but he did wish to return. In late January 1925 Cantú petitioned Governor Rodríguez that he might return to Baja California Norte to attend personally to his property there. Rodríguez forwarded the request to President Calles, who answered emphatically that Cantú not be allowed to set foot in the Northern District. The governor then responded that he did not see Cantú as any kind of threat or danger, and that his visit might be seen as a form of conciliation toward the expatriot elements of former days. Rodríguez was certain Cantú was planning no action against the government. Calles growled back at his fellow Sonoran that under no pretext was Cantú to be allowed to enter Mexico, and with regard to any political conciliation his presence in the country would lead to very bad results. At that moment it was not possible to allow Esteban Cantú to return to Mexicali or any other part of the nation.[8] Considering Cantú's attempts to seize Baja California Norte by force in the years following his removal from the governorship, one must agree with Calles's estimation of the situation—although Rodríguez, being closer to the scene, was probably also correct in seeing no threat or danger in Cantú's proposed visit.

Cantú eventually was able to return to Mexico City in October 1926. With some help from Francisco Serrano, it seems, he had petitioned to receive a commission from the Calles government to parcel out lands in Quintana Roo, but was disappointed in his quest. Calles continued to distrust the former governor of Baja California Norte. Cantú, disgusted at having received nothing from the Calles administration, celebrated his defeat in the cantina Broadway across from Alameda Park with his brother José and Federico Dato, all in a state of inebriation. There Cantú declared he would accept nothing from the "bolsheviks" who made up the current government. His friends urged him to be quiet before he drew attention to himself. After his brief stay at the Hotel Ritz, where he held fruitless meetings with ex-federal discontents, he returned to California.[9] Colonel Esteban Cantú's days of glory were over.

Cantú returned to Mexico City ten years later, in June 1936, and from his residence at 23 Calle Bolívar requested a copy of his military record of service that he might apply for a pension in his fifty-fifth year. The Secretary of War refused to grant his request because he recognized no *persona militar* in him. Shortly after the Japanese attack on Pearl Harbor, Cantú, now living in Mexicali, gallantly offered his services to the nation in view of the serious international moment and perhaps in an effort to gain sympathy for his request for a pension. The Ministry of National Defense thanked him for his patriotic offer, and there the matter rested for the moment.[10]

Cantú wrote to the Comisión Pro-Veteranos de la Revolución in July 1942 that his role in the revolution be recognized, as he believed his record of service demonstrated. Although the commission accepted his application, it informed him in May 1946 that it did not recognize him as a veteran of the revolution because he had served the usurper Victoriano Huerta with *"armas en la mano."*[11] Indeed, Carranza had ordered that all members of the federal army who had served under Huerta were to be disarmed. The commission further noted that Huerta had promoted Cantú to lieutenant colonel and awarded him *La Cruz de Valor y Abnegación* for his victory over Rodolfo Gallego at La Islita on the Río Colorado on November 14, 1913. In 1947 Cantú finally received the extract of his record of service that he had requested years before.[12]

After Cantú was elected senator from the new State of Baja California in 1953, he wrote to President Adolfo Ruiz Cortinez in November 1955 that he had always been loyal to the revolution and President Carranza. He noted that he had fought against the *filibusteros* who invaded Baja California Norte in 1911. Cantú reminded the president that other military men caught on the wrong side of the revolution had been reinstated in the army, and that was now his desire as well. The Ministry of National Defense, however, found no document in Cantú's record of service proving that he had fought against the *filibusteros* in 1911 or that he had ever resigned from the army, and therefore he could not be reinstated nor receive the retirement he wanted and perhaps now needed.[13]

Cantú's persistence in pursuing a pension from the Mexican government over a period of more than twenty years suggests he was in financial constraints. One can only wonder what happened to the millions of dollars Cantú had deposited in United States and Canadian banks during the years of his governorship. A sizable portion of it was certainly spent on the several efforts to regain control of Baja California Norte, which ended in failure after failure. His brother-in-law, Federico Dato, most likely absconded with a goodly sum, but what of the rest? Cantú owned property in the Northern District as well as in California and was a wealthy man when he left the governorship. Did he simply fritter it away? In 1926 the government of Mexico granted Cantú the right to establish a lottery in the Northern District, the proceeds of which were to maintain the national road linking Ensenada, Tijuana, and Mexicali. Tickets were to be sold in Tijuana only with the top prize being $10,000 pesos. Cantú had to deposit $30,000 gold pesos with the treasury of Baja California Norte before tickets could be sold and then had to pay 15 percent of the ticket sales to the treasury. The scheme failed, as Cantú was unable to cover the debt he owed the treasury, his deposit with the treasury was embargoed, and the lottery failed.[14] Yet this still does not explain the relative poverty of his later years.

Cantú's luck began to change for the better in 1946, when he was named purveyor for the government of Baja California Norte at a salary of $582 pesos a month. Not a great sum, but in 1950 he became the administrative inspector for the territory at $1,000 pesos monthly, which alleviated his former penury. After he returned to Mexicali following his term in the Senate in Mexico City, the State of Baja California granted Cantú a life pension of $2,000 pesos a month. Colonel Esteban Cantú, once governor of Baja California Norte and now a relatively poor man, died of a heart attack in his beloved Mexicali on March 15, 1966.[15]

From the day in June 1911 when Cantú, then a major, arrived in Mexicali with a detachment of federal troops until the day he was forced from the governorship in August 1920, he had acted independently of the government in Mexico City. He made a pretense of bowing to federal authority, when in actuality he was a law unto himself.[16] While he seemingly recognized the government of the usurper Victoriano Huerta by willingly accepting a promotion to the rank of colonel, he later had no compunctions about accepting appointment to the governorship from Pancho Villa, Eulalio Gutiérrez of the Convention government, and the First Chief of the Constitutionalist forces, Venustiano Carranza.[17] Following Carranza's victory, Cantú feigned loyalty to the Constitutionalist leadership, promulgated the 1917 Constitution in Baja California Norte, and cast that territory's vote for the First Chief in the presidential election that followed.[18] Juan Velázquez, the *cantuista* representative in the Cámara de Diputados, declared that his chief obeyed and complied with all laws emanating from the national government and was one of the most loyal servants of the republic.[19] Cantú himself invoked the 1917 Constitution when it suited his purposes, and on occasion wrote the First Chief regarding his compliance with federal laws.[20]

The actual condition of affairs in Baja California Norte was quite another matter. Esteban Cantú accepted few of the federal appointees Carranza sent to the territory and often ignored the laws proclaimed by the Constitutionalist government.[21] After the fall of Carranza in 1920, Cantú claimed he followed the orders of Interim President Adolfo de la Huerta, but refused to deliver the governorship into the hands of de la Huerta's appointee, and then refused to visit the nation's capital to explain the situation prevailing in Baja California.[22] It was immaterial to Cantú who happened to be president; he had generally acted independently of Carranza and at times made statements that should have come only from the nation's executive.[23] *El Heraldo de México* was on the mark in reporting that the *ex-federal* Cantú had run Baja California Norte like a fief. Having outwitted all his rivals for the gubernatorial chair, he only pretended to bow to the central government. The paper further noted that the government sent agents to investigate the real situation in the Northern District, but Cantú showered them with banquets, dances, and trips around the country in his Packard, so that when they returned to the capital they painted a rosy picture of the situation.[24]

Teodoro Frezieres, Mexican Consul at San Diego, believed Cantú was especially dangerous because he was out of reach of the government, and through his farming of the vice trade in Tijuana and Mexicali, possessed funds enough to win the good will of his followers. *El Heraldo de México* repeatedly lamented the lack of a rail link to Baja California Norte via Sonora and the abandonment of the peninsula by the central government. According to the newspaper and if one could rely on Alexander von Humbolt, the mail between the peninsula and the mainland was swifter during the colonial era than in 1919.[25] Cantú was simply beyond the military reach of the central government, and Sonora, from which an invasion could be launched, was often in turmoil itself. Carranza never governed a Mexico completely at peace with itself. Moreover, Baja California Norte could be reached via Sonora only by sea or the railroads of the United States; there was no railroad that crossed Sonora to the Northern District. Any army would have to cross the desert. If he enriched himself while governor, his behavior was not terribly different from that of other military chieftains during these years; he was merely more orderly and businesslike. Thus Cantú was able to enjoy an unchallenged neutrality in his island of tranquility as the revolution and civil war raged on the mainland.[26] While he governed Baja California Norte as he pleased, the territory became a refuge for anti-Constitutionalists of all stripes who despised the First Chief personally and denigrated his rule freely and publicly, but after the First Chief's death on May 21 of that year Cantú openly declared his loyalty to the regime of the assassinated president.[27] He soon adhered to the interim government of Adolfo de la Huerta, but when he refused to turn the governorship over to the appointee of that government, the leaders of the Agua Prieta revolt which ended

Carranza's rule determined to unseat the insubordinate governor with military force. Although Cantú made public his intention of resisting, he had in fact lost much support in Baja California Norte.

It may appear rather odd that Cantú would announce his loyalty to the fallen First Chief after so many years of political waywardness. Evidence indicates that he could have accommodated himself to the new order. United States Military Intelligence reported that he could have kept his governorship had he merely recognized the customs officials sent to the territory by the de la Huerta government. According to Consul Eduardo Ruiz at Los Angeles, the Sonorans assured Cantú that he could be used in a post of importance.[28] Why such seemingly unusual behavior? Perhaps Cantú doubted that de la Huerta and Obregón would be able to maintain themselves or that the storm of the revolution would finally give way to calm. Moreover, Cantú had earlier supported the *felicistas* in Sonora, a moment in his career that might now prove awkward in light of Agua Prieta. It had been Cantú's practice to give financial aid to any revolutionary movement in Sonora to prevent Carranza from having a base there from which to launch an attack on the Northern District. Even the *felicistas* understood this, realizing that they could only count on Cantú's aid if it aligned with his instincts for self-preservation.[29]

For the leaders of Agua Prieta, Baja California Norte was of special significance. It was Sonora's backyard and was becoming ever more important. Certainly they had their eyes on the vice revenue from Tijuana and Mexicali that formed the base of Cantú's power.

Despite his intelligence and political agility, Cantú did not have a firm grasp of the real political situation in Mexico as a whole. Nor did he seem to appreciate the political stature and popularity of Álvaro Obregón.[30] After his downfall, Cantú remained close to the *felicistas*, now his fellow exiles, and within a year announced his support for the restoration of the 1857 Constitution.[31] Writing to Félix Díaz in September 1921, Pedro del Villar informed the general that the ex-governor of Baja California was definitely in the Díaz group then planning a revolt in the Northern District, and that Cantú, its leader, believed the revolt should be based on the Constitution of 1857, not that of 1917. This caused Villar to ponder Cantú's support of Carranza after his assassination.[32] The "revolt" of November 1921 proved to be an absolute fiasco, discredited Cantú, and moved him completely into the Díaz camp.[33] Still one wonders, along with Pedro del Villar, about Cantú's rather easy adhesion to Félix Díaz and the 1857 Constitution after his heroic support of Carranza. Cantú's attitude toward the 1917 Constitution, however, suggests that he had always remained loyal to that of 1857.

In an apologia first published in 1920 after his fall from power and later reprinted in 1957, he painted a different picture of himself during the revolution. He claimed to be part of the revolutionary forces even before his arrival in Mexicali, gave the impression that he was a devout *maderista*, and claimed he brought the Constitutionalist regime to Baja California Norte when he seized power in 1914.[34] In the same apologia he referred to Venustiano Carranza as *"uno de los más grandes y mejores Presidentes que haya tenido nuestro país"* (one of the greatest and best presidents that our country has had).[35] How does one reconcile this with what we know of Esteban Cantú's attitude during the course of the revolution? One of the officers of the Twenty-Fifth Battalion, which arrived in Mexicali in 1911, related a different story. In a letter to Guillermo Rosas Jr., a dyed-in-the-wool *felicista*, Captain Carlos Vázquez wrote that the Twenty-Fifth Battalion was originally dispatched to Chihuahua to fight the Madero rebellion, but instead was diverted to Baja California to fight the *magonistas*, who had already been defeated and scattered before the battalion's arrival in Mexicali. There the Twenty-Fifth remained, vegetating for nearly ten years, despite all the changes in the National Palace.[36] It is perhaps worthwhile to note that the Twenty-Fifth Battalion was the only unit of the old federal army still extant when it was disbanded shortly after Cantú's removal from office. The new governor of Baja California Norte, Luis Mauricio Salazar, invited the men in the ranks to join the new revolutionary army, but none accepted.[37]

And so the Twenty-Fifth Battalion found itself stranded in Baja California Norte, insulated from the turmoil and the ideas of the revolution by geography and the political posture of Esteban Cantú, governor and military commander. Many changes occurred in the region during these years. Under Cantú the Northern District received its first network of roads, including the Camino de los Picachos linking Mexicali to Tijuana. Cantú gave a powerful impulse to education, increasing the pay and training of teachers and building schools in every community of the region, with the Escuela Cuauhtémoc as the crowning jewel. Hospitals were built and Mexicali was enlarged, beautified, and graced with Los Niños Héroes Park. There was a significant growth in population as the Northern District's inhabitants rose from ten thousand in 1910 to twenty-four thousand in 1920.

There was also a significant rise in vice. When he seized power, Cantú had to make a choice; either let the vice in Mexicali, Tijuana, and elsewhere run rampant, or exercise control over it for the benefit of Baja California Norte and himself. He chose the latter path, which enabled him to launch an unprecedented growth of the region's infrastructure and assured his independence from the central government. One might deplore the vice, but given the economic disparity that existed along the border, it would have developed in any case. Cantú did not initiate the vice; it was already in place when he took power. He simply moved the dens of iniquity somewhat out of sight, regulated and taxed them, and for that won the applause of the upright citizens of Mexicali as well as those of Calexico.

While Cantú's grip on the Northern District was firm, Mexico's hold on Baja California was weak. Although this was a problem for the central government, it paled in comparison to Chihuahua until Villa agreed to lay down his arms. With all the talk of purchasing or annexing the peninsula among the citizens and public figures of California and Arizona, there was a very real concern that it could be lost, especially given Mexico City's feeble control of the several outlying regions of the country. Only with the triumph of Agua Prieta and the arrival of Abelardo Rodríguez's troops in Mexicali did the central government exert its power over Baja California Norte. But despite all his public statements about the neutrality or independence of the Northern District during the civil wars raging on the mainland, and General John J. Pershing's fox hunt in Chihuahua, there is no evidence that Esteban Cantú ever considered the traitorous act of seceding from Mexico. Rather, the peaceful order that Cantú maintained in Baja California Norte gave Washington no excuse to intervene in the territory.

When the revolution burst forth Esteban Cantú found himself on an island of tranquility in comparison to the tempest that was raging elsewhere in Mexico. A federal officer trained at the military academy at Chapultepec, he had little use for the ideas of Francisco Madero, but easily adhered to Victoriano Huerta, like himself a federal officer. It was rather like a comfortable return to the *Porfiriato* during which Cantú had begun his career.[38] Consul Enrique González learned from one of Cantú's own officials that he was "in agreement with Huerta in everything," and that the exiled former president was on his way to confer with Cantú when he was arrested in El Paso, Texas.[39] Like many of the officers of the old federal army as well as those of the new revolutionary officer corps, Cantú was an opportunist. He outmaneuvered all his rivals in Baja California Norte, seized power, and was recognized as governor by every administration in Mexico City. With the country in chaos and finding himself in control of the Northern District with all the vice revenue at his fingertips, Cantú decided to remain in Mexicali and become the father of Baja California Norte. Only with the victory of Agua Prieta did his judgment falter.

NOTES

Chapter I

1. Esteban Cantú Jiménez, *Apuntes históricos de Baja California Norte* (México: n.p., 1957), p. 11. Cantú's *Apuntes históricos* was originally published during his exile in Los Angeles, California, on September 3, 1920. See Enrique Aldrete, *Baja California heroica* (México: n.p., 1958), p. 384; Marco Antonio Samaniego, "La Revolución Mexicana en Baja California: maderismo, magonismo, filibusterismo y la pequeña reveulta local," *Historia Mexicana* 56, no. 4 (abril-junio 2007): pp. 1254-57; Lowell L. Blaisdell, *The Desert Revolution, Baja California, 1911* (Madison: University of Wisconsin Press, 1962), p. 175; Lowell L. Blaisdell, "Was It Revolution or Filibustering? The Mystery of the Flores Magón Revolt in Baja California," *Pacific Historical Review* 23, no. 2 (May 1954): pp. 163-64.

2. Samaniego, "La Revolución Mexicana," pp. 7, 11.

3. Pablo L. Martínez, *Historia de Baja California* (2nd ed.; México: Editorial Baja California, 1956), pp. 500-501; Jesus Silva Herzog, *Breve historia de la Revolución Mexicana* (México: Fondo de Cultura Económico, 1960), 1:152; José Alfredo Gómez Estrada, *Gobierno y casinos: El origen de la riqueza de Abelardo L. Rodríguez* (México: Instituto Mora, 2007), p. 43; William Dirk Raat, *Revoltosos: Mexico's Rebels in the United States, 1903-1923* (College Station: Texas A&M University Press, 1981), p. 241; Justo Sierra, *The Political Evolution of the Mexican People* (Austin: University of Texas Press, 1969), pp. 365-66; Luis G. Zorrilla, *Historia de las relaciones entre México y los Estados Unidos de América, 1800-1958* (2nd ed.; México: Editorial Porrua, 1966), 2:214; William Dirk Raat, "The Diplomacy of Suppression: *Los Revoltosos*, Mexico, and the United States, 1906-1911," *Hispanic American Historical Review* 56, no. 4 (November 1976): pp. 532-33.

4. Archivo de Cancelados, Expediente XI/111/ 2-755, vol. 1, folios 20, 22-23, 3v., 36, 84, 153-66, vol. 3, folios 653, 661, vol. 4, folio 826, Archivo Histórico de la Defensa Nacional, Mexico City (hereafter cited as AHDN, Cancelados); *Calexico Chronicle* Feb. 21, 1911; *Jefe Político*, Ensenada, to Secretario de Gobernación, Jan. 29, 1911, Celso Vega to Miguel S. Macedo, Feb. 1, 1911, *Presidente Municipal*, Ensenada, to Secretario de Gobernación, Feb. 14, 1911, Caja 13, exp. 13, Fondo Distrito Norte, Archivo Histórico Estatal de Baja California (hereafter cited as AHEBC).

5. Cantú, *Apuntes históricos*, pp. 13-15; Eric Michael Schantz, "From the *Mexicali Rose* to the Tijuana Brass: Vice Tours of the United States-Mexico Border" (Los Angeles: PhD diss., University of California, 2001), pp. 77, 88.

6. *Los Angeles Times*, Aug. 19, 1920; Martínez, *Historia de Baja California*, p. 501.

7. Cantú, *Apuntes históricos*, pp. 12-17; Berta Ulloa, *La Revolución intervenida. Relaciones diplomáticas entre México y Estados Unidos (1910-1914)* (México: El

Colegio de México, 1971), p. 82; *El Diario* (Mexico City), July 4, 1911; Antonio Ponce Aquilar, *El Coronel Esteban Cantú en el Distrito Norte de Baja California, 1911-1920* (Mexicali: Dhiré, 2010), pp. 15-16.

8. *Calexico Chronicle*, July 20, 1911.

9. Cantú, *Apuntes históricos*, pp. 20-23; Finis C. Farr, *The History of Imperial County California* (Berkeley, California: Elms and Franks, 1918), pp. 301-304.

10. Cantú, *Apuntes históricos*, p. 30.

11. Lista nominal...del Cuerpo Auxiliar de Voluntarios, Caja 17, exp. 6, Fondo Distrito Norte, AHEBC; Alfonso Salazar Rovirosa, *Cronología de Baja California: Del territorio y del estado, de 1500 a 1956*, 10 vols. (México: Litografía Artística, 1956), 8:21, 28.

12. Cantú, *Apuntes históricos*, pp. 23-7; Oscar J. Martínez, *Fragments of the Mexican Revolution: Personal Accounts From the Border* (Albuquerque: University of New Mexico Press, 1968), p. 39.

13. AHDN, Cancelados, XI/111/4-1122, vol. 1, folios 7, 331, 330v., 172v., 481v., 434, 436, 427v., 428, 444, 50v., 17v., 51v. The folios in vol. 1 are not in sequential order; *Calexico Chronicle*, Nov. 27, 1917; Claire Kenamore, "The Principality of Cantú," *The Bookman* 46 (September 1917): pp. 23-27.

14. AHDN, Cancelados, XI/111/4-1122, vol. 1, folios 449, 445, 448, 443, 457, 455, 454, 440, 430-31; Gabriel Luján, *Coronel Esteban Cantú Jiménez: Benefactor de Baja California. México, vida y obra* (Mexicali, Baja California, México: AR Impresiones, 2009), pp. 26-27.

15. AHDN, Cancelados, XI/111/4-1122, vol. 1, folios 84-106, 61, 81, vol. 2, folio 445, vol. 3, folios 512, 532. The folios in vol. 3 are not in sequential order.

16. Agustín Martínez to General en Jefe de la 2/a Zona Militar, Oct. 1, 1909, Aug. 11, 1910, AHDN, Cancelados, XI/111/4-1122, vol. 3, folios 559, 618, 561, 573, 629-710, vol. 2, folios 218, 361, 364. The folios in vol. 2 are not in sequential order; Edwin Lieuwen, *Mexican Militarism: The Political Rise and Fall of the Revolutionary Army, 1919-1940* (Albuquerque: University of New Mexico Press, 1968), pp. xi-xii, 4-5.

17. Martínez, *Historia de Baja California*, p. 521; Joaquín Maass to Secretaría de Guerra, Aug. 5, 1911, AHDN, Cancelados, XI/111/2-326, vol. 3, folio 581.

18. AHDN, Cancelados, XI/111/4-1122, vol. 1, folios 341, 419, vol. 2, folio 404.

19. Gordillo Escudero to Secretaría de Gobernación, Dec. 21, 1912, AHDN, Cancelados, XI/111/2-326, vol. 3, folios, 613-18; A. G. Peña to Secretaría de Guerra, Jan. 3, 1913, AHDN, Cancelados, folio 609; *La Nación* (Mexico City), June 23, 1912.

20. *San Diego Union*, Sep. 7, Dec. 17, 1912.

21. AHDN, Cancelados, XI/111/2-326, vol. 1, folios 6v., 8v., 10v., 12v., 14v., 16v., 17v., 18, 67-79, 101-102, 127, 135-36, vol. 2, folios 393, 476, 481, 499, vol. 3, folios 514, 602, vol. 4, 844.

22. Martínez, *Historia de Baja California*, pp. 521-22; Tenorio to Venustiano Carranza, Aug. 15, 1915, AHDN, Cancelados, XI/111/3-1961, vol. 3, folios 503-506.

23. J. Isaac Aceves to Miguel de Diebold, May 28, 1913, Archivo de Embajadas de México en los Estados Unidos de America (hereafter cited as AEMEUA), leg. 412, exp. 1, Archivo de la Secretaría de Relaciones Exteriores (hereafter cited as ASRE).

24. Álvaro Obregón, *Ocho mil kilómetros en campaña* (México: Librería de la Vda. de Ch. Bouret, 1917), pp. 120-21. José María Maytorena thought Obregón's book

should be cited 8000 minutes per kilometro"; Maytorena to Luis Vargas Piñera, Nov. 11, 1938, Box VI, José María Maytorena Papers, Pomona College Library, Claremont, California; Aceves to Embajada de México, Sep. 1, 1913, Alfredo Margaín to Sr. Encargado de Negocios, Sep. 11, 1913, AEMEUA, leg. 417, exps. 1, 2, ASRE; El Inspector de Consulados to Sr. Encargado de Negocios, July 12, 1913, AEMEUA, leg. 435, exp. 1, ASRE; Martínez, *Historia de Baja California*, pp. 522-23; *Calexico Chronicle*, Aug. 19, Aug. 26, Sep. 5, 1913.

25. Cantú, *Apuntes históricos*, pp. 19-20.

26. El Inspector de Consulados to Sr. Encargado de Negocios, Sep. 6, Oct. 21, Nov. 19, Dec. 2, 1913, Jan. 7, 1914, AEMEUA, leg. 417, exp. 1, leg. 419, exp. 4, 6, leg. 435, exp. 1, ASRE; Martínez, *Historia de Baja California*, pp. 523-24; Cantú, *Apuntes históricos*, pp. 19-20; Ulloa, *La Revolución intervenida*, pp. 124-125; Juan B. Hernández, ed., *Pasajes de la Revolución Mexicana en el Distrito Norte de la Baja California* (n.p.:1956), p. 71; Rodolfo Gallego later fought in the Cristero Rebellion in which he was killed, Lieuwin, *Mexican Militarism*, pp. 84-85.

27. AHDN, Cancelados, XI/111/4-1122, vol. 2, folios 340, 345; *San Diego Union*, June 2, 1920; Ulloa, *La Revolución intervenida*, p. 82.

28. Martínez, *Historia de Baja California*, p. 525; *Calexico Chronicle*, Aug. 25, Sep. 1, 1914; Salazar Rovirosa, *Chronología de Baja California*, 7:48; Paul J. Vanderwood, *Disorder and Progress: Bandits, Police and Mexican Development* (Lincoln: University of Nebraska Press, 1981), p. 58.

29. *San Diego Union*, Dec. 13, 1914; Martínez, *Historia de Baja California*, p. 525.

30. *Calexico Chronicle*, Aug. 21, 25, 28, Sep. 4, 1914; Cantú, *Apuntes históricos*, pp. 37-9; AHDN, Cancelados, XI/111/4-277, vol. 1, folios 9, 36, 48, 51; Hernández, *Pasajes de la Revolución*, pp. 73-5; Salazar Rovirosa, *Cronología de Baja California*, 7:54-5; Alan Knight, *The Mexican Revolution*, 2 vols. (Lincoln and London: University of Nebraska Press, 1986), 1:148-49, 437.

31. AHDN, Cancelados, XI/111/3-1961, vol. 2, folios 333-4, 337v., vol. 3, folios 633, 707; José María Maytorena to Avilés, Sep. 3, 1914, AHDN, Cancelados, XI/111/4-7003, folio 8; Maytorena to Cantú, AHDN, Cancelados, XI/111/4-1122, vol. 4, folio 895; Francisco Villa to Maytorena, Aug. 30, 1914, Box IV, Maytorena Papers; Martínez, *Historia de Baja California*, p. 525; Antonio G. Rivera, *La revolución en Sonora* (México: n.p., 1969), p. 393; John Womack, *Zapata and the Mexican Revolution* (New York: Alfred A. Knopf, 1969), p. 148; *Calexico Chronicle*, Sep. 11, 14, 18, 1914; Silva Herzog, *Breve historia de la Revolución Mexicana*, 2:115; Friederich Katz, *The Life and Times of Pancho Villa* (Stanford: Stanford University Press, 1998), p. 279; Linda B. Hall, *Álvaro Obregón: Power and Revolution in Mexico, 1911-1920* (College Station: Texas A&M University Press, 1981), p. 74; Francisco R. Almada, *La Revolución en el Estado de Sonora* (México: Talleres Gráficos, 1971), pp. 136-37; Adolfo Gilly, comp., *Felipe Ángeles en la Revolución* (México: Ediciones Era, 2008), pp. 72, 87, 91, 93; Bernardino Mena Brito, *Carranza: Sus amigos, sus enimigos* (México: Ediciones Botas, 1935), p. 129.

32. AHDN, Cancelados, XI/111/3-1961, vol. 1, folios 18, 23, 26, 75, 85, 85v., 87, 89, 91, 108-109, 198-198v., vol. 2, folios 264, 367-68, 496, Report of Gordillo Escudero, June 30, 1912, vol. 2, folio 288.

33. Maytorena to Ángeles, Dec. 3, 1914, Box IV, Maytorena Papers; *San Diego Union*, Dec. 2, 1914; Martínez, *Historia de Baja California*, pp. 526-27; Hernández, *Pasajes de la Revolución*, pp. 77-80; Almada, *La Revolución en el Estado de Sonora*, p. 154; Susan M. Deeds, "José María Maytorena and the Mexican Revolución in Sonora (Part I)," *Arizona and the West* 18, no. 1 (Spring 1976): pp. 138-42.

34. Lowell L. Blaisdell, "Harry Chandler and Mexican Border Intrigue, 1914-1917," *Pacific Historical Review* 35, no. 4 (November 1966): p. 386; Cantú, *Apuntes históricos*, p. 39.

35. Maytorena to Ángeles, Dec. 3, 1914, Box IV, Maytorena Papers; *San Diego Union*, Dec. 2, 1914.

36. Martínez, *Historia de Baja California*, p. 528; Maytorena to Ángeles, Dec. 3, 1914, Box IV, Maytorena Papers; *San Diego Union*, Dec. 2, 8, 9, 10, 18, 1914; *New York Times*, Dec. 2, 1914; Almada, *La Revolución en el Estado de Sonora*, p. 160.

37. Blaisdell, *The Desert Revolution*, p. 387; Enrique A. González to Jorge U. Orozco, Dec. 31, 1914, AEMEUA, leg. 442, exp. 14, ASRE; AHDN, Cancelados, XI/111/3-1961, vol. 2, folio 425v.; Martínez, *Historia de Baja California*, p. 530; Adolfo Labastida to Carranza, Jan. 2, 1915, carp. 24, leg. 2325, Carranza Papers, Archivo de Venustiano Carranza, Centro de Estudios de Historia de México, Carso, Fundación Carlos Slim, México (hereafter cited as AVC); *New York Times*, Feb. 20, 1915.

38. Maytorena to Ángeles, Dec. 3, 1914, Box IV, Maytorena Papers; Adolfo Carrillo to Carranza, Apr. 9, 1915, carp. 35, leg. 3717, Carranza Papers, AVC.

39. Barry Carr, "Las perculiaridades del norte mexicano, 1880-1927: ensayo de interpretación," *Historia Mexicana* 22, no. 3 (*enero-marzo* 1973), pp. 321-323, 327; Ángela Moyano Pahissa, *California y sus relaciones con Baja California* (México: Fondo de Cultura Económico, 1983), p. 17.

40. P. L. Bell and H. Bentley Mackenzie, *Mexican West Coast and Lower California, a Comercial and Industrial Survey* (Washington, DC: G.P.O., 1923), pp. 281-83, 300-307; Dorothy Pierson Kerig, "Yankee Enclave: The Colorado River Land Company and Mexican Agrarian Reform in Baja California, 1902-1944" (Irvine: PhD diss., University of California, 1988), pp. 38, 97, 122; Aurelio de Vivanco, *Baja California al Día* (n.p.: 1924), p. 410; Edna Aidé Grijalva Larrañaga, "La Colorado River Land Company," in David Piñera Ramírez, *Panorama histórico de Baja California* (Tijuana: Centro de Investigaciones Históricas, UNAM-UABC, 1983), pp. 350-61; Moyano Pahissa, *California y sus relaciones con Baja California*, pp. 97-9.

41. Samuel G. Vázquez to Cándido Aguilar, Feb. 16, 1918, AEMEUA, leg. 533, exp. 44, anexo no. 5, ASRE; Adolfo Carrillo to Subsecretario Encargado del Despacho de Fomento, Apr. 10, 1915, exp. 17-20-156, ASRE; Modesto C. Rolland, *Informe sobre el Distrito Norte de la Baja California*, (México: Universidad Autónoma de Baja California, 1993), p. 166. Rolland made his report on December 19, 1919.

42. Bell and Mackenzie, *Mexican West Coast and Lower California*, pp. 285-88; J. R. Southworth, *El territorio de la Baja California: su agricultura, comercio, minería é industrias* (México: Gob. del Territorio, 1899), pp. 12-13; José Vasconcelos, *La tormenta*, (México: Fondo de Cultura Económico, 1982), p. 890.

43. Bell and Mackenzie, *Mexican West Coast and Lower California*, pp. 285-88; Southworth, *El territorio de la Baja California*, pp. 12-13.

44. "Breve resumen histórico geográfico del Distrito Norte, 1920," Caja 5, exp. 19, Fondo Distrito Norte, AHEBC; Vivanco, *Baja California al día*, pp. 315-16.

45. David E. Lorey, ed., *United States-Mexico Border Statistics Since 1900* (Los Angeles: UCLA Latin American Center, 1990), p. 11; *Calexico Chronicle*, Apr. 23, 1910, Feb. 11, 1911; Kerig, "Yankee Enclave," pp. 118-20; Knight, *The Mexican Revolution*, 1:30; Schantz, "From the *Mexicali Rose* to the Tijuana Brass," p. 66.

46. Francisco Álvarez, "La Situación Real de la Baja California," a report to the President of the Republic, published in *Nueva Era* (Mexico City), June 8, 1912,

Fideicomiso Archivos Plutarco Elías Calles y Fernando Torreblanca (hereafter cited as FAPEC), Archivo Plutarco Elías Calles (hereafter cited as APEC), exp. 9, inv. 460, leg. 1.

47. *San Diego Union*, Dec. 13, 1914.

Chapter II

1. Esteban Cantú, "A Manifesto to the Nation [in English]," Oct. 15, 1915, Caja 5, exp. 15, Fondo Distrito Norte, AHEBC; Harry Carr, "The Kingdom of Cantú: Why Lower California is an Oasis of Perfect Peace in Bloody Mexico," *Sunset* 37, no. 3 (April 1917): p. 33.

2. Martínez, *Historia de Baja California*, pp. 528-29; González to Agente Confidencial del Gobierno de México, Dec. 31, 1914, AEMEUA, leg. 466, exp. 5, ASRE; Cantú, "A Manifesto to the Nation;" Salazar Rovirosa, *Cronología de Baja California*, 7:57; *Calexico Chronicle*, Jan. 26, 1915.

3. González to Agente Confidencial del Gobierno de México, Dec. 31, 1914, AEMEUA, leg. 466, exp. 5; González to Subsecretario de Relaciones, Feb. 25, July 7, 1915, AEMEUA, leg. 467, exp. 13 and leg. 476, exp. 2; González to Consul, Los Angeles, Dec. 31, 1914, AEMEUA, leg. 470, exp. 12, (quotation) ASRE.

4. Carrillo to Carranza, Feb. 1, 1915, AEMEUA, leg. 450, exp. 6, Samuel G. Vázquez to Cándido Aguilar, Feb. 16, 1918, AEMEUA, leg. 533, exp. 44, anexo no. 5; Manuel G. Paredes to Edgar E. Howe, July 30, 1915, AEMEUA, leg. 474, exp. 4, ASRE; Adolfo Carrillo to Subsecretario de Fomento, Apr. 10, 1915, Frezieres to Aguilar, May 9, 1916, Frezieres to Arredondo, May 19, 1916, Frezieres to Carranza, May 22, 1916, all in AEMEUA, leg. 494, exp. 5, ASRE; Gómez Estrada, *Gobierno y Casinos*, p. 63-64; L. A. Peredo to Obregón, Oct. 2, 1916, AHDN, Cancelados, XI/111/4-1122, vol. 4, folios 796, 854; FAPEC, Archivo Fernando Torreblanco, Fondo Álvaro Obregón (hereafter cited as FAO), exp. 2, inv. 57, leg. 1; Aguilar to Obregón, Aug. 15, 1916, AHDN, Cancelados, XI/III/4-1122, vol. 2, folio 512, FAPEC, FAO.

5. *Baltimore Evening Sun*, [about Dec. 30, 1914?], in Frezieres to Arredondo, Dec. 31, 1914, AEMEUA, leg. 450, exp. 6, ASRE; Frezieres to Aguilar, May 9, 1916, Frezieres to Arredondo, May 19, 1916, Frezieres to Carranza, May 22, 1916, AEMEUA, leg. 494, exp. 5, ASRE.

6. Tenorio to Carranza, Aug. 15, 1915, AHDN, Cancelados, XI/111/3-1961, vol. 3, folios 503-506; Edmundo F. Cota to De Negri, June 12, 1916, AHDN, Cancelados, XI/4-1122, vol. 3, folio 747; Esteban Cantú, *Circular*, Feb. 25, 1915, FAPEC, FAO, exp. 3, inv. 58, leg. 1; Rolland, *Informe sobre el Distrito Norte de la Baja California*, pp. 116, 119; San Diego Union, Oct. 19, 1915.

7. De Negri to Arredondo, July 18, 1915, AEMEUA, leg. 456, exp. 1; Arredondo to González, July 19, 1915, AEMEUA, leg. 456, exp. 1; González to Subsecretario de Relaciones, March 20, 1915, AEMEUA, leg. 472, exp. 4; González to Carranza, July 14, Aug. 5, 1915, AEMEUA, leg. 474, exp. 3, leg. 475, exp. 1; González to Jesús Acuña, Aug. 3, 1915, AEMEUA, leg. 475, exp. 1; González to Subsecretario de Relaciones, July 17, 31, 1915, AEMEUA, leg. 474, exp. 3, 4; De Negri to Arredondo, July 22, 1915, AEMEUA, leg. 474, exp. 4; González to De Negri, July 21, 1915, AEMEUA, leg. 474, exp. 4; González to United States Marshall, Sep. 3, 1915, AEMEUA, leg. 475, exp. 4; [?] to Robert Lansing, July 19, 1915, AEMEUA, leg. 462, exp. 2; González to Subsecretario de Relaciones, Sep. 7, 1915, AEMEUA, leg. 475, exp. 4, ASRE; Rolland, *Informe sobre el Distrito Norte de la Baja California*, p. 173.

8. Paredes to De Negri, May 15, 1915, De Negri to Carranza, May 20, 1915, exp. 11-4-92, ASRE; Carrillo to Carranza, Apr. 9, 1915, carp. 35, leg. 3717, Carranza Papers, AVC; Paredes to De Negri, Apr. 9, 1915, carp. 35, leg. 3752, AVC, De Negri to Carranza, Apr. 9, 1915, González to Carranza, Oct. 28, 1915, carp. 57, leg. 6449, AVC; De Negri to Carranza, Apr. 2, 1915, AEMEUA, leg. 473, exp.1, ASRE; Pedro Castro, *Álvaro Obregón: Fuego y cenizas de la Revolución Mexicana* (México: Ediciones Era, 2009), p. 308; Knight, *The Mexican Revolution*, 1:230; John Reed, *Insurgent Mexico* (New York: Appelton, 1914), pp. 64-5, 71-2; Frank Tannenbaum, *Peace by Revolution: An Interpretation of Mexico* (New York: Columbia University Press, 1933), p. 120; Paul J. Vanderwood, "Response to Revolt: The Counter-Guerrilla Strategy of Porfirio Díaz," *Hispanic American Historical Review* 56, no. 4 (November 1976), p. 573.

9. De Negri to Arredondo, Dec. 3, 1915, Arredondo to De Negri, Dec. 3, 1915, Arredondo to Lansing, Dec. 4, 1915, Alvey A. Adee to Arredondo, Dec. 14, 1915, AEMEUA, leg. 483, exp. 4, ASRE.

10. González to Subsecretario de Relaciones Exteriores, Jan. 23, 1915, González to American Consul, Ensenada, Jan. 29, 1915, AEMEUA, leg. 470, exp. 12, Paredes to González, Mar. 17, 1915, González to Carranza, Mar. 17, 1915, AEMEUA, leg. 472, exp. 3, González to Pan American News Service, Feb. 3, 1915, AEMEUA, leg. 467, exp. 13, ASRE; Manuel L. Velarde to Celestino Ruiz, Feb. 5, 1915, carp. 38, leg. 3746, Félix Díaz Papers, AVC; *El Pueblo* (Mexico City), Dec. 11, 1915; Marco Antonio Samaniego López, *Los gobiernos civiles en Baja California, 1920-1923: Un estudio sobre la relación entre los poderes local y federal* (Mexicali: Instituto de Cultura de Baja Califorrnia, 1998), pp. 30-31, 34, 66.

11. Adee to Arredondo, July 22, 1915, AEMEUA, leg. 480, exp. 8, ASRE; *El Demócrata* (Mexico City), Sep. 28, 1916; Arredondo to Paredes, July 26 1915, AEMEUA, leg. 474, exp. 4, ASRE; Paredes to Rafael E. Múzquiz, May 5, 1915, Múzquiz to Arredondo, June 22, 1915, Arredondo to C. M. Dávalos, July 12, 1915, Paredes to Galen Nichols, Apr. 26, 1915, Nichols to Paredes, Apr. 29, 1915, exp. 16-15-14, ASRE; Carrillo to Jesús Urueta, Feb. 3, 1915, AEMEUA, leg. 450, exp. 6, ASRE.

12. Paredes to Arredondo, July 7, 1915, AEMEUA, leg. 474, exp. 2, ASRE, González to Subsecretario de Relaciones, Oct. 13, 1915, AEMEUA, leg. 480, exp. 8, ASRE; *Calexico Chronicle*, Aug. 28, Oct. 21, 1915.

13. González to Subsecretario de Relaciones, Oct. 13, 1915, AEMEUA, leg. 480, exp. 8, ASRE; González to Carranza, Oct. 25, 1915, carp. 57, leg. 6393, Carranza Papers, AVC; Knight, *The Mexican Revolution*, 2:104; Lieuwin, *Mexican Militarism*, pp. 34-36; Thomas Benjamin, *La Revolución: Mexico's Great Revolution as Memory, Myth, and History* (Austin: University of Texas Press, 2000), p. 51.

14. Genaro G. Cota to Carranza, Sep. 23, 1915, carp. 52, leg. 5804, Carranza Papers, AVC; *Calexico Chronicle*, Oct. 24, Nov. 11, 1915; *San Diego Union*, Oct. 24, 1915; *New York Times*, Nov. 7, 1915.

15. Martínez, *Historia de Baja California*, pp. 532-33; Frezieres to Arredondo, AEMEUA, Apr. 24, 1916, leg. 494, exp. 5, ASRE; *Calexico Chronicle*, Dec. 24, 1915, Jan. 25, Feb. 5, 13, 1916; Secretaría del Ejército del Noreste to Cantú, Apr. 1, 1916, AHDN, Cancelados, XI/111/4-1122, vol. 2, folio 492.

16. [?] to Pablo González, Jan. 4, 1916, carp. 65, leg. 7163, Carranza Papers, AVC; Hall, *Álvaro Obregón*, p. 184; Castro, *Álvaro Obregón*, pp. 50, 55-56; Douglas Richmond, "The First Chief and Revolutionary Mexico: The Presidency of Venustiano Carranza, 1915-1920" (PhD diss., University of Washington, 1976),

pp. 352-54; "Mi Gobierno en Sonora: informc quc rindi al pucblo del Estadu el general José María Maytorena...en el cuadrienio de 1911 a 1915," p. 49, Box VII, Maytorena Papers; *El Heraldo de México* (Mexico City), Sep. 15, 1919; Almada, *La Revolución en el Estado de Sonora*, p. 105; M. D. To Carranza, June 14, 1916, carp. 83, leg. 92, 93, Carranza Papers.

17. Enrique Barrera to Obregón, June [?] 1920, FAPEC, FAO, exp. 158, inv. 3034, leg. 1; *El Heraldo de México* (Mexico City), Sep. 15, 1919.

18. Frezieres to Arredondo, Apr. 24, 1916, AEMEUA, leg. 494, exp. 5, ASRE; Cantú to Obregón, Mar. 11, 1916, Cándido Aguilar to Obregón, Sep. 21, 1916, AHDN, Cancelados, XI/111/4-1122, vol. 2, folios 488-91, 647; Luis G. Beltrán to Tomás Ojeda, June 22, 1916, Ojeda to De Negri, June 7, 1916, AHDN, Cancelados, XI/111/4-1122, vol. 4, folios 770, 754, 788; Obregón to Secretaría de Comunicaciones y Obras Públicas, May 19, 1916, AHDN, Cancelados, XI/111/4-1122, vol. 2, folio 506; *Periódico Oficial* (Mexicali), Aug. 31, 1916; *La Crónica* (San Francisco), n.d.; Martínez, *Historia de Baja California*, p. 532.

19. Tenorio to Carranza, Aug. 15, 1915, AHDN, Cancelados, XI/111/3-1961, vol. 3, folios 503-506; Zárate to Carranza, Oct. 13, 1916, carp. 99, leg. 11233. Carranza Papers, AVC; AHDN, Cancelados, XI/111/4-1122, folio 788.

20. *Calexico Chronicle*, Sep. 9, 1916.

21. *El Heraldo de México* (Mexico City), Sep. 14, 1919.

22. Zárate to Carranza, Oct. 13, 1916, carp. 99, leg. 11233, Carranza Papers, AVC; Frezieres to Aguilar, Nov. 16, 1916, exp. 16-20-149, ASRE.

23. Frezieres to Arredondo, Aug. 22, 1916, AEMEUA, leg. 494, exp. 6, ASRE; Aguilar to Obregón, Aug. 30, Sep. 26, 1916, AHDN, Cancelados, XI/111/4-1122, vol. 2, folio 521, 23, vol. 4, folios 792, 801; E. Garza Pérez to Obregón, Sep. 6, 1916, AHDN, Cancelados, XI/111/4-1122, vol. 2, folios 515, 525-26, "Mas datos sobre la preparación militar de Esteban Cantú...," AHDN, Cancelados, XI/111/4-1122, vol. 4, folio 798; Tenorio to Carranza, Aug. 15, 1915, XI/111/3-1961, vol. 3, folios 503-506; David Gershon to the Department of State, Dec. 24, 1916, Records of the Department of State Relating to Internal Affairs of Mexico, 1910-29, Microcopy No. 274, Record Group 59, National Archives, 812.00 (hereafter cited as RDS No. 274, NA); Martínez, *Historia de Baja California*, p. 533.

24. "Mas datos sobre la preparación militar de Esteban Cantú...,"AHDN, Cancelados, XI/111/4-1122, vol. 4, folio 798; Aguilar to Obregón, Nov. 7, 1916, AHDN, Cancelados, XI/111/4-1122, vol. 4, folio 813; Aguilar to Obregón, Sep. 21, 1916, AHDN, Cancelados, XI/111/4-1122, vol. 2, folio 528; Jesús Rocha to Adolfo Gómez, May 16, 1916, Edmundo F. Cota to De Negri, June 12, 1916, AHDN, Cancelados, XI/111/4-1122, vol. 3, folios 746-48; Frezieres to Aguilar, Oct. 31, 1916, AEMEUA, leg. 502, exp. 1, ASRE; Gershon to the Department of State, May 9, 1918, RDS, No. 274, 812.00, NA.

25. Aguilar to Obregón Nov. 7, 1916, AHDN, Cancelados, XI/111/4-1122, vol. 4, folios 810, 816; Frezieres to Carranza, Oct. 6, 1916, carp. 98, legs. 11,152; Carranza Papers, AVC; Consul, San Diego to Aguilar, Oct. 7, 1916, AEMEUA, leg. 480, exp. 8, ASRE; De Negri to Aguilar, Oct. 28, 1916, exp. 16-20-149, ASRE.

26. *El Universal* (Mexico City), Mar. 5, June 25, Aug. 31, Sep. 10, 1917; Cantú to Garza Pérez, May 8, 1917, exp. 20-22-37, ASRE; *Calexico Chronicle*, Feb. 16, 1917.

27. Paredes to Garza Pérez, Oct. 5, 1917 (second, third and fourth quotations), Andrés G. García to Garza Pérez, Oct. 8, 1917 (first quotation), Juan B. Vegas to Paredes, Oct. 20, 1917, exp. 11-18-171, ASRE.

28. Vasconcelos, *La tormenta*, pp. 865, 872, 890; Jorge Vera Estañol, *Historia de la Revolución mexicana: Orígenes y resultados* (3rd ed.; México: Editorial Porrúa, 1976), pp. 377, 437; Decree signed by Cantú, June 10, 1917, Caja 18, exp. 30, Fondo Distrito Norte, AHEBC.

29. De Negri to Aguilar, Mar. 2, 1918, Genaro G. Cota to De Negri, Feb. 27, 1918, De Negri to Garza Pérez, Jan. 3, 1917, Feb. 14, 1919, legs. 17-14-51, 17-8-130, 17-16-141, ASRE; *El Heraldo de México* (Los Angeles), Feb. 27, 1918, Feb. 14, 1919.

30. De Negri to Garza Pérez, Jan. 3, 1917, leg. 17-8-130, ASRE; Manuel García Rubio to Carranza, July 8, 1916, carp. 82, leg. 9,148, Carranza Papers, AVC; De Negri to Calles, Feb. 16, 1918, FAPEC, Anexo, Fondo Elías Calles (hereafter cited as FEC), exp. 25, inv. 1,051, leg. 1; Michael C. Meyer, *Huerta: A Political Portrait* (Lincoln: University of Nebraska Press, 1972), pp. 159-63.

31. Knight, *The Mexican Revolution*, 2:447-48; Michael C. Meyer, *Mexican Rebel: Pascual Orozco and the Mexican Revolution, 1910-1915* (Lincoln: University of Nebraska Press, 1967), p. 89.

32. De Negri to Salvador Diego Fernández, Mar. 21, Apr. 2, 1919, exp. 17-16-141, ASRE; *Los Angeles Times*, Aug. 5, 1920; *Excelsior* (Mexico City), Feb. 13, 1920; Testimony of Charles E. Jones, May 17, 1920, US Senate, 66th cong., 2nd sess., *Senate Executive Document* no. 285 (7665-6), "Investigation of Mexican Affairs," pp. 2,994, 2,998. Jones was a journalist who worked for the Bureau of Investigation of the United States Justice Department. At the same time he was an agent of Mexico employed to keep watch on Mexican revolutionaries in the United States; *El Heraldo de México* (Mexico City), Sep. 15, 1919; Ben Franklin Fly to Captain McNamee, June 3, 1918, RDS No. 274, 812.00, NA (quotation).

33. Lieuwin, *Mexican Militarism*, pp. 36-37.

34. Edmundo F. Cota to De Negri, Feb. 27, 1918, exp. 17-14-51, ASRE; Ageo Meneses to Carranza, Oct. 2, 1917, carp. 117, leg. 13, 310, Carranza Papers, AVC.

35. José Montes, Luis H. Vega and J. Jesús Carranza to Carranza, Aug. 6, 1916, carp. 90, leg. 10,156, Carranza Papers, AVC; Genaro C. Cota to Carranza, Sep. 23, 1915, carp. 52, leg. 5804, Carranza Papers, AVC.

36. Tomás Ojeda to Calles, Sep. 3, 1917, Calles to Ojeda, Sep. 12, 1917, FAPEC, FEC, exp. 138, inv. 993, leg. 1.

37. W. F. Fullam to the Secretary of the Navy, May 29, 1918, RDS No. 274, 812.00, NA; Ponce Aguilar, *El Colonel Esteban Cantú*, p. 99.

38. *Los Angeles Times*, Aug. 5, 19, 1920; *Calexico Chronicle*, Sep. 9, 1916; *San Diego Union*, Dec. 18, 1914; Edmundo F. Cota to De Negri, Feb. 27, 1918, exp. 17-14-51, ASRE; Esteban Cantú, *Circulars*, Jan. 21, Apr. 7, 1915, FAPEC, FAO, exp. 3, inv. 58, leg. 1; Antimaco Sax, *Los Mexicanos en el destierro* (San Antonio, Texas: n.p., 1916), pp. 39-41; Celso Aguirre Bernal, *Breve historia del Estado de Baja California* (México: Ediciones Quinto Sol, 1987), p. 96.

39. Edmundo F. Cota to De Negri, Apr. 7, 1918, leg. 17-14-51, ASRE; Montes, Vega and J. Carranza to Carranza, Aug. 6, 1916, carp. 90, leg. 10,156, Carranza Papers, AVC; Cresse [Charles E. Jones] to the Secretary of State, Sep. 29, 1918, RDS No. 274, 812.00; Obregón, *Ocho mil kilometros*, p. 372; *Excelsior* (Mexico City), Aug. 27, 1920; Testimony of Jones, May 17, 1920, *Sen. Ex. Doc.* no. 285 (7665-6), p. 2, 998; Knight, *The Mexican Revolution*, 1:473.

40. Ramón Araiza and José Rivero to Carranza, May 8, 1917, telegram, Carranza Papers, AVC; José Cantú to Obregón, Mar. 24, 1917, Bruno García Lozano to

Comandante Militar de la Plaza, May 10 , 1917, AHDN, Cancelados, XI/111/5-1272, folios 1-2; *El Demócrata* (Mexico City), Jan. 4, 5, 1916; Frezieres to Arredondo, Dec. 2, 1916, AEMEUA, leg. 494, exp. 1, Vázquez to Bonillas, June 1, 1918, AEMEUA, leg. 591, exp. 20, ASRE; Katz, *Pancho Villa*, pp. 314-15; Friederich Katz, *The Secret War in Mexico: Europe, The United States and the Mexican Revolution* (Chicago: University of Chicago Press, 1981), pp. 305, 490.

41. Creese [Charles E. Jones] to the Secretary of State, Sep. 4, 27, 1918, RDS No. 274, 810.00, NA; Testimony of Jones, May 17, 1920, *Sen. Ex. Doc.* No. 285 (7665-6), p. 3,051; RDS No. 274, 812.00; Katz, *Pancho Villa*, pp. 222, 315.

42. Frezieres to Carranza, Apr. 25, 1918, in Testimony of Jones, May 17, 1920, *Sen. Ex. Doc.* No. 285 (7665-6), pp. 3,014-16; Carr, "Las peculiaridades del norte mexicano," pp. 321, 326-27; Thomas Benjamin and Mark Wassermann, eds., *Provinces of the Revolution: Essays on Regional Mexican History, 1910-1929* (Albuquerque: University of New Mexico Press, 1990), p. 20; Jürgen Buchenau, *Plutarco Elías Calles and the Mexican Revolution* (Lanham: Rowman and Littlefield, 2007), pp. 56-58.

43. Frezieres to Carranza, Apr. 25, 1918, in Testimony of Jones, May 17, 1920, *Sen. Ex. Doc.* No. 285, pp. 2, 997-98.

44. Carranza to José J. Pesquiera, Teodoro Frezieres and Manuel G. Paredes, Jan. 24, 1917, José Garza Zertuche to Juan B. Rojo, June 24, 1919, Rojo to Salvador Diego Fernández, June 28, 1919, De Negri to Garza Pérez, Mar. 8, Garza Pérez to De Negri, Apr. 24, 1919, exps. 16-20-149, 17-20-105, 17-18-60, ASRE.

Chapter III

1. De Negri to S. D. Fernández, May 21, 1919, exp. 17-16-141, ASRE.

2. *Calexico Chronicle*, Nov. 12, 1915, Jan. 4, 1916; Esteban Cantú, *Circulars*, Oct. 1, Nov. 29, 1915, FAPEC, FAO, exp. 3, inv. 58, leg. 1.

3. *San Diego Union*, Aug. 19, 1915, July 6, 1917.

4. Paredes to Juan N. Amador, Mar. 31, 1915, Paredes to Jesús Urueta, Mar. 19, 30, 1915, González to Subsecretario de Relaciones Exteriores, Mar. 22, 1915, AEMEUA, leg. 472, exp. 4, ASRE; *Washington Post*, Apr. 7, 1915.

5. Marshall to Prieto, Apr. 12, 1915, Prieto to Arredondo, Jan. 5, Apr. 15, 1915, Prieto to Marcelino Dávalos, 28 Dec. 1914, AEMEUA, leg. 450, exp. 9, ASRE.

6. González to Subsecretario de Relaciones Exteriores, Mar. 22, 1915, AEMEUA, leg. 472, exp. 4, ASRE.

7. *San Diego Union*, Apr. 28, June 24, 1917.

8. *Calexico Chronicle*, Jan. 25, 1918.

9. *San Diego Union*, June 24, 1918.

10. *San Diego Union*, May 27, Aug. 13, 1917, June 24, 1918; *El Heraldo de México* (Mexico City), Apr. 22, 1920; Luis G. Beltrán to Tomás Ojeda, June 22, 1916, AHDN, Cancelados, XI/111/4-1122, vol. 4, folio 769.

11. Hugo H. Johnstone to W. F. Fullam, June 24,1918, RDS No. 274, 812.00, NA; *El Universal* (Mexico City), June 27, 1918; Knight, *The Mexican Revolution* 1:278, 2:220, 474-75; *Diccionario Porrúa de historia, biografía y geografía de México.* Tercera ed. (México: Editorial Porrúa, 1971), 2:1,809; Salvador Cruz, *Vida y obra de Pastor Rouaix* (México: Instituto National de Antropogía e Historia, 1980), pp. 25, 28, 32, 38, 42; Hall, *Álvaro Obregón*, pp. 174, 179.

12. Fullam to the Secretary of the Navy, June 24, 1918, RDS No. 274, 812.00, NA.

13. Boyle to the Secretary of State, Aug. 25, 1920, RDS No. 274, 812.00/24495, NA.

14. Gershon to the Department of State, May 9, 1918, RDS No. 274, 812.00, NA; Hutchinson to the Director of Naval Intelligence, Sep. 11, 1918, RDS No. 274, 812.00, NA; Testimony of Jones, May 17, 1920, *Sen. Ex. Doc.*, No. 285 (7665-6), p. 3,017.

15. *San Diego Union*, Sep. 28, 1914, Nov. 4, 1917; Hutchinson to the Director of Naval Intelligence, Oct. 15, 1918, RDS No. 274, 812.00, NA; Robert Lansing to the President, Apr. 18, 1917, Records of the Department of State Relating to Political Relations between the United States and Mexico, 1910-1929, Microcopy No. 314, Record Group 59, National Archives, 711.12/43 A (hereafter cited as RDS No. 314, NA).

16. Hutchinson to the Director of Naval Intelligence, May 13, 1918, RDS No. 274, 812.00, NA.

17. Roger Wells to Leland Harrison, June 5, 1918, RDS No. 274, 812.00, NA.

18. W. C. Van Antwerp to Naval Intelligence, June 18, 1918, RDS No. 274, 812.00, NA; Leroy Holt to T. S. Jevans Mar. 19, 1918, RDS No. 274, 812.00/0070, NA; Cantú to Secretario de Gobernación, Apr. 29, June 28, 1918, Caja 21, exp. 16, Fondo Distrito Norte, AHEBC; *Excelsior* (Mexico City), Jan. 26, 1919; Edward McCauley, Jr., to Harrison, Apr. 27, 1918, RDS No. 274, 812.00, NA; Harrison to Auchinloss, May 14, 1918, RDS No. 274, 812.00, NA.

19. Testimony of Jones, Oct. 23, 1918, *Sen. Ex. Doc.* No. 285 (7665-6), p. 3,017; Gershon to the Department of State, May 9, 1918; *San Diego Union*, Nov. 4, 29, 1917.

20. Cantú to Fly, Feb. 20, 1918, RDS No. 274, 812.00, NA; Fletcher to the Secretary of State, Apr. 29, 1918, RDS No. 274, 812.00, NA.

21. Charles B. Parker to Aguilar, Jan. 14, 1917, Aguilar to Parker Jan. 16, 1917, Aguilar to Obregón, Jan. 16, 1917, Obregón to Aguilar, Jan. 16, 1917, Aguilar to Paredes, Jan. 17, 1917, Frezieres to Aguilar, Jan. 15, 1917, Parker to Aguilar, Feb. 13, 1917, Aguilar to Carranza, Feb. 21, 1917, Carranza to Aguilar, Feb. 28, 1917, Garza Pérez to Parker, Feb. 28, 1917, Adolfo de la Huerta to Garza Pérez, Mar. 5, 1917, Garza Pérez to de la Huerta, Feb. 28, 1917, all in exp. 17-10-12, ASRE.

22. Office of the Military Attaché, American Embassy, Mexico City to Director of Military Intelligence, Sep. 1, 29, Oct. 6, 1919, Military Intelligence Branch, Executive Division, Washington, DC, US Military Intelligence Reports: Mexico, 1919-1941, Reel 1 (Frederick, MD: University Publications of America). Hereafter cited as Intelligence Reports, Mexico.

23. Pedro R. Mejía to De Negri, Feb. 21, 1919, De Negri to Garza Pérez, Feb. 21, 1919, exp. 17-18-56, ASRE; *El Heraldo de México* (Mexico City), Mar. 19, 1920.

24. *Excelsior* (México City), Sep. 26, 1919.

25. *New York Times*, Mar. 29, Oct. 18, 1914; *Calexico Chronicle*, Oct. 20, 1914; González to Carranza, Oct. 25, 1915, carp. 57, leg. 6393, Carranza Papers, AVC.

26. *Calexico Chronicle*, Jan. 25, 1916; Cantú to Obregón, Mar. 11, 1916, AHDN, Cancelados, XI/111/4-1122, vol. 2, folios 488-91.

27. Martínez, *Historia de Baja California*, p. 532; Aguilar to Obregón, Apr. 19, 1916, Pesqueira to Aguilar, May 8, 1916, AHDN, Cancelados, XI/111/4-1122, vol. 2, folios 495-96. Santa Ysabel is present day General Trías in honor of Ángel Trías, a famous nineteenth century governor of Chihuahua.

28. *Calexico Chronicle*, Mar. 18, 1916.

29. González to Aguilar, June 13, 1916, Frezieres to Cantú, June 19, 1916, [Aguilar] to Frezieres, June [?] 1916, AEMEUA, leg. 494, exp. 5, ASRE.

30. *San Diego Sun*, June 19, 1916; *Los Angeles Times*, June 19, 1916; *Evening Tribune* (San Diego), June 20, 1916; *San Diego Union*, June 20, 1916; Aguilar to Obregón, Aug. 8, 1916, Frezieres to Aguilar, July 27, 1916, AHDN, Cancelados, XI/111/4-1122, vol. 4, folio 778; *El Paso Democrat*, July 19, 1916; *New York Times*, June 19, 1916.

31. De Negri to Garza Pérez, Dec. 27, 1917, exp. 17-14-34, ASRE; Fullam to the Secretary of the Navy, May 29, 1918, RDS No. 274, 812.00, NA.

32. *El País* (Mexico City), July 6, 17, 1911; Paredes to Arredondo, Jan. 10, 1916, exp. 17-9-208, ASRE; *Calexico Chronicle*, Jan. 6, 1916; Marco Antonio Samaniego, "El norte revolucionario. Diferencias regionales y sus paradojas en la relación con Estados Unidos," *Historia Mexicana* 40, no. 2 (*octubre-diciembre* 2010): pp. 966-67, 973-74; Paredes to Arredondo, Jan. 10, 1916, exp. 17-9-208, ASRE.

33. *Arizona Daily Star* (Tucson), Jan. 8, 1919; *The Congressional Record*, 65th cong., 3rd sess., Jan. 1, 1919, p. 249; *New York Times*, Jan. 8, 1919.

34. *The Congressional Record*, 65th cong., 3rd sess., Jan. 7, 1919, p. 1,098; *Arizona Republican* (Phoenix), Jan. 10, 1919; George F. Sparks, *A Many-Colored Toga: The Diary of Henry Fountain Ashurst* (Tucson: University of Arizona Press, 1962), pp. 74, 91, 93; *El Heraldo de México* (Mexico City), Sep. 13, Nov. 6, 1919; *San Francisco Bulletin*, Jan. 24, 29, 1919; Zorrilla, *Historia de las relaciones entre México y los Estados Unidos* 2:333.

35. *Excelsior* (Mexico City), Jan. 28, 1919; Cantú, *Apuntes históricos*, pp. 31-4.

36. González to Subsecretario de Relaciones, Mar. 22, 1915, AEMEUA, leg. 472, exp. 4, ASRE; *Excelsior* (Mexico City), Apr. 1, 2, 1919; *El Correo de la Tarde* (Mazatlán), Aug. 19, 21, 1919.

37. Hobby to Lansing, Aug. 25, 1919, RDS No. 314, 711.12/210, NA; Hall, *Oil, Banks and Politics*, p. 47.

38. *San Diego Union*, Jan. 14, 1919; Karl M. Schmitt, *Mexico and the United States, 1821-1973* (New York: John Wiley & Sons, 1974), p. 156; *Sen. Ex. Doc.* No. 285 (7665-6) "Investigation of Mexican Affairs," 2 vols., Washington, DC, 1920; Hall, *Oil, Banks and Politics*, p. 47; Katz, *The Secret War in Mexico*, pp. 165-66.

39. *San Diego Union*, Apr. 28, 1913; Paredes to Jesús Urueta, Mar. 31, 1915, AEMEUA, leg. 473, exp. 1, ASRE; *El Heraldo de México* (Mexico City), July 30, 1920; De Negri to Jesus Urueta, Feb. 25, 1915, B. J. Viljoen to Maytorena, Feb. 27, 1915 (quotation), Box V, Maytorena Papers; Luján, *Coronel Esteban Cantú*, pp. 208-209; Frezieres to Ignacio Bonillas, Sep. 25, 1917, AEMEUA, leg. 509, exp. 8, ASRE; Cantú, *Apuntes históricos*, pp. 17-19.

40. De Negri to Garza Pérez, Jan. 6, 1918, Garza Pérez to De Negri, Jan. 7, 1918, exp. 17-14-34, ASRE; *San Francisco Examiner*, Dec. 31, 1917, Jan. 1, 1918; *San Diego Union*, Dec. 18, 31, 1917; Martínez, *Historia de Baja California*, pp. 533-34.

41. Cantú, *Apuntes históricos*, p. 32; De Negri to Fernández, Mar. 29, 1919, exp. 17-16-141, ASRE.

42. De Negri to Fernández, Mar. 29, 1919, exp. 17-16-141, ASRE; De Negri to Garza Pérez, Mar. 1, 1919, exp. 17-18-51, ASRE; Ignacio Bonillas to Garza Pérez, Jan. 5, 1919, exp. 17-16-143, ASRE.

43. De Negri to Hilario Medina, Mar. 5, 1920, exp. 17-17-346, ASRE; J. J. Favela to Medina, Mar. 19, 1920, exp. 17-17-345, ASRE; Cantú, *Apuntes históricos*, pp.16-19.

44. Gómez Estrada, *Gobierno y casinos*, pp. 49-50; Cantú, *Apuntes históricos*, pp. 16-17.

45. Montes, Vega, and J. Jesús Carranza to Carranza, Aug. 6, 1916, carp. 90, leg. 10,156, Carranza Papers, AVC; *San Diego Union*, Aug. 21, 1916, Jan. 2, 6, 1918.

46. Bonillas to Cantú, Jan. 29, 1920, Cantú to Bonillas, Jan. 30, 1920, AEMEUA, leg. 573, exp. 6, ASRE; *San Diego Union*, Jan. 17, 1919, *Excelsior* (Mexico City), Jan. 7, 8, 1918, July 27, Oct. 1, 1919; *El Universal* (Mexico City), Jan. 7, 1918.

47. "Carta abierta al pueblo y al gobierno de los Estados Unidos," Feb. 2, 1919, in Cantú, *Apuntes históricos*, pp. 31-34.

48. *Excelsior* (Mexico City), Sep. 14, 1919; *El Universal* (Mexico City), June 12, 1920; *El Heraldo de México* (Mexico City), Sep. 13, 1919.

49. Burdett to the Secretary of State, July 28, 1920, RDS No. 314, 711.12/284, NA; R. Velasco Ceballos, *¿Se apoderará los Estados Unidos de América de la Baja California?* (México: Imp. Nacional, 1920).

50. *Excelsior* (Mexico City), Aug. 4, 1920.

51. Rolland, *Informe sobre el Distrito Norte de la Baja* California, pp. 130-31, 166; *El Diario* (Mexico City), June 17, 1911; De Negri to Carranza, Apr. 2, 1915, González to Subsecretario de Relaciones Exteriores, Apr. 9, 1915, AEMEUA, leg. 473, exp. 1, ASRE; Luis G. Beltrán to Tomás Ojeda, June 22, 1916, AHDN, Cancelados, XI/111/4-1122; Ageo G. Meneses to Carranza, Oct. 2, 1917, carp. 117, leg. 13,310, Carranza Papers, AVC; *Excelsior* (Mexico City), Apr. 2, 1919; Calles to Carranza, Sep. 8, 1919, FAPEC, Archivo Plutarco Elías Calles Anexo, Fondo Presidentes, exp. 1, inv. 710, leg. 1; De Negri to Garza Pérez, Mar. 8, 1919, Garza Pérez to De Negri, Apr. 24, 1919, exp. 17-18-60, ASRE.

52. Knight, *The Mexican Revolution* 1: 374-80.

Chapter IV

1. *Calexico Chronicle*, May 25, 1915; Testimony of Jones, May 17, 1920, *Sen. Ex. Doc.* No. 285 (7665-6), pp. 3,018, 3,020, 3,023; E. M. Blandford to the Secretary of State, Apr. 24, 1917, RDS No. 274, 812.00, NA.

2. Testimony of Jones, May 17, 1920, *Sen. Ex. Doc.* No. 285 (7665-6), pp. 3,017, 3,025-6; Mark T. Gilderhus, *Diplomacy and Revolution: U.S.-Mexican Relations under Wilson and Carranza* (Tucson: University of Arizona Press, 1977), p. 65; Vasconcelos, *La Tormenta*, pp. 866-7, 894-5.

3. Testimony of Jones, May 17, *Sen. Ex. Doc.* No. 285 (7665-6), pp. 3,017, 3,020-21; *Calexico Chronicle*, Oct. 12, 14, 1916; Frezieres to Alfonso M. Siller, Dec. 23, 1916, exp. 16-20-149, ASRE; El Primer Secretario to Secretaría de Relaciones Exteriores, July 31, 1920, AEMEUA, leg. 676, exp. 5, ASRE; Vasconcelos, *La Tormenta*, p. 867; Katz, *The Secret War in Mexico*, p. 515; Buchenau, *Plutarco Elías Calles*, p. 76; Joseph A. Stout, Jr., *Spies, Politics, and Power: El Departamento Confidencial en México, 1922-1946* (Fort Worth: TCU Press, 2012), pp. 19, 21; Richmond, "The First Chief," pp. 288-89.

4. Henry Prather Fletcher to the Secretary of State, Mar. 30, June 3, 5, 1917, RDS No. 314, 711.12/49, NA; Gilderhus, *Diplomacy and Revolution*, p. 32; Richmond, "The First Chief," pp. 310-15.

5. *San Diego Union*, Sep. 28, 1914, Nov. 4, 1917; Robert Lansing to the president, Apr. 18, 1917, RDS No. 314, 711.12/43A, NA; C. Sheldon to N. L. Windslow, Oct. 4, 1918, Joseph K. Hutchinson to Director of Naval Intelligence, May 13, 1918, RDS, No. 274, 812.00, NA; Katz, *The Secret War in Mexico*, p. 433; Clair Kenamore, "What is Germany doing in Mexico?" *The Bookman* 44 (June 1917): pp. 342-46.

6. Hutchinson to Naval Intelligence, Oct. 15, 1918, RDS No. 2/4, 812.00, NA.

7. De Negri to Garza Pérez, Jan. 26, 1918, exp. 17-14-36, ASRE.

8. Hutchinson to Naval Intelligence, Sep. 11, Oct. 15, 16, 1918, Hutchinson to Leland Harrison, Aug. 27, 1918, Admiral Fullam to Opnav, Sep. 10, 1918, Harrison to Flournoy, Nov. 19, 1918, RDS No. 274, 812.00, NA; Testimony of Jones, May 17, 1920, *Sen. Ex. Doc.* No. 285 (7665-6), p. 3,017.

9. *San Diego Union*, Apr. 4, 1918; Testimony of Jones, *Sen. Ex. Doc.* No. 285 (7665-6), p. 3,048.

10. De Negri to Aguilar, Apr. 12, 1918, exp. 17-14-51, ASRE.

11. Gershon to the Department of State, May 9, 1918, RDS No. 274, 812.00, NA; Katz, *The Secret War in Mexico*, p. 562; Charles H. Harris and Louis R. Sadler, "The Witzke Affair: German Intrigue on the Mexican Border, 1917-18," *Military Review* 59, no. 2 (February 1979): p. 44.

12. Knight, *The Mexican Revolution* 1:185, 208; *El Correo de la Tarde* (Mazatlán), Aug. 21, 1919; *Excelsior* (Mexico City), Aug. 1, 1919; *El Imparcial* (Mexico City), June 28, 1911; Buchenau, *Plutarco Elías Calles*, p. 78; Dorothy Pierson Kerig, *El valle de Mexicali y la Colorado River Land Company, 1902-1946* (Mexicali: Baja California: Universidad Autónoma de Baja California, 2001), pp. 136-7; Richmond, "The First Chief," pp. 120-21.

13. *El Diario* (Mexico City), June 17, 1911; *El Heraldo de México* (Mexico City), Sep. 22, 1919; *Calexico Chronicle*, Oct. 24, 1919; *Excelsior* (Mexico City), June 8, 1919.

14. *El Heraldo de México* (Mexico City), Apr. 25, 1920; *San Diego Union*, Sep. 9, 1919; Ponce Aguilar, *El Coronel Esteban Cantú*, p. 110.

15. Ricardo Covarubias to Obregón, May 2, 1924, exp. 104-CH-1, Ramo Presidentes, Obregón/Calles, AGN (hereafter cited as O/C, AGN).

16. Robert Chao Romero, *The Chinese in Mexico, 1882-1940* (Tucson: University of Arizona Press, 2010), pp. 148-52; Robert H. Duncan, "The Chinese and the Economic Development of Northern Baja California, 1889-1929," *Hispanic American Historical Review* 74, no. 4 (November 1994): pp. 615-16, 638, 647; William H. Beezley, *Insurgent Governor: Abraham González and the Mexican Revolution in Chihuahua* (Lincoln: University of Nebraska Press), pp. 96-7; Katz, *Pancho Villa*, pp. 597, 604, 626, 630; Oscar J. Martínez, *Fragments of the Mexican Revolution: Personal Accounts From the Border* (Albuquerque: University of New Mexico Press, 1968), pp. 46-7; Robert E. Quirk, *The Mexican Revolution, 1914-1915: The Convention of Aguascalientes* (Bloomington: Indiana University Press, 1960), p. 284.

17. Serafín Equihua Ballesteros, "El Puerto de San Felipe," in Piñera Jiménez, *Panorama histórico*, pp. 509-510.

18. Kerig, "Yankee Enclave," p. 152; Pedro F. Pérez y Ramírez, "Panorama de Mexicali, 1915-1930," in Piñera Ramírez, *Panorama histórico*, pp. 408-410; Paredes to Urueta, Mar. 17, 1915, AEMEUA, leg. 472, exp. 3, ASRE.

19. Chao Romero, *The Chinese in Mexico*, pp. 14-15, 21-27; Rolland, *Informe sobre el Distrito Norte de la Baja California*, pp. 153-54.

20. Boyle to the Department of State, Aug. 25, 1920, RDS No. 274, 812.00, NA; Rolland, *Informe sobre el Distrito Norte de la Baja California*, p. 41.

21. Boyle to the Department of State, Aug. 25, 1920, RDS No. 274, 812.00, NA; De Negri to Aguilar, Feb. 19, 1919, L. Monroy Baigén to Jefe del Departamento Consular, Feb. 26, 1920, Monroy Baigén to De Negri, Feb. 28, 1920, exps. 17-14-

42, 16-26-87, ASRE; Pérez y Ramírez, "Panorama de Mexicali," in Piñera Ramírez, *Panorama histórico*, pp. 405-406.

22. Bell and Mackenzie, *Mexican West Coast and Lower California*, pp. 294-95; Eugene Keith Chamberlin, "Mexican Colonization versus American Interests in Lower California," *Pacific Historical Review* 20, no. 1 (February 1951): p. 45; Evelyn Hu-DeHart, "The Chinese of Baja California Norte, 1910-1934," *Proceedings of the Pacific Coast Council on Latin American Studies: Baja California and the North American Frontier* 12 (1985-1986): pp. 10-11; Kerig, *El valle de Mexicali*, pp. 133-48; Peter Johannes Watry, "The Economic Development of Baja California, Mexico" (PhD diss., University of Missouri-Columbia, 1970), pp. 30-31.

23. Cantú to Carranza, Feb. 17, 1916, FAPEC, FAO, exp. 2, inv. 57, leg. 1.

24. Bell and Mackenzie, *Mexican West Coast and Lower California*, pp. 294-95, 331-32; Vivanco, *Baja California al Día*, pp. 193, 198; Kerig, *El valle de Mexicali*, p. 160; Duncan, "The Chinese and the Economic Development of Northern Baja California, 1889-1929, pp. 635-39; Chao Romero, *The Chinese in Mexico*, p. 130.

25. Evelyn Hu-DeHart, "Immigrants to a Developing Society: The Chinese in Northern Mexico, 1875-1932," *The Journal of Arizona History* 21, no. 3 (Autumn 1980): pp. 276-77; Duncan, "The Chinese and the Economic Development of Northern Baja California, 1889-1929," pp. 638-41.

26. *Calexcio Chronicle*, Sep. 16, 1919; Chao Romero, *The Chinese in Mexico*, p. 135.

27. *Le Courier du Mexique* (Mexico City), Sep. 15, 1919; Chamberlin, "Mexican Colonization," p. 47; *El Heraldo de México* (Mexico City), Jan. 2, 1920.

28. Simon to Aguilar, Apr. 8, 1916, Aguilar to Simon, Apr. 9, 1916, Aguilar to Jesús Acuña, Apr. 9, 1916, Acuña to Aguilar, Apr. 11, 1916, exp. 16-16-197, ASRE.

29. Fong Tsiang Kwang to Fernández, Oct. 7, 1919, Secretaría de Gobernación to Hilario Medina, Oct. 15, 1919, Summerlin to Medina, Nov. 3, 1919, exp. 16-29-42, ASRE; *Calexico Chronicle*, Nov. 4, 1919; Chao Romero, *The Chinese in Mexico*, pp. 6, 57, 64; *El Heraldo de México* (Mexico City), Nov. 1, 1919.

30. Hu-DeHart, *The Chinese of Baja California Norte*, p. 18.

31. Vivanco, *Baja California al Día*, p. 269; *Excelsior* (Mexico City), Nov. 16, 1919; *El Heraldo de México* (Mexico City), Nov. 22, 1919, Jan. 24, 1920; Rolland, *Informe sobre el Distrito Norte de la Baja California*, p. 132; Luján, *Coronel Esteban Cantú*, pp. 141-44, 148-49, 158; Cantú, *Apuntes históricos*, p. 40.

32. Kerig, *"Yankee Enclave,"* pp. 161-62; Pablo Herrera Castillo, *Colonización del Valle de Mexicali* (Mexicali, Baja California, México: Universidad Autónoma de Baja California, 1976), pp. 114, 125-29, 136-37.

33. Enrique M. Terrazas to Cantú, Dec. 8, 1916, Cantú to Terrazas, Dec. 9, 1916, H. Castelum to Cantú, Dec. 5, 1916, Cantú to Castelum, Dec. 12, 1916, Salvador Bracamontes to Cantú, Dec. 8, 1916, Cantú to Bracamontes, Dec. 13, 1916, Hipólito Chávez to Cantú, Dec. 12, 1916, Cantú to Chávez, Dec. 13, 1916, Guadalupe Sandoval to Cantú, Dec. 14, 1916, Cantú to Sandoval, Dec. 15, 1916 and *passim* Caja 21, exp. 14, Fondo Distrito Norte, AHEBC.

34. Carrillo to Jesús Urueta, May 25, 1915, AEMEUA, leg. 458, exp. 1, ASRE; Knight, *The Mexican Revolution* 2:99; *Diccionario Porrúa*, 2:2,247.

35. Scretario de Relaciones Exteriores to Obregón, Mar. 28, 1916, Obregón to Cantú, Mar. 30, 1916, Secretaría del Cuerpo de Ejército del Noreste to Cantú, Apr. 1, 1916, AHDN, Cancelados, XI/111/4-1122, vol. 2, folios, 482, 484, 492.

36. Carrillo to Urueta, May 25, 1915, AEMEUA, leg. 458, exp. 1, ASRE; Katz, *The Secret War in Mexico*, p. 507.

37. Eugene Keith Chamberlin, "The Japanese [illegible] of Magdalena Bay," *Pacific Historical Review* 24, no. 4 (November 1955): pp. 345-56.

38. Raat, *Revoltosos*, pp. 238, 267; *San Francisco Examiner*, Jan. 31, Feb. 1, 1912; *Kansas City Star*, Jan. 31, 1912; *Washington Post*, Jan. 31, 1912; Gilberto Crespo y Martínez to Secretaría de Relaciones Exteriores, Feb. 2, 1912, exp. 30-16-1, ASRE.

39. Bonillas to Cantú, Jan. 29, 1918, AEMEUA, leg. 573, exp. 6, ASRE.

40. *Excelsior* (Mexico City), Apr. 11, 1919.

41. *New York Times*, Mar. 22, 1919.

42. *Excelsior* (Mexico City), Apr. 1, 2, 1919.

43. *New York Times*, Aug. 13, 1920; Richmond, "The First Chief," pp. 319-22.

44. *Excelsior* (Mexico City), Apr. 11, 1919; *El Heraldo de México* (Mexico City), Sep. 15, 1919; José Cantú to Obregón, Dec. 8, 1922, July 27, 1923, Secretario de Industria, Comercio y Trabajo to José Cantú, Jan. 4, 1923, exp. 422-S-9, O/C, AGN.

45. Celso Aguirre Bernal, "El ferrocarril y el crecimiento de Mexicali," in Piñera Jiménez, *Panorama histórico*, pp. 500-501; Martínez, *Historia de Baja California*, pp. 544-47.

46. Enrique Krauze, *Mexico, Biography of Power: A History of Modern Mexico, 1801-1996* (New York: Harper, 1998), p. 545.

Chapter V

1. Conrado Acevedo Cárdenas, David Piñera Ramírez, and Jesús Ortiz, "Semblanza de Tijuana, 1915-1930," in Piñera Ramírez, *Panorama histórico*, p. 433; David M. Kennedy, ed., *Progressivism: The Critical Issues* (Boston: Little, Brown and Co., 1971), pp. 25-26, 69-73, 82, 110-113, 120; Arthur S. Link and Richard L. McCormick, *Progressivism* (Arlington Heights, Illinois: Harlan Davidson, 1983), pp. 15, 22, 69, 79; George E. Mowry, "The Progressive Era. 1900-20: The Reform Persuasion," *American Historical Association* (1958), AHA Pamphlet No. 212, pp. 6-9; Richard Hofstadter, *The American Political Tradition* (New York: Alfred A. Knopf, 1948), pp. 225, 259; Marco Antonio Samaniego López, "Formación y consolidación de las organizaciones obreras en Baja California, 1920-1930," *Mexican Studies/Estudios Mexicanos* 14, no. 2 (Summer 1998): p. 333; David E. Lorey, *The U.S.-Mexican Border in the Twentieth Century* (Wilmington: Scholarly Resources, 1999), p. 45-48.

2. Acevedo Cárdenas, Piñera Ramírez and Ortiz, "Semblanza de Tijuana," in Piñera Ramírez, *Panorama histórico*, p. 433; Gómez Estrada, *Gobierno y casinos*, p. 53; Vasconcelos, *La Tormenta*, p. 866.

3. *San Diego Union*, June 19, Oct. 3, 1915, Jan. 2, 1916, Sep. 12, 1916; Concession to H.A. Houser and H.J. Moore, Mar. 2, 1915, FAPEC, FAO, exp. 2, inv. 57, leg. 1; Avcevedo Cárdenas, Piñera Ramírez and Ortiz, "Semblanza de Tijuana," in Piñera Ramíez, *Panorama histórico*, pp. 433-35; Gómez Estrada, *Gobierno y casinos*, pp. 53, 55; T. D. Proffitt, *Tijuana: The History of a Mexican Metropolis* (San Diego: San Diego University Press, 1994), p. 190.

4. González to Director General de Consulados, Jan. 3, 1916, AEMEUA, leg. 481, exp. 4, ASRE; *San Diego Union*, Oct. 19, 1915; Samaniego López, *Los gobiernos civiles*, p. 57.

5. Willard Brown Thorp to Lansing, Jan. 24, 1920, RDS No. 274, 812.4065/0128, NA; Acevedo Cárdenas, Piñera Ramírez and Ortiz, "Semblanza de Tijuana," in Piñera Ramírez, *Panorama histórico*, pp. 435-36; Eric Michael Schantz, "All Night

at the Owl: The Social and Political Relations of Mexicali's Red-Light District, 1913-1925," *Journal of the Southwest* 43, no. 4 (Winter 2001): p. 554; Lorey, *The U.S.-Mexican Border*, p. 45; Vivanco, *Baja California al día*, p. 263.

6. Almada, *La Revolución en el Estado de Sonora*, pp. 231-32; Beezley, *Insurgent Governor*, pp. 103-05; Buchenau, *Plutarco Elías Calles*, pp. 59-60; Krause, *Mexico, Biography of Power*, pp. 409-10; Richmond, "The First Chief," pp. 132-33.

7. Uribe to de la Huerta, June 6,1920, exp. 243-B-1, O/C, AGN.

8. Salazar Rovirosa, *Cronología de Baja California* 8:25-6; *San Diego Union*, Apr. 20, 1915.

9. *Excelsior* (Mexico City), Feb. 13, July 17, 19, 20, 30, Aug. 6, 1920.

10. John B. Elliot to William McAdoo, June 8, 1916, Edwin T. Earl to Lansing, July 12, 1916, RDS No. 274, 812.4065/0002, /0031, NA.

11. Frederich Simpich to the Department of State, Apr. 16, 1917, RDS No. 274, 812.113/6580, NA; "Informe que rinde el Señor coronel Esteban Cantú, al CU Venustiano Carranza...," Dec. 24, 1915, exp. 1, inv. 56, leg. 1, FAPEC, FAO; Rolland, *Informe sobre el Distrito Norte de la Baja California*, p. 41; Schantz, "From the *Mexicali Rose* to the Tijuana Brass," p. 116.

12. Reglamento de Sanidad para el Distrito Norte de la Baja California, 1915, Caja 10, exp. 3, Registro de meretrices en Mexicali, Feb. 17, 1919, Caja 12, exp. 1, Fondo Distrito Norte, AHEBC.

13. Schantz, "All Night at the Owl," pp. 577-79.

14. *Calexico Chronicle*, Jan. 5, May 29, 1915; *San Diego Union*, Apr. 19, 1915; Schantz, "All Night at the Owl," pp. 562-63.

15. *Calexico Chronicle*, May 23, 1910, Jan. 2, 1914.

16. William Jennings Bryan to Claude Guyant, Jan. 20, 21, 1914, Guyant to Francisco Vázquez, Jan. 22, Feb. 14, 1914, Vázquez to Secretario de Gobernación, Jan. 23, 1914, Vázquez to Guyant, Apr. 26, 1914, Caja 24, exp. 14, Vázquez to Jefe Político, Feb. 16, 1914, Caja 6, exp. 12, Fondo Distrito Norte, AHEBC; *Calexico Chronicle*, May 23, 1910, Jan. 2, 6, 30, Feb. 6, 17, Mar. 17, 1914.

17. *San Diego Union*, July 31, 1920; *Calexico Chronicle*, Aug. 27, 1920; Schantz, "All Night at the Owl," p. 571.

18. *Excelsior* (Mexico City), July 17, 19, Aug. 6, 1920; *San Diego Union*, Apr. 19, 20, 28, 1915.

19. Boyle to the Department of State, Aug. 25, 1920, RDS No. 274, 812.00/24495, NA.

20. Schantz, "All Night at the Owl," pp. 557-58, 569; *San Diego Union*, Apr. 28, 1915, Sep. 9, 1919; *Calexico Chronicle*, June 8, 1916, June 10, 1920.

21. Cantú, *Apuntes históricos*, p. 39; Martínez, *Historia de Baja California*, p. 529.

22. Gómez Estrada, *Gobierno y casinos*, pp. 57-58; Chao Romero, *The Chinese in Mexico*, p. 59; Schantz, "From the *Mexicali Rose* to the Tijuana Brass," pp. 33, 136-38.

23. Paredes to De Negri, May 15, 1915, De Negri to Carranza, May 20, 1910, exp. 11-4-92, ASRE.

24. Paredes to Urueta, Mar. 17, 1915, AEMEUA, leg. 472, exp. 3, ASRE.

25. Schantz, "From the *Mexicali Rose* to the Tijuana Brass," pp. 43, 170-78.

26. F. E. Johnson to Los Angeles Collector of Customs, Sep. 29, 1916, RDS No. 274,

812.00/0994, 14A.

27. W. B. Evans to Los Angeles Collector of Customs, Oct. 12, 1916, RDS No. 274, 812.114/0340, NA; Cantú to Carranza, May 12, Sep. 23, 1915, FAPEC, FAO, exp. 2, inv. 57, leg. 1.

28. M. P. Wolburn to the Department of State, Apr. 28, 1916, Elliott to McAdoo, Oct. 4, 1916, Johnson to Los Angeles Collector of Customs, Oct. 30, 1916, RDS No. 274, 812.114/0321, /0333, /0349, NA; Gómez Estrada, *Gobierno y casinos*, pp. 48, 51-52, 59-60; Pedro Castro, *Adolfo de la Huerta: La integradad como arma de la revolución* (México: Universidad Autónoma Metropolitana, 1998), p. 101; Esteban Cantú, *Circular*, Jan. 21, 1915, FAPEC, FAO, exp. 3, inv. 58, leg. 1.

29. Esteban Cantú, *Circular*, June [?] 1916, AHDN, Cancelados, XI/111/4-1122, vol. 4, folio 854; Gómez Estrada, *Gobierno y casinos*, pp. 59-60.

30. González to Subsecretario de Relaciones Exteriores, Sep. 11, 1915, De Negri to Arrendondo, Oct. 15, 25, 1915, AEMEUA, leg. 480, exp. 8, ASRE.

31. Adolfo Carrillo to Juan N. Amador, Oct. 29, 1915, González to Refael E. Múzquiz, Oct. 29, 1915, AEMEUA, leg. 480, exp. 8, ASRE.

32. Paredes to Amador, n.d., De Negri to Amador, Nov. 5, 1915, Paredes to Arredondo, n.d., AEMEUA, leg. 480, exp. 8, ASRE.

33. Edward B. Browne to Edwin T. Earl, July 8, 1916, Earl to Lansing, July 12, 1916, RDS No. 274, 812.4065/0031, /0032, NA; Aguilar to Obregón, May 9, Aug. 15, 1916, AHDN, Cancelados, XI/111/4-1122, vol. 2, folios 500, 512; Frezieres to Arredondo, Apr. 24, 1916, González to Secretaría de Relaciones Exteriores, Aug. 1, 1916, AEMEUA, leg. 494, exps. 5, 6, ASRE.

34. Boyle to the Secretary of State, Aug. 25, 1920, RDS No. 274, 812.00/24495, NA.

35. Gershon to the Department of State, Jan. 11, 1917, F. P. Webster to the Department of State, Jan. 15, 1917, RDS No. 274, 812.00, NA; Simpich to the Secretary of State, Apr. 16, 1917, RDS No. 274, 812.113/6580, NA; Piñera Ramírez, *Panorama histórico*, pp. 477-79; Farr, *The History of Imperial County*, p. 298; Bell and Mackenzie, *Mexican West Coast and Lower California*, pp. 328-29; Luján, *Coronel Esteban Cantú*, p. 207; Vivanco, *Baja California al día*, pp. 404-407; Esteban Cantú, "Breve apuntes complimentarios del informe rendido al ciudadano Primer Jefe...24 de diciembre de 1915," Informe de Jan. 12, 1916, FAPEC, FAO, exp. 1, inv. 56, leg. 1.

36. Serafín Equihua Ballesteros, "El Puerto de San Felipe," in Piñera Ramírez, *Panorama histórico*, p. 510; Excelsior (Mexico City), Jan. 29, 1918; *Calexico Chronicle*, Dec. 14, 1918; Vivanco, *Baja California al día*, p. 407; Bell and Mackenzie, *Mexican West Coast and Lower California*, p. 329.

37. Cantú to Fly, Feb. 20, 1918, RDS No. 274, 812.00, NA; Fletcher to the Secretary of State, Apr. 29, 1918, RDS No. 274, 812.00, NA; Vivanco, *Baja California al día*, p. 412; Cantú, "Breve apuntes complimentarios...," Jan. 12, 1916, FAPEC, FAO, exp. 1, inv. 56, leg. 1; Esteban Cantú, *Circular*, Jan. 10, 1916, Esteban Cantú, Concession to J. W. Hackworth, Dec. 6, 1915, Esteban Cantú, Concession to Manuel P. Barbachano, June 4, 1915, FAPEC, FAO, exp. 2, inv. 57, leg. 1.

38. Martínez, *Historia de Baja California*, p. 529; Adalberto Walther Meade, "Características generales de los régimenes de Cantú y Rodríguez," in Piñera Ramírez, *Panorama histórico*, p. 391; *Excelsior* (Mexico City), Sep. 5, 1919.

39. Vivanco, *Baja California al día*, p. 317; Schantz, "All Night at the Owl," p. 563; *San Diego Union*, May 27, 1917; Pérez y Ramírez, "Panorama de Mexicali," in Piñera Ramírez, *Panorama histórico*, pp. 399-400.

40. Bell and Mackenzie, *Mexican West Coast and Lower California*, p. 296; Vivanco,

Baja California al día, pp. 316-18, 325 (quotation).

41. Bell and Mackenzie, *Mexican West Coast and Lower California*, p. 296.

42. Vivanco, *Baja California al día*, pp. 321-25; *El Heraldo de México* (Mexico City), Jan. 23, 1919.

43. Pérez y Ramírez, "Panorama de Mexicali," in Piñera Ramírez, *Panorama histórico,* p. 402; Rolland, *Informe sobre el Distrito Norte de la Baja California*, p. 160; Vivanco, *Baja California al día*, p. 187; Farr, *The History of Imperial County*, p. 298; *Excelsior* (Mexico City), Sep. 5, 1919; *Calexico Chronicle,* Jan. 25, 1916.

44. Vivanco, *Baja California al día*, p. 258; Farr, *The History of Imperial Country*, p. 298.

45. *San Diego Union,* May 5, 27, 1917; *Informe que rinde el C. Francisco Bórquez, Presidente Municipal de Mexicali...en el año 1916-17 sobre las labores llegadas a cabo por el Ayuntaminto saliente,* Caja 10, exp. 6, Fondo Distrito Norte, AHEBC.

46. Licence to José María Flores, May 7, 1910, Licence to Carlos E. Gale, Sep. 2, 1910, Licence to Angelo Cugñago, Nov. 29, 1910, Caja 8, exp. 12, Fondo Distrito Norte, AHEBC.

47. Rolland, *Informe sobre el Distrito Norte de la Baja California*, pp.104-107.

48. Rolland, *Informe sobre el Distrito Norte de la Baja California*, pp. 160-61.

Chapter VI

1. Charles C. Cumberland, *Mexican Revolution: The Constitutionalist Years* (Austin: University of Texas Press, 1972), pp. 408, 411; Martínez, *Historia de Baja California*, pp. 535-36; Hall, *Álvaro Obregón*, pp. 163, 200, 203, 228, 234-36; *El Heraldo de México* (Mexico City), Mar. 12, 1920; Buchenau, *Plutarco Elías Calles,* p. 83; Álvaro Matute, *Historia de la Revolución Mexicana*, vol. 8, *La carrera del caudillo, 1917-1924* (México: El Colegio de México, 1980), pp. 84-85; John W. F. Dulles, *Yesterday in Mexico: A Chronicle of the Revolution, 1919-1936* (Austin: University of Texas Press, 1961), p. 22; Miguel Alessio Robles, *Historia política de la Revolución*, 2nd ed. (México: Ediciones Botas, 1938), pp. 286-87.

2. Castro, *Adolfo de la Huerta*, pp. 11-12, 20, 31; Hall, *Álvaro Obregón*, pp. 242-46; Juan de Dios Bojorquez (Djed Borquez), *Forjadores de la Revolución mexicana* (México: Talleres Gráficos de la Nación, 1960), p. 40; J. Ruben Romero, *et. al., Obregón: Aspectos de su vida* (México: Editorial "Cvltvra," 1935), p. 163.

3. *Calexico Chronicle*, Apr. 12,1920; *New York Times,* Apr. 13, 1920; Cantú to Obregón, May 19, 1920, Obregón to Cantú, May 26, 1920, FAPEC, FAO, exp. 124, inv. 2140, leg. 1; Matute, *La carrera del caudillo*, p. 150 (quotation); Cantú, *Apuntes históricos*, p. 42; De Dios Bojorquez, *Forjadores*, pp. 64-5.

4. Martínez, *Historia de Baja California*, p. 536; Burdett to the Secretary of State, July 23, 1920, RDS No. 274, 812.00/24403, NA; Cantú to Obregón, June 3, 1920, FAPEC, FAO, exp. 124, inv. 2140, leg. 1; *San Diego Union*, June 2, 5, 1920; *Excelsior* (Mexico City), June 12, 21, 1920; *New York Times*, July 29, 1920; *Calexico Chronicle*, June 2, 4, 1920; Castro, *Álvaro Obregón*, p. 91.

5. Uribe to de la Huerta, June 6, 1920, exp. 243- B1- B4, O/C, AGN; *Calexico Chronicle*, June 7, 18, 1920; Enrique Barrera to Obregón, June [?], 30, 1920, FAPEC, FAO, exp. 158, inv. 3034, leg. 1; *Excelsior* (Mexico City), June 21, 1920; *San Diego Union*, June 7, 15, 1920; *The San Francisco Call and Post*, Aug. 20, 1920; Cantú to Obregón, June 6, 1920, FAPEC, FAO, exp. 124, inv. 2140, leg. 1; Samaniego López, *Los gobiernos civiles*, pp. 78-81.

6. Martínez, *Historia de Baja California*, p. 536; *New York Times*, July 30, 1920

(quotation).

7. *Los Angeles Times*, Aug. 5, 1920; *Excelsior* (Mexico City), July 24, 29, Aug. 4, 5, 1920.

8. *La Prensa* (San Antonio, Texas), Sep. 16, 1919; *New York Times*, May 4, July 30, 31, 1920; *San Diego Union*, Aug. 2, 1920; Luis Pinal to Obregón, June 16, 1920, FAPEC, FAO, exp. 641, inv. 2657, leg. 1; Burdett to the Secretary of State, July 23, 1920, RDS No. 274, 812.00/24403, NA; Rafael Conrado Silver to de la Huerta, July 6, 8, 1920, FAPEC, FAO, exp. 441, inv. 4314, leg. 1; Bernstein to Cantú, Dec. 12, 1916, Cantú to Bernstein, Dec. 18, 1916, Caja 21, exp. 14, Fondo Distrito Norte, AHEBC; Gómez Estrada, *Gobierno y casinos*, pp. 64-65.

9. Miguel Alesio Robles to Iglesias Calderón, Aug. 2, 1920, AEMEUA, leg. 676, exp. 5, ASRE; *El Heraldo de México* (Mexico City), July 29, 1920; Esteban Cantú, *A los Habitantes del Distrito Norte de la Baja California y al Pueblo Mexicano en General*, July 28, 1920, carp. 2, leg. 179, Félix Díaz Papers, AVC. The manifesto may also be found in AEMEUA, July 28, 1920, leg. 666, exp. 2, ASRE, and Caja 5, exp. 15, Fondo Distrito Norte, AHEBC; Boyle to the Secretary of State, July 28, 1920, RDS, No. 274, 812.00/24402, NA; *Excelsior* (Mexico City), Aug. 3, 1920.

10. *Los Angeles Times*, July 29, 1920.

11. Cantú to Obregón, Mar. 11, 1916, AHDN, Cancelados, XI/111/4-1122, vol. 2, folios 488-91; M. D. [?] to Carranza, June 14, 1916, carp. 83, leg. 9293, Carranza Papers, AVC; Hall, *Álvaro Obregón*, p. 184.

12. Iglesias Calderón to de la Huerta, Aug. 2, 1910, AEMEUA, leg. 672, exp. 4, ASRE; *Calexico Chronicle*, Jul. 31, Aug. 10, 1920; *Washington Post*, Aug. 1, 1920; *El Heraldo de México* (Mexico City), Aug. 4, 5, 1920; Quirk, *The Mexican Revolution*, p. 84.

13. T.O. Paine to the Secretary of State, July 31, 1920, RDS No. 274, 812.00/24428, NA; W. A. Weymouth, to the Secretary of State, Feb. 19, 1919, RDS No. 274, 812.00, NA; A. Ruiz Sandoval to Iglesias Calderón, Aug. 6, 1920, El Primer Secretario de la Embajada Mexicana to Sandoval, Aug. 14, 1920, AEMEUA, leg. 666, exp. 2, ASRE; Luis Montes de Oca to Calles, Aug. 3, 1920, Calles to Montes de Oca, Aug. 4, 1920, AHDN, Cancelados, XI/111/4-1122, vol. 2, folios 478, 579; Obregón to Calles, July 13, 1920, FAPEC, FAO, exp. 104, inv. 2120, leg.½.

14. Boyle to the Secretary of State, July 29, 30, Aug. 4, 1920, Summerlin to the Secretary of State, Aug. 10, 1920, RDS No. 274, 812.00/24405, /24427, /24435, /24474, NA; *New York Times*, Aug. 9, 1920; El Primer Secretario to Subsecretario de Relaciones Exteriores, Aug. 6, 1920, AEMEUA, leg. 666, exp. 2, ASRE; Genero G. Cota to Obregón, July 11, 1920, FAO, exp. 362, inv. 3202, leg. 1; *El Heraldo de México* (Mexico City), Aug. 8, 12, 1920.

15. Boyle to the Secretary of State, July 28, 1920, William C. Burdett to the Secretary of State, July 28, Aug. 2, 1920, RDS No. 274, 812.00/24401, /24402, /24430, NA; *El Heraldo de México* (Mexico City), July 28, 31, 1920; Boyle to the Secretary of State, July 31, 1920, *Papers Relating to the Foreign Relations of the United States, 1920* (Washington, DC: GPO, 1936), Vol. 3, 246; *New York Times*, Aug. 6, 1920; *San Diego Tribune*, Aug. 5, 1920; *San Diego Union*, Aug. 9, 1920.

16. Boyle to Bainbridge Colby, Aug. 4, 9, 1920, RDS No. 274, 812.00/24435, /24448, NA; Obregón to Pesqueira, Aug. 8, 1920, Obregón to W. J. Hunsaker, Aug. 8, 1920, Louis Hostetter to Obregón, Aug. 18, 19, 1920, FAPEC, FAO. exp. 383, inv. 2399, leg. 1; *El Heraldo de México* (Mexico City), Aug. 29, 1920; *New York Times*, Aug. 3, 5, 1920; [?] to de la Huerta, Aug. 18, 1920, AEMEUA, leg. 630, exp. 18, ASRE; P. J. Sepúlveda to Obregón, Aug. 6, 1920, FAPEC, FAO, exp.

1431, inv. 4304, leg. 1.

17. Iglesias Calderón to de la Huerta, Aug. 2, 1920, AEMEUA, leg. 672, exp. 4, ASRE; *El Heraldo de México* (Mexico City), Aug. 1, 4, 1920; *New York Times*, Aug. 2, 5, 14, 1920; *Excelsior* (Mexico City), Aug. 1, 1920; P. J. Sepúlveda to Obregón, Aug. 6, 1920, FAPEC, FAO, exp. 1431, inv. 4304, leg.1.

18. *El Heraldo de México* (Mexico City), 3, 4 (quotation), Aug. 7, 8, 1920; *Excelsior* (Mexico City), Aug. 5, 1920; Knight, *The Mexican Revolution* 2:493; Castro, *Adolfo de la Huerta*, pp. 82-83.

19. *Excelsior* (Mexico City), Aug. 10, 1920; Burdett to the Secretary of State, July 30, 1920, RDS No. 274, 812.00/24439, NA; *Calexico Chronicle*, Aug. 6, 7, 1920.

20. *Washington Post*, July 31, 1920; *Diccionario Porrúa*, 1:65.

21. *Excelsior* (Mexico City), July 30, 1920; *El Heraldo de México* (Mexico City), Aug. 5, 1920; Zorrilla, *Historia de las relaciones entre México y los Estados Unidos*, 2:355.

22. General Ramón Rodríguez F., "La Pacificación de Baja California," *Excelsior* (Mexico City), Feb. 13, 1958; Abelardo Rodríguez, *Autobiografía de Abelardo Rodríguez*, pp. 99-101, 103; Martínez, *Historia de Baja California*, pp. 537-38.

23. Gómez Estrada, *Gobierno y casinos*, pp. 115-18; Rodríguez, *Autobiografía*, pp. 19-61, 103; Oscar J. Martínez, *U.S.- Mexico Borderlands: Historical and Contemporary Perspectives* (Wilmington: Scholarly Resources, 1996), p. 93.

24. Calles to Subsecretario de Guerra, Aug. 22, 1917, AHDN, Cancelados, XI/111/1-449, vol. 1, folios 14, 21, 37, 37v., 38v., 50, 53, 84, 92, 180-81, 195, 237; Calles to Subsecretario de Guerra, Aug. 22, 1917, AHDN, Cancelados, XI/111/1-449, vol. 3, folio 653; Rodríguez to Secretario de Guerra, May 17, 1930, AHDN, Cancelados, XI/111/1-449, vol. 4, folios 801, 827, 917.

25. Rodríguez F., "La Pacificación de Baja California," *Excelsior* (Mexico City), Feb. 13, 1958; Rodríguez to Francisco Serrano, Feb. 15, 1921. A typographical error reads 1922, "Informe de las operaciones militares de tropas puestas a las ordenes del Gral. Brigadier A. L. Rodríguez," AHDN, Cancelados, XI/111/1-449, vol. 8, folios 1956-58; Summerlin to the Secretary of State, July 28, Aug. 17, 1920, RDS No. 274, 812.00/24400, NA.

26. Martínez, *Historia de Baja California*, p. 538; *Excelsior* (Mexico City), Aug. 6, 7, 1920; Rodríguez to Serrano, Feb. 15, 1921, "Informe de las operaciones...," AHDN, Cancelados, XI/111/1-449, vol. 8, Anexo # 1, Anexo # 2, folios 1977-80; Hernández, ed., *Pasajes de la Revolución*, pp. 20-21; Chapman to the Secretary of State, Aug. 5, 1920, RDS No. 274, 812.00/24441, NA.

27. Rodríguez F., "La Pacificación de Baja California,*" Excelsior* (Mexico City), Feb. 13, 1958; Iglesias Calderón to Secretario de Relaciones Exteriores, n. d., AEMEUA, leg. 676, exp. 5, ASRE; Martínez, *Historia de Baja California*, p. 538; Rodríguez to Serrano, Feb. 15, 1921, "Informe de las operaciones...," AHDN, Cancelados, XI/111/1-449, vol. 8, folios 1957-60, telegram, Calles to Rodríguez, Aug. 8, 1920. A typographical error reads 1922, Anexo # 3, vol. 8, folio 1981; B. F. Yost to Colby, Aug. 15, 1920. There are two separate dispatches of the same date, RDS No. 274, 812.00/24462, /24487, NA; Obregón to Secretario de Relaciones Exteriores, Apr. 19, 1922, exp. 121-W-B-3, O/C, AGN; Rodríguez, *Autobiografía*, pp. 102-105. In his "Informe de las operaciones...," Rodríguez places the landing at Mazatlán on August 2, in his *Autobiografía* at August 6.

28. The Secretary of State to Boyle, July 31, 1920, *Papers Relating to the Foreign Relations of the United States, 1920*, p. 158; Colby to Boyle, July 30, 1920, RDS No. 274, 812.00/24402, NA; *New York Times*, Aug. 7, 1920; El Primer Secretario

to Occretaria de Relaciones Exteriores, Aug. 3, 1920, Iglesias Calderón to Secretario de Relaciones Exteriores, Aug. 5, 1920, AEMEUA, leg. 6/6, exp. 3, ASRE.

29. *San Diego Union*, Aug. 12, 1920; *Excelsior* (Mexico City), Aug. 13, 1920; *El Heraldo de México* (Mexico City), Aug. 5, 1920; Lelevier to Pesqueira, Aug. 12, 1920, Caja 17, exp. 13, Fondo Distrito Norte, AHEBC.

30. *Washington Post*, Aug. 2, 1920; *Excelsior* (Mexico City), Aug. 8, 9, 1920; *El Universal* (Mexico City), Aug. 8, 9, 1920; *El Heraldo de México* (Mexico City), Aug. 9, 1920.

31. Rodríguez to Serrano, Feb. 15, 1921, "Informe de las operaciones...," AHDN, Cancelados, XI/111/1-449, vol. 8, folios 1958-59; *Excelsior* (Mexico City), Aug. 19, 1920; Castro, *Adolfo de la Huerta*, pp. 102-103.

32. Adolfo de la Huerta, *Memorias de don Adolfo de la Huerta* (México: Ediciones "Guzmán," 1957), pp. 168-73; *New York Times*, July 29, 1920; Castro, *Adolfo de la Huerta*, p. 71; Katz, *Pancho Villa*, pp. 721-29; *El Heraldo de México* (Mexico City), July 29, 1920.

33. Esteban Cantú, *A los Habitantes del Distrito Norte, Mexicali*, July 28, 1920, carp. 2, leg. 179, Félix Díaz Papers, AVC.

34. Abelardo Rodríguez, *A los Habitantes del Distrito Norte de la Baja California*, n. p., n. d., AHDN, Cancelados, XI/111/1-449, vol. 1, folio 146. Also found in AEMEUA, leg. 666, exp. 2, ASRE; *El Heraldo de México* (Mexico City), Aug. 9, 1920.

35. Ciudadanos de Baja California, *A los Habitantes del Distrito Norte de la Baja California*, Mexicali, July 31, 1920, AEMEUA, leg. 666, exp. 2, ASRE.

36. *San Diego Union*, July 30, Aug. 2, 1920; *El Heraldo de México* (Mexico City), Aug. 5, 7, 10, 11, 13, 14, 1920; Lelevier to Roberto Pesqueira, Aug. 12, 1920, AEMEUA, leg. 666, exp. 2, ASRE; Rafael González A. to Obregón, Aug. 17, 1920, FAPEC, FAO, exp. 650, inv. 3526, leg. 1; Samaniego López, *Los gobiernos civiles*, p. 30; *Excelsior* (Mexico City), Aug. 10, 13, 1920; *San Diego Tribune*, Aug. 14, 1920.

37. Esteban Cantú, "Consideraciones que tuve en cuenta para hacer entrega del gobierno del Distrito Norte de la Baja California...," Sept. 3, 1920, in Cantú, *Apuntes históricos*, pp. 42-46.

38. Terrazas to Guillermo Rosas, Jr., Aug. 22, 1920, Félix Díaz Papers, AVC, carp. 2, leg. 183; Cantú, "Consideraciones...," in Cantú, *Apuntes históricos*, pp. 42-46; Boyle to the Secretary of State, Aug. 25, 1920, RDS No. 274, 812.00/24495; Rodríguez F., "La Pacificación de Baja California," *Excelsior* (Mexico City), Feb. 13, 1958.

39. *El Heraldo de México* (Mexico City), Aug. 10, 15, 1920; Lelevier to Pesqueira, Aug. 12, 1920, Caja 17, exp. 13, Fondo Distrito Norte, AHEBC; José Alfredo Gómez Estrada, *Lealtades divididas: camarrillas y poder en México, 1913-1932*, (México: Instituto Mora, 2012), pp. 103, 108, 110.

40. Summerlin to the Secretary of State, Aug. 11, 1920, RDS No. 274, 812.00/24477, NA; De la Huerta, *Memorias*, pp. 173-74; Obregón to Thomas E. Campbell, Aug. 3, 1920, FAPEC, FAO, exp. 638, inv. 2654, leg. 1/3; Paredes to Rodríguez, Aug. 15, 1920, Caja 17, exp. 13, Fondo Distrito Norte, AHEBC; *El Heraldo de México* (Mexico City), Aug. 15, 29, 1920; *El Universal* (Mexico City), Aug. 29, 1920; Martínez, *Historia de Baja California*, p. 538; Matute, *La carrera del caudillo*, pp. 150-54. Samaniego López, *Los gobiernos civiles*, p. 92, places Vito Alessio Robles's arrival on August 18 after the pact with Cantú had already been agreed upon but does not provide a source for that date.

41. *El Heraldo de México* (Mexico City), Aug. 15, 16, 1920; Samaniego López, *Los gobiernos civiles*, p. 178.

42. Cambio de Gobierno del Distrito Norte de la B. C. donde entrega el poder el Sr. Coronel Esteban Cantú a Sr. C. Luis Salazar, Aug. 18, 1920, Caja 5, exp. 17, Fondo Distrito Norte, AHEBC.

43. Boyle to the Secretary of State, Aug. 18, 1920, Zach Lamar Cobb to G. Howland Shaw, Aug. 19, 1920, RDS No. 274, 812.00/24471, /24472, /24480, NA; *Excelsior* (Mexico City), Aug. 20, 1920; *El Heraldo de México* (Mexico City), Aug. 20, 29, 1920; Rodríguez to Serrano, Feb. 15, 1921, "Informe de las operaciones...," AHDN, Cancelados, XI/111/1-449, folios 1956-67; Telegram, Salazar to Rodríguez, Aug. 19, 1920, AHDN, Cancelados, XI/111/1-449, Anexo # 6, Vol. VIII, folio 1985.

44. *Excelsior* (Mexico City), Aug. 29, 1920.

Chapter VII

1. Ibarra to El Presidente, Apr. 9, 1921, Obregón to Calles, Apr. 21, 1921, exp. 243-B-1-A, Ibarra to Frank Terrazas, Apr. 20, 1921, exp. 243-B1-A-2, Calles to Secretaría de Relaciones, Mar. 26, 1921 (quotation), Adolfo Labastida to Obregón, Nov. 8, 11, 1921, Obregón to Rodríguez, Mar. 4, 1921, exp. 425-T-7, all in O/C, AGN; Martínez, *Historia de Baja California*, p. 540; Knight, *The Mexican Revolution*, 1:174, 2:258, 475.

2. Luis M. Salazar to Obregón, Feb. 24, 1921, exp. 711-S-1, O/C, AGN.

3. Report of Abelardo Rodríguez, n.d., AHDN, Cancelados, XI/111/1-449, vol. 8, folios 1966-69; "Informe de las operaciones militares de...Gral. Brigadier A. L. Rodríguez," Feb. 15, 1922, APEC, exp. 189, inv. 5010, leg. 2/11.

4. Memo from Agent Torres, May 20, 25, 1921, AEMEUA, leg. 623, exp. 4, ASRE; Iglesias Calderón to Secretaría de Relaciones Exteriores, Oct. 1, 1920, Manuel Tellez to Mexican Consul, New York, Oct. 14, 1920, AEMEUA, leg. 630, exp. 18, ASRE; Enrique D. Ruiz to Obregón, May 12, 1921, exp. 101-R-1-A-1, O/C, AGN; Uriburu to Félix Díaz, Sep. 30, 1921, carp. 3, leg. 243, Félix Díaz Papers, AVC; ES [?] to Díaz, Jan. 26, 1920, carp. 2, leg. 157, Félix Díaz Papers, AVC; Arnulfo R. Gómez to Joaquín Amaro, Apr. 12, 1921, FAPEC, Archivo Joaquín Amaro, exp. 1, inv. 57, leg. 4/7.

5. Luis Licéaga, *Félix Díaz* (México: Editorial Jus, 1958), pp. 687-90, 694-95; Ferreira to Secretaría de Relaciones Exteriores, Sep. 9, 1921, exp. 429-S-7, O/C, AGN; Rafael Ochoa Ramos to Díaz, Aug. 22, 1921, Escudero to Díaz, Nov. 6, 1921, carps. 2, 7, legs. 230, 656, Félix Díaz Papers, AVC; Pedro del Villar to Díaz, Sep. 8, 1921, Uriburu to Díaz, Oct. 18, 1921, carp. 3, legs. 232, 249, Félix Díaz Papers, AVC.

6. F. C. Drew to Obregón, Oct. 26, 1921, exp. 425-T-7, El Subsecretario de Relaciones to Fernando Torreblanca, Oct. 21, 1921, exp. 429-S-7, O/C, AGN; Uriburu to Díaz, Oct. 20, 1921, carp. 3, leg. 250, Félix Díaz Papers, AVC; Pesqueira to Calles, Aug. 25, 1920, Caja 17, exp. 13, Fondo Distrito Norte, AHEBC.

7. Mexican Consul, Los Angeles, to Secretaría de Relaciones Exteriores, Oct. 28, Nov. 14, 1921, Memorandum, Nov. 17, 1921, Garza Zertuche to Embajada Mexicana, Nov. 23, 1921, Tellez to Secretaría de Relaciones Exteriores, Jan. 6, 1922, AEMEUA, leg. 673, exp. 8, ASRE; F. W. Becker to Lugo, May 1, 1922, APEC, exp. 127, inv. 3316, leg. 4/12; Manuel P. Cubillas to Calles, Dec. 20, 1921,

APEC, cxp. 233, inv. 1749, leg. 1, pp. 12-15; Ibarra to Obregón, rec. Nov. 2, 1921, exp. 243-B-1-A-2, O/C, AGN; Labastida to Obregón, Nov. 8, 1921, exp. 425-1-7, O/C, AGN; Schantz, "All Night at the Owl," p. 581.

8. Ferreira to Secretaría de Relaciones Exteriores, Nov. 9, 1921, Tellez to Secretaría de Relaciones Exteriores, Nov. 10, 16, 1921, Garza Zertuche to Legación de México, Nov. 15, 1921, Ferreira to Embajada de México, Nov. 18, 1921, AEMEUA, leg. 673, exp. 8, ASRE; AHDN, Cancelados, XI/111/1-449, vol. 3, folio 583.

9. Uriburu to Díaz, Nov. 16, 1921, carp. 3, leg. 267, Félix Díaz Papers, AVC; Roster, *Regimiento de Caballería "Esteban Cantú,"* FAPEC, FAO, exp. 6, inv. 61, leg. 1; Gómez Estrada, *Lealdades divididas,* p. 87.

10. "Informe de las operaciones de...Gral. Brigadier A. L. Rodríguez," Feb. 15, 1922, Anexo no. 23, Rodríguez to Ángel Flores, Nov. 30, 1921, APEC, exp. 189, inv. 5010, leg. 2/11; *El Heraldo de México* (Mexico City), Dec. 23, 1921.

11. Eduardo Ruiz to Manuel Pérez Treviño, May 16, 1922, Ruiz to Obregón, May 17, 1922, exp. 429-S-7, Otts to Obregón, Dec. 6, 1923, exp. 101-R2-I-1-Anexo I, O/C, AGN; Frank C. Drew to Reed Smoot, Apr. 6, 1918, FAPEC, FAO, exp. 118, inv. 406, leg. 1.

12. Uriburu to Díaz, Nov. 9, 28, 30, 1921, Feb. 3, 1922, carp. 3, legs. 263, 275, 277, carp. 4, leg. 355, T. Castillo Corzo to Del Villar, Dec. [?] 1921, carp. 3. Leg. 302, Félix Díaz Papers, AVC; Almada, *La Revolución en el Estado de Sonora,* p. 34; Intelligence Officer, Fort Sam Houston to United States Army, Sep. 28, 1921, AEMEUA, leg. 673, exp. 10, ASRE; Licéaga, *Félix Díaz,* p. 703; Knight, *The Mexican Revolution* 1:195, 335-37; Evelyn Hu-DeHart, *Yaqui Resistance and Survival: The Struggle for Land and Autonomy, 1821-1910* (Madison: University of Wisconsin Press, 1984), pp. 9-11, 56, 93, 120, 204-207, 210-11; Katz, *The Secret War in Mexico,* p. 36; Héctor Aguilar Camín and Lorenzo Meyer, *In the Shadow of the Mexican Revolution: Contemporary Mexican History, 1910-1989* (Austin: University of Texas Press, 1993), p. 5; John Kenneth Turner, *Barbarous Mexico* (Austin: University of Texas Press, 1969), pp. 28-37; Peter V. N. Henderson, "Un gobernador maderista: José María Maytorena y la Revolución en Sonora," *Historia Mexicana* 51, no. 1 (*julio-septiembre* 2001): pp. 180-81; Deeds, "José María Maytorena," (Part I), *Arizona and the West* 18, no. 1(Spring 1976): pp. 35-6; Ignacio Almada, *Breve historia de Sonora* (México: El Colegio de México, 2000), pp. 133-34.

13. Caro to Díaz, Jan. 15, 1922, carp. 3, leg. 327, Félix Díaz Papers, AVC; Caro to García Naranjo, Nov. 29, 1921, in Licéaga, *Félix Díaz,* pp. 697-700; Uriburu to Díaz, Dec. 20, 1921, carp. 3, leg. 290, Félix Díaz Papers, AVC; Buchenau, *Plutarco Elías Calles,* pp. 51, 162; *New York Times,* Feb. 9, 1921; Brígido Caro, *Plutarco Elías Calles dictador bolsheviki de México: Episodios de la Revolución Mexicana, desde 1910 hasta 1924* (Los Angeles: Impreso de "*El Heraldo de México,*" 1924), pp. 161-62.

14. Memo, n.d., AEMEUA, leg. 673, exp. 7, ASRE; El Subsecretario de Relaciones Exteriores to Torreblanca, Oct. 21, 1921, exp. 429-S-7, O/C, AGN; *American National Biography* 7:696-98; Laton McCartney, *The Teapot Dome Scandal* (New York: Random House, 2008), pp. 31-32, 81-83; *El Heraldo de México,* Mar. 21, Apr. 9 (quotation), Apr. 10, 23, 1920; Albert B. Fall to Myron M. Parker, Oct. 7, 9, 1920, FAPEC, FAO, exp. 618, inv. 2634, leg. 2/2; Katz, *The Secret War in Mexico,* p. 536; Buchenau, *Plutarco Elías Calles,* pp. 85, 91; Linda B. Hall, *Oil, Banks and Politics: The United States and Postrevolutionary Mexico, 1917-1924* (Austin: University of Texas Press, 1995), pp. 37-38, 55-56; Katz, *Pancho Villa,* pp. 130, 144, 666-67; Aguilar Camín and Meyer, *In the Shadow of the Mexican Revolution,* p. 81.

15. Levi Eneas to "Muy querido Willie," Dec. 11, 1922, carp. 7, leg. 689, Uriburu to Rosas, Jan. 3, 1923, carp. 8, leg. 731, Mariano Viezca Arizpe to Díaz, Jan. 27, 1923, carp. 8, leg. 753, Félix Díaz Papers, AVC; Intelligence Officer, Fort Sam Houston to United States Army, Sep. 28, 1921, AEMEUA, leg. 673, exp. 10, ASRE; Gilderhus, *Diplomacy and Revolution*, pp. 73, 97, 107; William Weber Johnson, *Heroic Mexico: The Violent Emergence of a Modern Nation* (New York: Doubleday, 1968), p. 341.

16. Uriburu to Díaz, Nov. 30, 1921, Apr. 21, 1924, carps. 3, 10, legs. 277, 1017, Félix Díaz Papers, AVC.

17. Kosterlitzky to Secretaría de Guerra, June 9, 1883, Sep. 19, 1893, June 7, 1912, Bonifacio Topete to Secretaría de Guerra, June 11, 1883, AHDN, Cancelados, XI/111/4-3244, vol. 1, folios 2-3, 15, 21-22, 26, 28-30, 45, 68, 72, 160, 170; Ferreira to Consul, Los Angeles, July 26, 1924, exp. 101-R2-I-1, O/C, AGN; Knight, *The Mexican Revolution* 1:460; Linda B. Hall and Don M. Coerver, *Revolution on the Border: The United States and Mexico, 1910-1920* (Albuquerque: University of New Mexico Press, 1988), p. 32; Castro, *Álvaro Obregón*, pp. 26-27; Ulloa, *La Revolución Intervenida*, p. 143; Cornelius C. Smith, *Emilio Kosterlitzky: Eagle of Sonora and the Southwest Border* (Glendale: Arthur H. Clark, 1970), pp. 182-83.

18. F. W. Benteen to Whom it may Concern, Oct. 16, 1914, AZ-333, Box 1, Emilio Kosterlitzky Papers, University of Arizona, Special Collections.

19. Harrison Gray Otis to Kosterlitzky, Aug. 12, 1915, Feb. 11, 1916, Leonard Wood to Kosterlitzky, Jan. 17, Mar. 4, 1919, Kosterlitzky to Wood, Jan. 13, Feb. 12, 1919, Dec. 9, 1920, AZ-333, Box 1, Kosterlitzky Papers.

20. Caro to Díaz, Apr. 12, 1922, Federico García y Alba to Rosas, Sep. 23, 1922, carps. 5, 6, legs, 448, 609, Félix Díaz Papers, AVC; Ferreira to Consul, Los Angeles, Jul. 26, 1924, exp. 101-R2-I-1, O/C, AGN.

21. Uriburu to Díaz, Nov. 30, Dec. 12, 1921, carp. 3, legs. 277, 283, Félix Díaz Papers, AVC.

22. Rafael Ochoa Ramos to Díaz, Nov. 27, 1921, carp. 3, leg. 273, Félix Díaz Papers, AVC.

23. Uriburu to Díaz, Dec. 20, 21, 30, 1921, carp. 3, legs. 290, 291, 300, Félix Díaz Papers, AVC; Knight, *The Mexican Revolution* 1:66; Beezley, *Insurgent Governor*, p. 116; Anita Brenner, *The Wind that Swept Mexico* (New York: Harper Brothers, 1943), p. 31.

24. El Consul to Secretaría de Relaciones Exteriores, Dec. 7, 1921, AEMEUA, leg. 673, exp. 8, ASRE; Ferreira to Rodríguez, Dec. 19, 1921, exp. 243-B1-B4, O/C, AGN; Cubillas to Calles, Mar. 10, 1922, APEC, exp. 233, inv. 1249, leg. 1, p. 17; F. W. Becker to Lugo, May 10, 1922, APEC, exp. 127, inv. 3316, leg. 4/12.

25. Matthew E. Hanna to Tellez, Feb. 6, 1922, Memo 24-27 Dec. 1921, AEMEUA, leg, 673, exps. 8, 10, ASRE.

26. Caro to Díaz, May 14, 1922, carp. 5, leg. 480, Félix Díaz Papers, AVC; Del Villar to Díaz, Aug. 23, 1922, carp. 6, leg. 574, Félix Díaz Papers, AVC.

27. Uriburu to Díaz, Dec. 28, 1921, Feb. 27, 1922, Antonio Escobar to Díaz, Oct. 30, 192[2], carps. 3, 4, 7, legs. 299, 384, 647, Félix Díaz Papers, AVC; Knight, *The Mexican Revolution* 2:390; Report of United States Army Intelligence, Fort Sam Houston, Apr. 8-15, 1922, AEMEUA, leg. 673, exp. 10, ASRE; Ramón Eduardo Ruíz, *The Great Rebellion: Mexico, 1905-1924* (New York and London: Norton, 1980), pp. 193, 237; Dulles, *Yesterday in Mexico*, p. 74.

28. Esteban Ouuua, "Cunaiudadanof" n il , iaiu, 3, leg. 304, Félix Díaz Papers, AVC.

29. Caro to Felipe Mier, Dec. 26, 1921 (first and second quotations), Caro to Félix Díaz, Mar. 19, 1922 (third quotation), carps. 3, 4, legs. 297, 416, Félix Díaz Papers, AVC.

30. Peter V. N. Henderson, *Félix Díaz, the Porfirians, and the Mexican Revolution* (Lincoln: University of Nebraska Press, 1981), pp. 3, 55, 74, 96-98, 103-104, 134, 140-45; Katz, *The Secret War in Mexico*, p. 45; Vera Estañol, *Historia de la Revolución Mexicana*, pp. 267-68; Stanley R. Ross, *Francisco I. Madero: Apostle of Mexican Democracy* (New York: Columbia University Press, 1955), p. 268.

31. E. [Antonio Escobar] to Rosas, 5 Jan. 1922, carp. 3, leg. 312 (quotation), E. to Díaz, Jan. 31, 1922, carp. 4, leg. 351, Arturo A. Amaya to Rosas, Feb. 20, 1922, carp. 4, leg. 373, José Mina to R. W. Greer, Mar. 31, 1922, carp. 5, leg. 431, Ventura Anaya to Rosas, Apr. 10, June 8, 1922, carp. 5, legs. 444, 5509, E. to Rosas, June 2, 1922, carp. 5, leg. 500, all in Félix Díaz Papers, AVC.

32. E. [Antonio Escobar] to Díaz, Dec. 2, 19[22], carp. 7, leg. 684, Escudero to Suárez [Félix Díaz], Feb. 4, 1922, carp. 4, leg. 359, E. to Rosas, Feb. 7, 1922, carp. 4, leg. 364, L. [Lozano] to "Muy querido amigo," May 12, 1922, carp. 5, leg. 478, Félix Díaz Papers, AVC.

33. Escudero to Suárez [Félix Díaz], Mar. 29, 1922, carp. 2, leg. 204, E. [Antonio Escobar] to Rosas, Apr. 23, 1922, carp. 5, leg. 460, Uriburu to Díaz, Apr. 24, 1922, carp. 5, leg. 461, all in Félix Díaz Papers, AVC; Hall, *Oil, Banks, and Politics*, pp. 134-35; *Washington Post*, Sept. 9, 1920; *New York Tribune*, Jan. 7, 1921; *The Nation* (New York), June 1, 1921.

34. García y Alba to Díaz, Apr. 2, 1922, carp. 5, leg. 436, Escudero to Suárez [Félix Díaz], May 4, 1922, carp. 5, leg. 470, Félix Díaz Papers, AVC.

35. Lugo to Obregón, Mar. 2, 1922, exp. 243-B1-B, O/C, AGN; El Consul General, Laredo, to Sr. Encargado de Negocios, Washington, May 2, 1922, Report, United States Army Intelligence, May 1, 13, 1922, AEMEUA, leg. 673, exp. 10, ASRE; Uriburu to Díaz, Sep. 5, 1922, Félix Díaz Papers, AVC.

36. "Summary of the Principal Factors Menacing the Obregón Administration in Mexico, prepared by the Military Intelligence Division, G-2, General Staff, March 4, 1922," Intelligence Reports, Mexico, 1919-1941"; F. W. Becker to Obregón, June 21, 1922, exp. 243-B1-B4, O/C, AGN; Uriburu to Díaz, Sep. 5, 24, 1922, carp. 6, legs. 579, 610, Mariano Viesca Arizpe to Rosas, Aug. 15, 1922, carp. 6, legs. 569, 577, Félix Díaz Papers, AVC; Castro, *Álvaro Obregón*, pp. 116-17.

37. Juan Carrasco, "Manifiesto al Pueblo Mexicano," June 24, 1922, carp. 5, leg. 521, Thayer to Wilbur Bates, July 21, Aug. 2, 1922, Del Villar to Díaz, Aug. 10, 1922, carp. 6, leg. 562, Raymond Henri Bowles to Bates, Aug. 17, 1922, carp. 6, leg. 570, Uriburu to Rosas, Sept. 24, 1922, carp. 6, leg. 610, all in Félix Díaz Papers, AVC; Castro, *Álvaro Obregón*, pp. 118-19; Lieuwin, *Mexican Militarism*, p. 64; Hall, *Oil, Banks, and Politics*, p. 124; Dulles, *Yesterday in Mexico*, pp. 113-17; Katz, *Pancho Villa*, p. 738.

38. Uriburu to Díaz, Oct. 27, 1922, Carlos Vázquez to Rosas, Nov. 19, 1922, carp. 7, leg. 644, 670, Félix Díaz Papers, AVC; Jesús M. Ferreira to Francisco Serrano, Nov. 20, 1922, Obregón to Ferreira, Dec. 11, 1922, exp. 243-B1-B4, O/C, AGN.

39. Uriburu to Díaz, Aug. 14, 1922, carp. 6, leg. 568 (quotation), FedericoGarcía y Alba to Rosas, Nov. 25, 1922, carp. 7, leg. 671, Uriburu to Rosas, Sep. 24, 1922, carp. 6, leg. 610, Uriburu to Díaz, Oct. 18, Nov. 17, 1922, carp. 7, legs. 637, 668, 676, all in Félix Díaz Papers, AVC.

40. Aguilar to Obregón, May 31, 1916, AHDN, Cancelados, XI/111/4-1122, vol. 3, folio 743.

41. Otts to Obregón, Dec. 6, 11, 1923, 5 Apr., 17 Mar., E. Frezieres to Obregón, Jul. 26, Aug. 25, 1924, exp. 101-R2-I-1-Anexos I, II, V, O/C, AGN; Rodríguez, Memorandum, Nov. 20, 1924, exp. 243-B1-B4, AGN; J. Espinosa to "Mr. Richard Williams," Mar. 8, 1923, carp. 8, leg. 781, Carlos Vázquez to Rosas, Apr. 22, 1923, carp. 8, leg. 826, Ventura Anaya to Rosas, Aug. 6, 1923, carp. 9, leg. 903, Félix Díaz Papers, AVC.

42. Mariano Viesca Arizpe to Díaz, Aug. 12, 1923, Santos Cavazos to Rosas, Aug. 12, 1923, carp. 9 legs. 906, 907, Félix Díaz Papers, AVC.

43. Caro to Díaz, Sept. 2, 30, 1923, carps. 9, 10, legs. 920, 937, Teófilo Castillo Corzo to Rosas, Oct. 5, 1923, carp.10, leg. 941, Uriburu to Díaz, Dec. 5, 1923, carp. 10, leg. 970, Félix Díaz Papers, AVC.

44. Castro, *Álvaro Obregón*, pp. 238-80; Hall, *Oil, Banks, and Politics*, p. 166; Buchenau, *Plutarco Elías Calles*, pp. 105-107.

45. Castro, *Adolfo de la Huerta*, p. 275; Lieuwin, *Mexican Militarism*, pp. 73-76; Ruíz, *The Great Rebellion*, pp. 253, 256; *Diccionario Porrúa*, I, 739.

46. Lieuwin, *Mexican Militarism*, pp. 77-78; Ruíz, *The Great Rebellion*, p. 256; Rodríguez, Memorandum, May 15, 1924, Rodríguez to Obregón, n.d., 1924, exps. 243-B1-B4, 245-D1-P, O/C, AGN; Gómez Estrada, *Lealdades divididas*, pp. 93-94.

47. Castro, *Álvaro Obregón*, p. 275.

Chapter VIII

1. Martínez, *Historia de Baja California*, pp. 541-42; *passim*, exp. 424-A-9, O/C, AGN; Adalberto Walther Meade, "Caracteristicas generales de los regimenes de Cantú y Rodríguez," in Piñera Ramírez, *Panorama histórico*, pp. 393-95.

2. Gómez Estrada, *Gobierno y casinos*, pp. 71-73.

3. J. W. Sefton to Obregón, Dec. 14, 1920, Obregón to Sefton, Dec. 15, 1920, and *passim*, exp. 425-T-7, O/C, AGN.

4. Ibarra to Obregón, Mar. 18, 1921, exp. 243-B1-G1, O/C, AGN; Ibarra to Obregón, Dec. 29, 1920, Aug. 16, 1921, APEC, exp. 7, inv. 2872, leg. 1; Obregón to Ibarra, Jul. 18, 21, 1921, de la Huerta to Obregón, Jul. 19, 1921, Obregón to Secretaría de Hacienda, Aug. 6, 1921, Torreblanca to Ibarra, Aug. 15, 1921, exp. 816-B-10, O/C, AGN.

5. Gómez Estrada, *Gobierno y casinos*, pp. 76-83, 86, 90, 99, 137, 204; Schantz, "All Night at the Owl," pp. 580-84; Rodríguez to Obregón, n.d., 1924, exp. 245-D1-P, O/C, AGN; Rodríguez to Obregón, Feb. 15, Mar. 3, 7, 1924, Obregón to Rodríguez, Feb. 15, Mar. 4, 6, 1924, Obregón to Secretaría de Hacienda, Feb. 16, Mar. 4, 1924, AHDN, Cancelados, XI/111/1-449, Vol. V, folios 1049-51, 1057-61, 1188, Vol. VI, folios 1429-31.

6. Gómez Estrada, *Gobierno y casinos*, pp. 90, 165, 172, 208.

7. Schantz, "All Night at the Owl," pp. 580-84; Walter Meade, "Características generales de los regimenes de Cantú y Rodríguez," in Piñera Ramírez, *Panorama histórico*, pp. 393-95; Gómez Estrada. *Gobierno y casinos*, pp. 202-205.

8. Rodríguez to Calles, Jan. 18, 20, 1925, Calles to Gilberto Valenzuela, Jan. 20, 21, 1925, Calles to Rodríguez, Jan. 19, 21, 1925, exp. 121-G-C-1, O/C, AGN; Rodríguez to Obregón, Jan. 18, 20, 1925, Valenzuela to Obregón, Jan. 19, 1925, Valenzuela to Calles, Jan. 22, 1925, exp. 121-G-C-7, O/C, AGN.

9. *Informe Confidencial*," 22 Oct., Nov. 5, 1926, exp. 7, inv 1554, leg. 1 exp. 8 inv 1555, leg. 1, APEC, Anexo.

10. Cantú to Secretaría de Guerra y Marina, June 22, 1936, Blas Coral to Cantú, July 4, 1936, Cantú to Secretaría de la Defensa Nacional, Dec. 15, 1941, Florencio E. Anitúa Loy to Cantú, Dec. 27, 1941, AHDN, Cancelados, XI/111/4-1122, Vol. IV, folios 873-76; Castro, *Adolfo de la Huerta*, p. 264.

11. Rafael Moreno Ortega to Secretaría de la Defensa Nacional, Dec. 13, 1945, Cantú to Cristóbal Limón López, July 4, 1942, Limón López to Cantú, July 22, 1942, AHDN, Cancelados, XI/111/4-1122, Vol. IV, folios 894, 896, 898.

12. *The Mexican Herald* (Mexico City), Oct. 2, 1914; Moreno Ortega to Secretaría de la Defensa Nacional, Dec. 13, 1945, Moreno Ortega to Cantú, May 29, 1946, AHDN, Cancelados, XI/111/4-1122, Vol. IV, folios 898, 902.

13. Piñera Ramírez, *Panorama histórico*, pp. 401, 479; Moreno Ortega to Cantú, May 29, 1946, Juan García Rojas to Jefe de Estado Mayor, Feb. 28, 1947, Cantú to Adolfo Ruiz Cortinez, Nov. 20, 1955, AHDN, Cancelados, XI/111/4-1122, Vol. IV, folios 902, 925-27, 933.

14. Concesión otorgada al C. Esteban Cantú, Dec. 31, 1926, Fidel Favela to Tesorero del Districto Norte, Mar. 22, 1927, Lucas Rodríguez to Cantú, Apr. 28, 1927, Rodríguez to Governor, Baja California Norte, Jul. 1, 1927, all in Caja 18, exp. 53, Fondo Distrito Norte, AHEBC.

15. Luján, *Coronel Esteban Cantú*, pp. 270, 273, 304.

16. De Negri to Salvador Diego Fernández, April 2, 1919, leg. 17-16-141, ASRE; *Calexico Chronicle*, Sep. 9, 1916.

17. Werne, "Esteban Cantú," p.7.

18. Martínez, *Historia de Baja California*, pp. 530-33; *El Universal* (Mexico City), Mar. 5, 1917; Gershon to the Department of State, Feb. 24,1917, NA/RG 59, 812.00; T. R. de Esparza and J. Palacios to Carranza, n.d., carp.151, leg. 17216, Carranza Papers, AVC.

19. *El Universal* (Mexico City), Jun. 12, 1920.

20. Cantú to Carranza, Feb. 18, 1919, telegram, Carranza Papers, AVC.

21. Martínez, *Historia de Baja California*, pp. 532-34; *Calexico Chronicle*, Sept. 9, 1916.

22. *Excelsior* (Mexico City), Jul. 24, 29, 1920.

23. Gershon to the Department of State, Feb. 24, 1917, NA/RG 59, 812.00; Testimony of Jones, May 17, 1920, SED 285 (7665-66), p. 2, 994; De Negri to Fernández, Apr. 2, 1919, leg. 17-16-141, ASRE.

24. *El Heraldo de México* (Mexico City), Sept. 14, 1919.

25. *El Heraldo de México,* Nov. 5, 6, 19, 20, 1919.

26. Frezieres to Carranza, Apr. 25, 1918, in, Testimony of Jones, SED 285 (7665-66), pp. 2,997-98; Alessio Robles, *Historia política de la Revolución*, p. 276; Knight, *The Mexican Revolution*, II, 210, 275, 460.

27. José Montes, Luis H. Vega and J. Jesús Carranza to Carranza, Aug. 6, 1916, carp. 90, leg. 10156, Carranza Papers, AVC; Cantú, *Apuntes históricos*, p. 42.

28. "Summary of the Principal Factors...March 4, 1922," Intelligence Reports, Mexico, 1919-1941; *Los Angeles Times*, Jul. 30, 1920; *Excelsior* (Mexico City), Aug. 5, 1920; Castro, *Adolfo de la Huerta*, pp. 101-102.

29. SED 285 (7665-66), pp. 3014-15; Creese [Charles E. Jones] to the Secretary of

State, Sep. 27, 1918, NA/RG 59, 812.00.

30. Schantz, "All Night at the Owl," pp. 580-84; Ponce Aguilar, *El Coronel Esteban Cantú*, p. 146.

31. Uriburu to Díaz, 16 Aug. 1921, Ochoa Ramos to Díaz, Aug. 22, 1921, Esteban Cantú, "Conciudadanos," n.d., carp. 2, legs. 227, 230, carp. 3, leg. 304, Félix Díaz Papers, AVC

32. Villar to Díaz, Sep. 8, 1921, carp. 3, leg. 232, Félix Díaz Papers, AVC.

33. Uriburu to Díaz, Nov. 9, 1921, García y Alba to Díaz, April 2, 1922, carp. 3, leg. 263, carp. 5, leg. 436, Félix Díaz Papers, AVC; Rodríguez, *Autobiografía*, pp. 105-106.

34. Cantú, *Apuntes históricos*, pp. 5, 13, 36-37.

35. Cantú, *Apuntes históricos*, p. 41.

36. Carlos Vázquez to Rosas, May 20, 1922, carp. 5, leg. 488, Félix Díaz Papers, AVC.

37. *Excelsior* (Mexico City), Aug. 29, 1920.

38. Edward I. Bell, *The Political Shame of Mexico* (New York: McBride, Nast and Co., 1914), p. 223.

39. González to Subsecretario de Relaciones Exteriores, Jul. 7, 1915, AEMEUA, leg. 474, exp. 2, ASRE.

BIBLIOGRAPHY

ARCHIVES

Mexico:

Archivo General de la Nación, México, D.F.
  Ramo Presidentes, Obregón/Calles

Archivo Histórico de la Defensa Nacional, México, D.F.
  Archivo de Cancelados

Archivo de la Secretaría de Relaciones Exteriores, México, D.F.
  Archivo de Embajadas de México en los Estados Unidos

Centro de Estudios de Historia de México, CARSO, México, D.F.
  Félix Díaz Papers
  Venustiano Carranza Papers

Fideicomiso Archivos Plutarco Elías Calles y Fernando Torreblanca. México, D.F.
  Fondo: Plutarco Elías Calles
  Fondo: Álvaro Obregón

Archivo Histórico del Estado de Baja California, Mexicali, Baja California
  Fondo: Gobernación Distrito Norte

United States:

Records of the Department of State Relating to Internal Affairs of Mexico,
  Microcopy No. 274, Record Group 59

Records of the Department of State Relating to Political Relations between the
  United States and Mexico, 1910-1929, Microcopy No. 314, Record Group 59

The University of Texas, Austin
  The Nettie Lee Bensen Latin American Collection

Library of Pomona College, Claremont, California
  José María Maytorena Papers

University of Arizona, Tucson, Special Collections
  Emilio Kosterlitzky Papers

PUBLISHED PUBLIC DOCUMENTS

Bell, P. L. and H. Bently Mackenzie, *Mexican West Coast and Lower California, a Commercial and Industrial Survey.* Washington, DC: GPO, 1923.

The Congressional Record, 65th cong., 3rd sess.

Papers Relating to the Foreign Relations of the United States, 1920, III. Washington, DC: GPO, 1936.

Rolland, Modesto C., *Informe sobre el Distrito Norte de la Baja California.* México: Universidad Autónoma de Baja California, 1993.

U.S. Military Intelligence Reports: Mexico, 1919-1941, Military Intelligence Branch, Executive Division, Washington, DC.

US Senate, 66th cong., 2nd sess., *Senate Executive Document* No. 285 (7665-6), "Investigation of Mexican Affairs; 2 vols."

NEWSPAPERS

Los Angeles Times

Arizona Daily Star (Tucson)

Arizona Republican (Phoenix)

Calexico Chronicle

El Coreo de la Tarde (Mazatlán)

El Demócrata (Mexico City)

El Diario (Mexico City)

Evening Tribune (San Diego, CA)

Excelsior (Mexico City)

El Heraldo de México (Mexico City)

El Heraldo de México (Los Angeles, CA)

El Imparcial (Mexico City)

La Nación (Mexico City)

San Diego Union

San Francisco Examiner

New York Times

El País (Mexico City)

La Prensa (San Antonio, TX)

El Pueblo (Mexico City)

San Diego Tribune

El Universal (Mexico City)

Washington Post

BOOKS

Aguilar Camín, Héctor, and Lorenzo Meyer. *In the Shadow of the Revolution: Contemporary Mexican History, 1910-1989.* Austin: University of Texas Press, 1993.

Aguirre Bernal, Celso. *Breve historia del Estado de Baja California.* México: Ediciones Quinto Sol, 1987.

Aldrete, Enrique. *Baja California heroica.* México: printed by the author, 1958.

Alessio Robles, Miguel. *Historia política de la Revolución.* 2nd ed. México: Ediciones Botas, 1938.

Almada, Ignacio. *Breve historia de Sonora.* México: El Colegio de México, 2000.

Almada, Francisco R. *La Revolución en el Estado de Sonora.* México: Talleres Gráficos, 1971.

Beezley, William H. *Insurgent Governor: Abraham González and the Mexican Revolution in Chihuahua.* Lincoln: University of Nebraska Press, 1973.

Benjamin, Thomas. *La Revolución: Mexico's Great Revolution as Memory, Myth, and History.* Austin: University of Texas Press, 2000.

Benjamin, Thomas and Mark Wassermann, eds. *Provinces of the Revolution: Essays on Regional Mexican History, 1910-1929.* Albuquerque: University of New Mexico Press, 1990.

Blaisdell, Lowell L. *The Desert Revolution, Baja California, 1911.* Madison: University of Wisconsin Press, 1962.

Brenner, Anita. *The Wind that Swept Mexico.* New York: Harper Brothers, 1943.

Brown, Jonathan. *Oil and Revolution in Mexico.* Berkeley: University of California Press, 1993.

Buchenau, Jürgen. *Plutarco Elías Calles and the Mexican Revolution.* New York: Rowman and Littlefield, 2007.

Cantú Jiménez, Esteban. *Apuntes históricos de Baja California Norte.* México: self-published, 1957.

Caro, Brígido. *Plutarco Elías Calles, dictador bolsheviki de México: Episodios de la Revolución Mexicana, desde 1910 hasta 1924.* Los Angeles: Impresso de *El Heraldo de México*, 1924.

Castro, Pedro. *Álvaro Obregón: Fuego y cenizas de la Revolución Mexicana.* México: Ediciones Era, 2009.

———. *Adolfo de la Huerta: La integredad como arma de la revolución.* México: Universidad Autónoma Metropolitana, 1998.

Chao Romero, Robert. *The Chinese in Mexico, 1882-1940.* Tucson: University of Arizona Press, 2010.

Clendenen, Clarence C. *Blood on the Border: The United States Army and the Mexican Irregulars.* London: Macmillan, 1969.

Cruz, Salvador. *Vida y obra de Pastor Rouaix.* México: Instituto Nacional de Antropología e Historia, 1980.

Cumberland, Charles C. *Mexican Revolution: The Constitutionalist Years.* Austin: University of Texas Press, 1972.

Dios Bojorquez, Juan de (Djed Borquez). *Forjadores de la Revolución mexicana.* México: Talleres Gráficos de la Nación, 1960.

Dullas, John W. F. *Yesterday in Mexico: A Chronicle of the Revolution, 1919-1936.* Austin: University of Texas Press, 1961.

Farr, Finis C. *The History of Imperial County California.* Berkeley, Elms and Franks, 1918.

Gaxiola, Francisco Javier. *Memorias.* México: Porrúa, 1975.

Gilderhus, Mark T. *Diplomacy and Revolution: U.S.-Mexican Relations under Wilson and Carranza.* Tucson: University of Arizona Press, 1977.

Gilly, Adolfo, ed. *Felipe Ángeles en la Revolución.* México: Ediciones Era, 2008.

Gómez Estrada, José Alfredo. *Gobierno y casinos: El origen de la riqueza de Abelardo L. Rodríguez.* México: Instituto Mora, 2007.

———. *Lealtades divididas: Camarillas y poder en México, 1913-1932.* México: Instituto Mora, 2012.

Hall, Linda B. *Álvaro Obregón: Power and Revolution in Mexico, 1911-1920.* College Station: Texas A&M University Press, 1981.

———. *Oil, Banks, and Politics: The United States and Postrevolutionary Mexico, 1917-1924.* Austin: University of Texas Press, 1995.

Hall, Linda B., and Don M. Coerver, *Revolution on the Border: The United States and Mexico, 1910-1920.* Albuquerque: University of New Mexico Press, 1988.

Henderson, Peter V. N. *Félix Díaz, the Porfirians, and the Mexican Revolution.* Lincoln: University of Nebraska Press, 1981.

Hernández, Juan B., ed. *Pasajes de la Revolución Mexicana en el Distrito Norte de la Baja California.* Intstituto de Investigaciones Históricas del estado de Baja California, 1956.

Herrera Castillo, Pablo. *Colonización del Valle de Mexicali.* Mexicali: Universidad Autónoma de Baja California, 1976.

Hofstadter, Richard. *The American Political Tradition.* New York: Alfred A. Knopf, 1948.

Hu-DeHart, Evelyn. *Yaqui Resistance and Survival: The Struggle for Land and Autonomy, 1821-1910.* Madison: University of Wisconsin Press, 1984.

Huerta, Adolfo de la. *Memorias de don Adolfo de la Huerta.* México: Ediciones "Guzman," 1957.

Johnson, William Weber. *Heroic Mexico: The Violent Emergence of a Modern Nation.* New York: Doubleday, 1968.

Katz, Friederich. *The Life and Times of Pancho Villa.* Stanford: Stanford University Press, 1998.

———. *The Secret War in Mexico: Europe, The United States and the Mexican Revolution.* Chicago: University of Chicago Press, 1981.

Kennedy, David M., ed. *Progressivism: The Critical Issues.* Boston: Little, Brown and Co., 1971.

Kerig, Dorothy Pierson. *El Valle de Mexicali y la Colorado River Land Company, 1902-1946.* Mexicali, Baja California: Universidad Autónoma de Baja California, 2001.

Knight, Alan. *The Mexican Revolution.* 2 vols. Lincoln and London: University of Nebraska Press, 1986.

Krauze, Enrique. *Biography of Power: A History of Modern Mexico, 1801-1996.* New York: Harper, 1998.

Lieuwen, Edwin. *Arms and Politics in Latin America.* [illegible]

Lieuwen, Edwin. *Mexican Militarism: The Political Rise and Fall of the Revolutionary Army, 1919-1940.* Albuquerque: University of New Mexico Press, 1968.

López de Escalera, Juan. *Diccionario Biográfico y de Historia de México.* México: Editorial del Magisterio, 1964.

Lorey, David E. *The U.S.-Mexican Border in the Twentieth Century.* Wilmington: Scholarly Resources, 1999.

————. *United States-Mexico Border Statistics Since 1900.* Los Angeles: UCLA Latin American Center, 1990.

Luján, Gabriel. *Coronel Esteban Cantú Jiménez: Benefactor de Baja California. México, vida y obra.* Mexicali, Baja California, México: AR Impresiones, 2009.

Matute, Álvaro. *Historia de la Revolución Mexicana, 1917-1924: La carrera del caudillo.* México: El Colegio de México, 1980.

McCartney, Laton. *The Teapot Dome Scandal.* New York: Random House, 2008.

Martínez, Oscar J. *Fragments of the Mexican Revolution: Personal Accounts From the Border.* Albuquerque: University of New Mexico Press, 1968.

————, ed. *U.S.-Mexico Borderlands: Historical and Contemporary Perspectives.* Wilmington: Scholarly Resources, 1996.

Martínez, Pablo L. *Historia de Baja California.* 2nd ed. México: Editorial Baja California, 1956.

Mena Brito, Bernardino. *Carranza: Sus amigos, sus enemigos.* México: Ediciones Botas, 1935.

Meyer, Michael C. *Huerta: A Political Portrait.* Lincoln: University of Nebraska Press, 1972.

————. *Mexican Rebel: Pascual Orozco and the Mexican Revolution, 1910-1915.* Lincoln: University of Nebraska Press, 1967.

Moyano Pahissa, Ángela. *California y sus relaciones con Baja California.* México: Fondo de Cultura Económica, 1983.

Obregón, Álvaro. *Ocho mil kilómetros en campaña.* México: Librería de la Vda. De Ch. Bouret, 1917.

Piñera Ramírez, David. *Panorama histórico de Baja California.* Centro de Investigaciones Históricas, UNAM-UABC, 1983.

Porffitt, T. D. *Tijuana: The History of a Mexican Metropolis.* San Diego: San Diego University Press, 1994.

Ponce Aguilar, Antonio. *El Coronel Esteban Cantú en el Distrito Norte de Baja California, 1911-1920.* Mexicali: Dhiré, 2010.

Quirk, Robert E. *The Mexican Revolution, 1914-1915: The Convention of Aguascalientes.* Bloomington: Indiana University Press, 1960.

Raat, William Dirk. *Revoltosos: Mexico's Rebels in the United States, 1903-1923.* College Station: Texas A&M University Press, 1981.

Rivera, Antonio G. *La Revolución en* Sonora. México: self-published, 1969.

Rodríguez, Abelardo. *Autobiografía de Abelardo Rodríguez*. México: Novaro Editores, 1962.

Romero, Ruben, et. al. *Obregón: Aspectos de su vida*. México: Editorial "Cvltvra," 1935.

Ruíz, Ramón Eduardo. *The Great Rebellion: Mexico, 1905-1924*. New York and London: Norton, 1980.

Salazar Rovirosa, Alfonso. *Cronología de Baja California: Del territorio y del estado, de 1500 a 1956*. 10 vols. México: Litografía Artística, 1956.

Samaniego López, Marco Antonio. *Los gobiernos civiles en Baja California, 1920-1923: Un estudio sobre la relación entre los poderes local y federal*. Mexicali: Instituto de Cultura de Baja California, 1998.

Sax, Antimaco. *Los Mexicanos en el destierro*. San Antonio, Texas: n.p., 1916.

Sierra, Justo. *The Political Evolution of the Mexican People*. Austin: University of Texas Press, 1969.

Smith, Cornelius C., Jr. *Emilio Kosterlitzky: Eagle of Sonora and the Southwest Border*. Glendale: Arthur H. Clark, 1970.

Schmitt, Karl M. *Mexico and the United States, 1821-1973*. New York: John Wiley & Sons, 1974.

Silva Herzog, Jesús. *Breve historia de la Revolución Mexicana*. México: Fondo de Cultura Económica, 1960.

Southworth, J. R. *El territorio de la Baja California: Su agricultura, comercio, minería é industrias*. México: Gob. del Territorio, 1899.

Sparks, George F. *A Many-Colored Toga: The Diary of Henry Fountain Ashurst*. Tucson: University of Arizona Press, 1962.

Stout, Joseph A., Jr. *Spies, Politics, and Power: El Departamento Confidencial en México, 1922-1946*. Fort Worth: TCU Press, 2012.

Tannenbaum, Frank. *Peace by Revolution: An Interpretation of Mexico*. New York: Columbia University Press, 1933.

Turner, John Kenneth. *Barbarous Mexico* (Austin: University of Texas Press, 1969).

Ulloa, Berta. *La Revolución intervenida. Relaciones diplomáticos entre México y Estados Unidos (1910-1914)*. México: El Colegio de México, 1971.

Vanderwood, Paul J. *Disorder and Progress: Bandits, Police and Mexican Development*. Lincoln: University of Nebraska Press, 1981.

Vasconcelos, José. *La Tormenta*. México: Fondo de Cultura Económica, 1982.

Velasco Ceballos, R. *¿Se apoderará los Estados Unidos de América de la Baja California?* México: Imp. Nacional, 1920.

Vera Estañol, Jorge. *Historia de la Revolución Mexicana: Orígenes y resultados*. 3rd ed. México: Editorial Porrúa, 1976.

Verdugo Fimbres, Maria Isabel. *Frontera en el desierto, historia de San Luis Río Colorado*. Hermosillo, Sonora: Instituto Nacional de Antropología e Historia, 1983.

Vivanco, Aurelio de. *Baja California al día*. Wolfer Printing Company, 1924.

Womack, John. *Zapata and the Mexican Revolution*. New York: Alfred A. Knopf, 1969.

Zárate, David. *Bosquejo Histórico de la Peninsula de Baja California: Particularmente de la ciudad y puerto de Ensenada*. Ensenada: printed by author, 1948.

Zorrilla, Luis G. *Historia de las relaciones entre México y los Estados Unidos de América, 1800-1958*, II. México: Editorial Porrúa, 1966.

DISSERTATIONS

Henderson, Peter V. N. "Counterrevolution in Mexico: Félix Díaz and the Struggle for National Supremacy, 1910-1920." PhD diss., University of Nebraska, 1973.

Kerig, Dorthy Pierson. "Yankee Enclave: The Colorado River Land Company and Mexican Agrarian Reform in Baja California, 1902-1944." PhD diss., University of California, Irvine, 1988.

Richmond, Douglas. "The First Chief and Revolutionary Mexico: The Presidency of Venustiano Carranza, 1915-1920." PhD diss., University of Washington, 1976.

Schantz, Eric Michael. "From the *Mexicali Rose* to the Tijuana Brass: Vice Tours of the United States-Mexico Border, 1910-1965." PhD diss., University of California, Los Angeles, 2001.

Watry, James Peter. "The Economic Development of Baja California, Mexico." PhD diss., University of Missouri, Columbia, 1970.

ARTICLES

Blaisdell, Lowell L. "Harry Chandler and Mexican Border Intrigue, 1914-1917." *Pacific Historical Review*, XXXV (November 1966): 385-93.

———. "Was It Revolution or Filibustering? The Mystery of the Flores Magón Revolt in Baja California." *Pacific Historical Review*, XXIV (May 1954):147-64.

Chamberlin, Eugene Keith. "Mexican Colonization versus American Interests in Lower California." *Pacific Historical Review*, XX (February 1951): 43-55.

———. "The Japanese Scare at Magdalena Bay." *Pacific Historical Review*, XXIV (November 1955): 345-59.

Carr, Barry. "Las peculiaridades del norte mexicano, 1880-1927: ensayo de interpretación." *Historia Mexicana*, XXII (enero-marzo 1973): 320–46.

Carr, Harry. "The Kingdom of Cantú: Why Lower California is an Oasis of Perfect Peace in Bloody Mexico." *Sunset* 37, no. 3 (April 1917): 33-67.

Deeds, Susan M. "José María Maytorena and the Mexican Revolution in Sonora."

Arizona and the West, XVIII, Part I (Spring 1976): 21-40; Part II (Summer 1976): 125-48.

Duncan, Robert H. "The Chinese and the Economic Development of Northern Baja California, 1889-1929." *Hispanic American Historical Review*, LXXIV (November 1994): 615-47.

Harris, Charles H., and Louis R. Sadler. "The Witzke Afair: German Intrigue on the Mexican Border, 1917-18." *Military Review*, LIX (February 1979): 36-50.

Henderson, Peter V. N. "Un gobernador maderista: José María Maytorena y la Revolución en Sonora." *Historia Mexicana*, LI (julio-septiembre, 2001), pp. 151-85.

Hu-DeHart, Evelyn. "The Chinese of Baja California Norte, 1910-1934." Proceedings of the Pacific Coast Council on Latin American Studies: Baja California and the North American Frontier, XII (1985-1986), pp. 9-30.

_____. "Immigrants to a Developing Society: The Chinese in Northern Mexico, 1875-1932." *The Journal of Arizona History*, XXI (Autumn,1980), pp. 275-312.

_____. "Development and Rural Rebellion: Pacification of the Yaquis in the late *Porfiriato*." *Hispanic American Historical Review*, LIV (February, 1974), pp.72-93.

Kenamore, Claire. "The Principality of Cantú." *The Bookman*, 46 (September, 1917), pp. 23-28.

_____. "What is Germany doing in Mexico?" *The Bookman*, 44 (June, 1917), pp. 342-46.

Mowery, George E. "The Progressive Era, 1900-20: The Reform Persuasion." AHA Pamphlets No. 212 (1958).

Raat, William Dirk. "The Diplomacy of Suppression: *Los Revoltosos*, Mexico and the United States, 1906-1911." *Hispanic American Historical Review*, LVI (November, 1976), pp. 529-50.

Samaniego López, Marco Antonio. "Formación y consolidación de las organizaciones obreras en Baja California, 1920-1930." *Mexican Studies/ Estudios Mexicanos*, XIV (Summer, 1998), pp. 329-62.

_____. "El norte revolucionario. Diferencias regionales y sus paradojas en la relación con Estados Unidos." *Historia Mexicana*, LX (octubre-diciembre, 2010), pp. 961-1018.

_____. "La revolución Mexicana en Baja California: maderismo, magonismo, filibusterismo y la pequeña revuelta local." *Historia Mexicana*, LVI (abril-junio, 2007), pp. 1254-57.

Schantz, Eric Michael. "All Night at the Owl: The Social and Political Relations of Mexicali's Red-Light District, 1913-1925." *Journal of the Southwest*, XLIII (Winter, 2001), pp. 547-602.

Vanderwood, Paul J. "Response to Revolt: The Counter-Guerrilla Strategy of Porfirio Díaz." *Hispanic American Historical Review*, LVI (November, 1976), pp. 551-79.

_____. "Review of *Emilio Kosterlitzky: Eagle of Sonora and the Southwest Border*" by Cornelius C. Smith, Jr. *Hispanic American Historical Review*, LII (May, 1972), pp. 304-306.

Werne, Joseph Richard. "Esteban Cantú y la soberanía mexicana en Baja California." *Historia Mexicana*, XXX (julio-septiembre, 1980), pp.1-32.

INDEX

Agua Prieta revolt (1920), ix, xiii, 85–86,
96, 131–32, 134; Esteban Cantú on,
86, 89, 135; exiled rebels and, 123.
See also Plan of Agua Prieta (1920)
Aguascalientes, Convention of (1914), 8;
Esteban Cantú and, 17, 22, 40. See
also *carrancistas*
Aguilar, Cándido, 25, 38; on Esteban
Cantú's income, 75; on Esteban
Cantú's neutrality, 41; at San Antonio
revolutionary meeting (1923), 123;
support for Esteban Cantú from, 90
Aguirre Berlanga, Joaquín, 29, 39
airplanes: attempted purchase from the
United States by Esteban Cantú of,
25, 91
Alemán, Miguel, 63
Alessio Robles, Miguel, 95; on Esteban
Cantú's rebellion (1920), 100
Alessio Robles, Vito, 4; Esteban Cantú's
resignation as Baja California Norte
governor and, 103
alkaloids: importation fees on, 18, 74
Allen, Marvin, 67
Almada, Baldomero: appointed Baja
California Norte governor, 86–88
Amador, Juan Neftalí, 75
Anaya y Vasconcelos, Enrique, 8
Andrade, Alberto F., 34
Ángeles, Felipe, 9
anti-Constitutionalists: Esteban Cantú
established Baja California as a refuge
for, xiii, 27–28, 131. *See also* Consti-
tutionalists
Arizona Republican (Phoenix): on Mexico's uncontrollability, 42
Armenta, Anselmo, 108
arms smuggling: by Dato family, 50, 51;
by Esteban Cantú, xiii, 25, 25–26,
30–31, 50; in preparation for Esteban
Cantú's revolt (1920), 91, 104; in

preparation for Esteban Cantú's
revolt (1921), 109–10; in preparation
for Esteban Cantú's rebellion (1922)
and, 118
Arredondo, Eliseo, 21; appearance of,
22; on Esteban Cantú's extradition
agreement with Calexico authorities,
22; on Esteban Cantú's sale of Isla de
Guadalupe's goats, 19
Arriola, J. M.: on arms smuggling in Baja
California Norte, 26
Asama (ship), 61
Ashurst, Henry Fountain: on US annexation of Baja California Norte, 42–43,
45, 47
Asociación China de Mexicali, 57–58
Avilés, Baltasar: as Baja California Norte
governor, 8, 9, 9–11, 39; Baja California Norte treasury absconded by, 72,
82; during campaign against Guaymas
(1914), 9–11, 12; Esteban Cantú and,
10, 21–22, 73; as rumored member of
governing triumvirate in Baja California Norte's secession, 39–40

Baja California Norte: annexation by
United States of, rumored, 42–47,
134; anti-Chinese sentiment in, 54;
economic potential of (1912), 15;
Esteban Cantú as governor of, xii–
xiii, 12, 17–105; as Esteban Cantú's
fiefdom, 24–25; geographic isolation
of, xi, 37–38, 57; immunity from
Mexican Revolution of, xi–xii; as refuge for central government's political
opponents, 27–29, 131; secession of,
rumored, 39–40, 41–47, 134; situation in (1910), 13
Balarezo, Manuel: as Baja California
Norte governor, 107

Liga Protectora Mexicana de California,
27–28
Linares, Nuevo León: Esteban Cantú
born in, 4
Lindsay, Lycurgus, 45
Lodge, Henry Cabot, 61
Los Algodones, Baja California Norte:
Inter-California Railway in, 13;
schools constructed in, 80; telegraph
line to, 79; troop revolt in (1919), 54,
72, 89; vice trade in, 126, 127
Los Angeles, California: Esteban Cantú's
land ownership in, 75
Los Angeles Chamber of Commerce:
on US annexation of Baja California
Norte, 42
Los Angeles Times, 44, 116; on US annex-
ation of Baja California Norte, 42
Los Angeles Tribune: on Baja California
Norte's rumored secession, 39–40
Los Niños Héroes Park (Mexicali, Baja
California Norte), 81, 87, 133
Lugo, José Inocente, 63, 120; as Baja
California Norte governor, 107–8,
126–27; on vice trade, 126–27

Madden, W. D., 42
Madero, Francisco I., 1, 6, 65, 86, 119,
123; Abraham González appointed
secretary of education by, 117–18;
assassination of, 6, 96; Esteban Cantú
and, 134; on Japanese colony in Magdalena Bay, 61; José F. Gómez and, 48;
overtures about Baja California Norte's
sale to the United States made to, 44;
speech of (1910), disrupted by Brígido
Caro, 112; on vice trade, 67–68
Magdalena Bay, 10; rumored Japanese
takeover of, 43, 47, 61–62; suitability
as naval base of, 15;
magonistas: rebellion of (1911), in Baja
California Norte, 1, 2, 28, 39, 42, 133
Mann Act (1910), 71
Marshall, William Louis, 34; on Esteban
Cantú's political independence, 34–35
Martínez, Agustín, 5
Mascareñas, Alberto: *guano* exploitation
rights granted to, 18
Mateos, Juan A.: arrest of, 21
Maytorena, José María, 8, 100, 114;
Baja California Norte affairs arranged
by, 8–9; campaign against Guaymas
ordered by (1914), 9–10; Esteban

Cantú and, 12; Esteban Cantú's
loyalty questioned by, 10; Félix Díaz
and, 118, 119; at New York City
revolutionary meeting (1921), 109; in
Revolt of the Generals (1923–1924),
123–24; at San Antonio revolutionary
meeting (1923), 123; Yaquis and, 112
meerschaum, 18
Mena Brito, Bernardo: support for Esteban Cantú from, 90
Mexicali, Baja California Norte: Chinese
community in, 55–59; establishment
as municipality of, 81; Esteban Cantú
named military commander at, 9;
infrastructure of, improved, 79; population of (1910), 15; pictured, 31;
schools in, 80; as territorial capital, xii,
12, 76, 89; vice trade in, 72–73
Mexicali Valley: economic situation in
1910 of, 13–14
Mexican Land and Colonization
Company, 59–60; as Mexicali Valley
landowner, 13
Mexican Revolution: Abelardo Rodríguez
in, 96–97; Adolfo de la Huerta in, 86;
Esteban Cantú requests recognition
for service in, 128–29; xenophobia
exacerbated by, 53
Mexico City: Esteban Cantú's return from
exile to, 128
Meza y Salinas, Trinidad, 70–71
mica, 15
mining: in Baja California Norte, 15
Monroe Doctrine: Japanese Magdalena
Bay colony perceived as threat to, 62
Monterrey, Nuevo León, 8; Esteban
Cantú posted to, 4
Montes, Federico: in Agua Prieta revolt
(1920), 85
Moore, H. J., 66
Mora Nova, Jacinto, 3
morphine, xii, 74; in Tijuana, 69
Moyrón, Ramón: persecution of, 28
Murguía, Francisco, 108; on Constitution
of 1857, 120; death, 121; at New York
City revolutionary meeting (1921),
109; rebellion of (1922), 121

narcotics, 71–72; smuggling of, 74. *See
also specific narcotics*
National Preparatory School (Mexico
City), 6